D1738403

Linkography

Design Thinking, Design Theory

Ken Friedman and Erik Stolterman, editors

Design Things
A. Telier (Thomas Binder, Pelle Ehn, Giorgio De Michelis, Giulio Jacucci, Per Linde, and Ina Wagner), 2011

China's Design Revolution
Lorraine Justice, 2012

Adversarial Design
Carl DiSalvo, 2012

The Aesthetics of Imagination in Design
Mads Nygaard Folkmann, 2013

Linkography: Unfolding the Design Process
Gabriela Goldschmidt, 2014

Linkography

Unfolding the Design Process

Gabriela Goldschmidt

The MIT Press
Cambridge, Massachusetts
London, England

MIT Press books may be purchased at special quantity discounts for business or sales promotional use. For information, please email special_sales@mitpress.mit.edu.

Set in Stone Serif Std by Toppan Best-set Premedia Limited. Printed and bound in the United States of America.

Library of Congress Cataloging-in-Publication Data

Goldschmidt, Gabriela, 1942–
Linkography : unfolding the design process / Gabriela Goldschmidt.
pages cm.—(Design thinking, design theory)
Includes bibliographical references and index.
ISBN 978-0-262-02719-9 (hardcover : alk. paper) 1. Design—Methodology.
2. Design—Evaluation. I. Title.
NK1520.G64 2014
745.4—dc23
2013034867

10 9 8 7 6 5 4 3 2 1

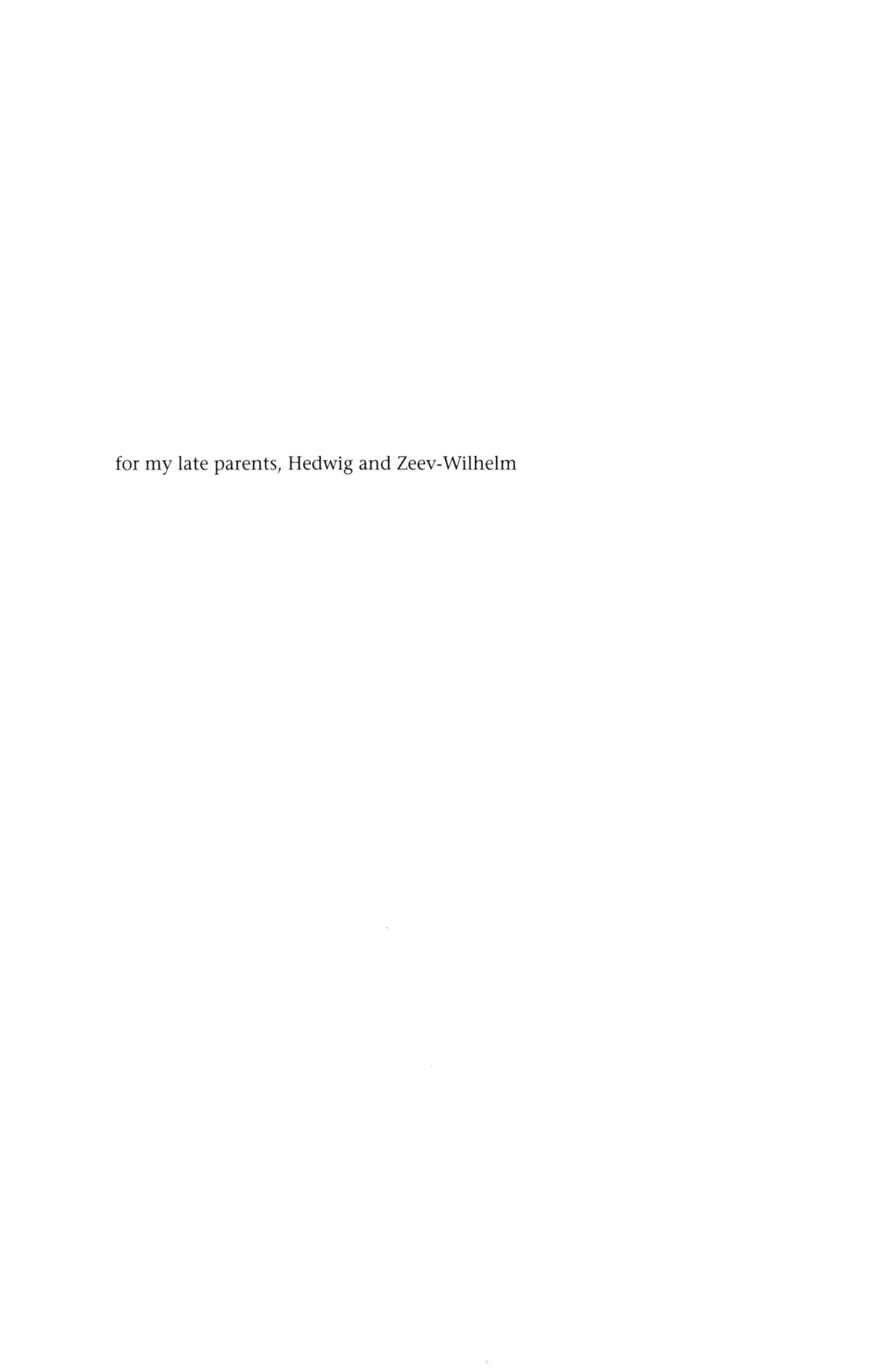

for my late parents, Hedwig and Zeev-Wilhelm

Contents

Series Foreword

As professions go, design is relatively young. The practice of design predates professions. In fact, the practice of design—making things to serve a useful goal, making tools—predates the human race. Making tools is one of the attributes that made us human in the first place.

Design, in the most generic sense of the word, began over 2.5 million years ago when *Homo habilis* manufactured the first tools. Human beings were designing well before they began to walk upright. Four hundred thousand years ago, they began to manufacture spears. By 40,000 years ago, they had moved up to specialized tools.

Urban design and architecture developed 10,000 years ago in Mesopotamia. Interior architecture and furniture design probably emerged with them. It was another 5,000 years before graphic design and typography got their start when Sumerians developed cuneiform.

Today all goods and services are designed. The urge to design—to consider a situation, imagine a better situation, and act to create that improved situation—goes back to our prehuman ancestors.

Today, the word "design" means many things. The common factor linking them is service. Designers engage in a service profession. Their work meets human needs.

Design is first of all a process. The word "design" entered the English language in the 1500s as a verb, and the first written citation of the verb is dated 1548. *Merriam-Webster's Collegiate Dictionary* defines the verb "design" as "to conceive and plan out in the mind; to have as a specific purpose; to devise for a specific function or end."

The first cited use of the noun "design" can be traced back to 1588. The *Collegiate Dictionary* defines the noun as "a particular purpose held in view by an individual or group; deliberate, purposive planning; a mental project or scheme in which means to an end are laid down." Today, we design large, complex processes, systems, and services, and to achieve this we design the organizations and structures that produce them. Design has changed considerably since our remote ancestors made the first stone tools.

At an abstract level, Herbert Simon's definition covers nearly all instances of design. To design, Simon writes, is to devise "courses of action aimed at changing existing situations into preferred ones" (*The Sciences of the Artificial*, second edition, MIT Press, 1982, 129). Design, properly defined, is the entire process across the full range of domains required for any outcome.

However, the design process is always more than a general, abstract way of working. Design takes concrete form in the work of the service professions that meet human needs. These professions include industrial design, graphic design, textile design, furniture design, information design, process design, product design, interaction design, transportation design, educational design, systems design, urban design, design leadership, and design management, as well as architecture, engineering, information technology, and computer science.

The various design professions focus on different subjects and objects. They have distinct traditions, methods, and vocabularies, used and put into practice by distinct and often dissimilar professional groups. Although the traditions dividing these professions are distinct, common boundaries sometimes form a border. Where this happens, they serve as meeting points where common concerns from two or more professions can lead to a shared understanding of design. Today, ten challenges uniting the design professions form such a set of common concerns.

Three performance challenges, four substantive challenges, and three contextual challenges bind the design disciplines and professions together as a common field. The performance challenges arise because all design professions act on the physical world, address human needs, and generate the built environment. In the past, these common attributes were not sufficient to transcend the boundaries of tradition. Today, objective changes in the larger world give rise to four substantive challenges that are driving convergence in design practice and research. These are increasingly ambiguous boundaries between artifacts, structure, and process; increasingly large-scale social, economic, and industrial frames; an increasingly complex environment of needs, requirements, and constraints; and information content that often exceeds the value of physical substance. These challenges require new frameworks of theory and method. In professional design practice, we often find that design requires interdisciplinary teams with a transdisciplinary focus. Fifty years ago, one designer and an assistant or two might have solved most design problems; today, we need skills across several disciplines, and the ability to work with, listen to, and learn from each other.

The first of the three contextual challenges is that design takes place in a complex environment in which many projects or products cross the boundaries of several organizations. The second is that design must meet the expectations of many organizations, stakeholders, producers, and users. Third, design has to deal with demands at every level of production, distribution, reception, and control. These ten challenges require a qualitatively different approach to professional design practice than was taken in earlier times, when environments were simpler. Individual experience and personal development were sufficient for depth and substance in professional practice. Though experience and development are still necessary, they are no longer sufficient. Most of today's design challenges require analytic and synthetic planning skills that cannot be developed through practice alone.

Professional design practice today involves advanced knowledge. This knowledge is not solely a higher level of professional practice. It is also a qualitatively different form of professional practice that emerges in response to the demands of the information society and the knowledge economy to which it gives rise.

In a recent article ("Why Design Education Must Change," *Core77*, November 26, 2010), Don Norman challenges the premises and practices of the design profession. In the past, designers operated on the belief that talent and a willingness to jump into problems with both feet gave them an edge in solving problems. Norman writes:

In the early days of industrial design, the work was primarily focused upon physical products. Today, however, designers work on organizational structure and social problems, on interaction, service, and experience design. Many problems involve complex social and political issues. As a result, designers have become applied behavioral scientists, but they are woefully undereducated for the task. Designers often fail to understand the complexity of the issues and the depth of knowledge already known. They claim that fresh eyes can produce novel solutions, but then they wonder why these solutions are seldom implemented, or if implemented, why they fail. Fresh eyes can indeed produce insightful results, but the eyes must also be educated and knowledgeable. Designers often lack the requisite understanding. Design schools do not train students about these complex issues, about the interlocking complexities of human and social behavior, about the behavioral sciences, technology, and business. There is little or no training in science, the scientific method, and experimental design.

This is not industrial design in the sense of designing products, but industry-related design—design as thought and action for solving problems and imagining new futures.

The Design Thinking, Design Theory series emphasizes strategic design to create value through innovative products and services, emphasizing design as service through rigorous creativity, critical inquiry, and sustainable ethics. This rests on a sense of understanding, empathy, and appreciation for people, for nature, and for the world we shape through design. Our goal as editors is to develop a series of conversations that help designers and researchers to serve business, industry, and the public sector for positive social and economic outcomes.

The idea of this series is to present books that bring a new sense of inquiry to design, helping to shape a more reflective and stable design discipline able to support a stronger profession grounded in empirical research, generative concepts, and the solid theory that gives rise to what W. Edwards Deming described as profound knowledge in his 1993 book *The New Economics for Industry, Government, Education*. For Deming, a physicist, engineer, and designer, profound knowledge comprised systems thinking and the understanding of processes embedded in systems; an understanding of variation and the tools we need to understand variation; a theory of knowledge; and a foundation in human psychology. This is the beginning of "deep design"—the union of deep practice with robust intellectual inquiry.

A series on design thinking and theory faces many of the same challenges as the design professions themselves. On one level, design is a general human process that we use to understand and to shape our world. Nevertheless, we cannot address this process or the world in its general, abstract form. Rather, we seek to meet the challenges of design in specific challenges, addressing problems or ideas in a situated context. The challenges we face as designers today are as diverse as the problems our clients bring us. We are involved in design for economic anchors, economic continuity, and economic growth. We design for urban needs and rural needs, for social development, and for creative communities. We are involved with environmental sustainability, with economic policy, with agriculture, with competitive crafts for export, with competitive products and brands for micro-enterprises, with developing new products for bottom-of-pyramid markets, and with redeveloping old products for mature or wealthy markets. Within the framework of design, we are also challenged to design for extreme situations, for biotech, nanotech, and new materials, and for social business, as well as facing conceptual challenges for worlds that do not yet exist, such as the world beyond the Kurzweil singularity—and for new visions of the world that does exist.

The Design Thinking, Design Theory series explores these issues and others—meeting them, examining them, and helping designers to address them.

Join us in this exploration.

Ken Friedman
Erik Stolterman

Preface

This book has been very long in the making. My work on linkography was initiated in 1988 while I was at MIT, on leave from the Technion—the Israel Institute of Technology. After further development of the concept, a first paper on linkography was presented at the Tenth European Meeting on Cybernetics and Systems Research in Vienna in 1990. Much to my surprise, the paper was received very well and was honored as one of the two best papers presented at the conference. This was encouraging, of course, and in the next few years two more papers about linkography and its use as a research method were written. One of these was honored as the best paper published in the journal *Design Studies* in 1995.

For more than a decade now, colleagues have been encouraging me to write a more comprehensive text. Some years ago, I wrote a few dozen pages. That beginning was not followed through, however, because I felt that something was still missing; that more work would have to be done before a book could be undertaken. Only quite recently have I been able to convince myself that I am as ready as I will ever be to finally write the book, though clearly more work still remains to be done on many aspects of linkography.

Portions of the studies featured in this book have been published as journal papers, by me and by others, but the book is in no way a compendium of papers. Rather, existing publications served as inputs to the book. The original empirical research that informed the studies described in the book (excluding chapter 7) is briefly reported in the appendix.

Although I cannot point to a specific influence that led to this book, there are certainly people and institutions that contributed indirectly by shaping my thinking and serving as intellectual stimulation. First and foremost among them was my teacher, and later colleague and dear friend, the late Abraham Wachman, whose morphology classes were exciting and thought provoking, and who set me on a path of scholarly pursuit. He challenged me more than once with his demands for precision and clarity, which were lessons for life. Donald Schön was a valuable source of inspiration, and during my time at MIT he was helpful in serving as a model for inquiry and providing critical feedback, which was invaluable to me while I was struggling to turn from a practitioner to a researcher. A two-year stay at MIT in this crucial phase of my life was a wonderful opportunity to be exposed to academic pursuit at its best. I consider myself very fortunate for having had the opportunity to gain inspiration and insights from countless formal and informal encounters with great thinkers whom I met at MIT. I would like to single out John Habraken, William Porter, and Larry Bucciarelli, who remain close colleagues to this very day. I am grateful to MIT for instilling in me values and passions that have guided my academic pursuits.

Another institution to which I am grateful is the Delft University of Technology, in particular the Department of Product Innovation Management in the Faculty of Industrial Design Engineering. I have been associated with this school for two decades, and I spent a sabbatical year there in 2005–06. The friendship I encountered there, the encouragement, and the openness to new ideas made for an ideal work environment. In particular, Petra Badke-Schaub was a wonderful hostess, fully supportive of the linkography enterprise. Thanks to the faculty members and students who were so kind and supportive, Delft has become another home away from home, as MIT had been.

Howard Gruber, Tamar Globerson, and Bernard Kaplan, and later Sidney Strauss, helped me come to grips with questions related to developmental psychology and creativity. Danny Gopher provided an introduction to experimental cognitive psychology, and the seminar on Human Factors Research he headed at the Technion, which I attended for years, was both instructive and a model of exacting research standards.

Sincere thanks are extended to the many participants in the empirical studies reported in this book. They volunteered their time and were patient with occasional mishaps that prolonged the experimental sessions. Where names of participants are mentioned, they are fictitious.

I also want to thank the many students who took part in my graduate seminar Cognitive Aspects of the Design Process, wherein linkography was introduced as a possible addition to "classical" protocol analysis. Their challenging questions and comments forced me to think of new ways to develop the theory and application of linkography. Some of the students went on to write brilliant term papers, and in some cases master's theses, using linkography. They taught me that there is no limit to inventiveness and creativity, and what they did with linkography was always a refreshing and pleasant surprise.

I am grateful to Eilam Tycher for his kind, careful, and patient work in upgrading many of the figures. I would like to extend my heartiest thanks to the individuals who wrote the code that made digital production of linkographs possible. The first version, meant for Macintosh computers, was called MacLinkograph. It was written by Shahar Dumai, then a teenager, who also wrote a manual for it. Later a new version was written on a Java platform. The budget allowed for only a very limited amount of development, but we still use this application, called Linkographer, which was written by Konstantin Zertsekel, Robert Sayegh, and Hanna Mousa. Hanna Mousa has been a talented and kind savior angel ever since, solving sticky problems that came up occasionally. Many thanks also to Doug Sery, my editor at the MIT Press.

I am also indebted to the National Endowment for the Arts for research grant 87-4251-0169 at the outset of this endeavor, which allowed for an incubation period that was crucial to the formation of the initial concepts of linkography.

1 Beginnings

Beginnings, I

Linkography is the outcome of a long chain of experiences that can be pinpointed only partially and only with hindsight. Some of these experiences can be described only in general terms; others have a precise timing attached to them. The very first of these events took place a long time ago, but the exact date can still be cited: On November 17, 1964, I happened to notice a copy of Christopher Alexander's book *Notes on the Synthesis of Form* in a small bookstore in my home city, Jerusalem. Attracted to the book beyond resistance, I purchased it. The sales receipt is reproduced here as figure 1.1.

I was a beginning architecture student at the time, and I understood only part of what Alexander wrote, but it was reassuring to get a sense that designing is a structured process that can be explained and analyzed. Years later, I returned to *Notes on the Synthesis of Form* and reread it in its entirety. Decades later, I can now explain precisely what I found—and still find—so attractive about the book. I cannot, however, fully account for my intuitive response to it then, nor is there an explanation for the fact that the book had reached that little bookstore, in what was then a small, isolated, and rather provincial city, so soon after its publication.

In architecture school we learned how to design by doing it. We would come to class with our ideas drawn up, and we would get feedback from our teachers before making the next step or going back to modify our drawings. Alexander's book revealed to me that designing can be clarified—that there is a logic to it, and that it is not pure magic. Furthermore, the process of designing can be researched. I will discuss Alexander's contribution at

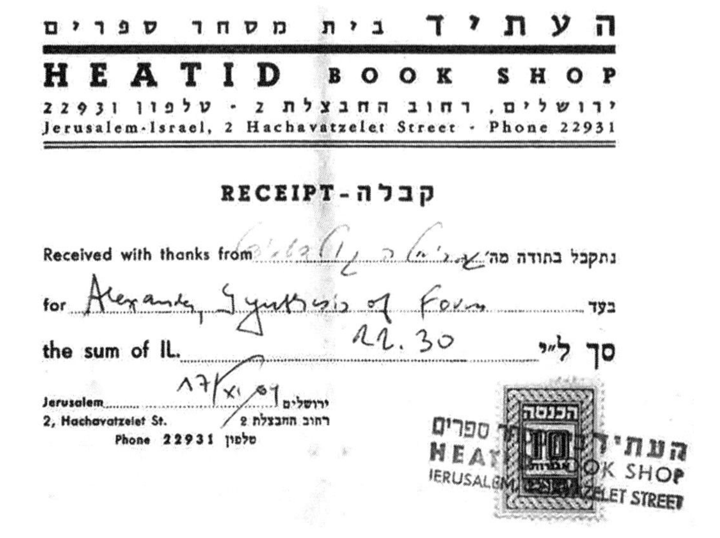

העתיד בית מסחר ספרים

HEATID BOOK SHOP

ירושלים, רחוב החבצלת 2 · טלפון 22931

Jerusalem-Israel, 2 Hachavatzelet Street · Phone 22931

RECEIPT - קבלה

Received with thanks from .... נתקבל בתודה מה'

for Alexander, Synthesis of Form .... בעד

the sum of IL. 22.30 .... סך ל"י

Jerusalem .... ירושלים

2, Hachavatzelet St. רחוב החבצלת 2

Phone 22931 טלפון

Figure 1.1

Sales receipt for Alexander's *Notes on the Synthesis of Form*, dated November 17, 1964.

some length in chapter 2; here I only want to make the point that when I first came across it I had a strong intuition that it was important and that I should make an effort to understand it.

Beginnings, II

A decade later, already an architect with some experience, I began to teach design. I spent many hours in the studio, trying to help students with their design projects. In my first few years of teaching, I taught students at different levels, mostly in first-year and second-year studios. It was impossible not to notice how their rates of learning, their thinking, and their reasoning varied, and how comments that were useful to one student were not necessarily helpful to another. This variation raised a lot of questions about thinking, reasoning, and learning in design, a field in which no amount of declarative knowledge can seriously shape the process of idea generation and in which procedural knowledge is mostly accumulated individually with experience. I knew I wanted to know more about how designers—novice and experienced—think, how they generate ideas, and how they put ideas to the test, combine them into something meaningful. Why are some designers better and more creative than others? What is it that a good or an experienced designer does that a less brilliant or novice designer does not do?

My experience in a design workshop for children in 1985 (see Goldschmidt 1994a) led to a number of insights into individual differences and about reasoning in general. It seemed that the children's reasoning was not entirely different from that of professional designers, although the knowledge they possessed and used was obviously not the same. I realized that I would have to turn to psychology for some of the answers. I approached developmental psychologists, and discovered a fascinating world of research. Little by little, though, I came to realize that *cognitive* psychology was really the field I should look into. That realization opened a vast and wonderful treasure box.

At the same time, I reflected on my own design processes as a practitioner and, before that, as a student. Why was it sometimes difficult to generate good ideas? What was I doing right on some occasions and less so on others? The "front edge" of the design process—the race to secure good design ideas that are capable of "carrying" a design solution—became the topic I wanted to focus on.

Beginnings, III

On a summer's day in 1988, I was sunbathing next to the small swimming pool of the condo in which I was living in the Brighton neighborhood of Boston, Massachusetts. I was on sabbatical at MIT and was working on my research for the National Endowment for the Arts, which was titled "Notation Systems for Processes of Designing." I had the background written up, but an actual notation was yet to be devised. Hoping that the refreshing poolside environment would also refresh my thoughts, I sat there with my papers and stared at the water. The only precedent I could think of for the notation I had in mind was a notation my former student Eduardo Naisberg had developed for the purpose of representing students' design decisions in the course of a short design process (see Naisberg 1986). An example of Naisberg's notation is shown here in figure 1.2.

It was clear that Naisberg's notation, elegant as it was, was not the solution to what I had been trying to achieve, but for a long time my experimentation with various other notations was unsatisfactory. I had been introduced

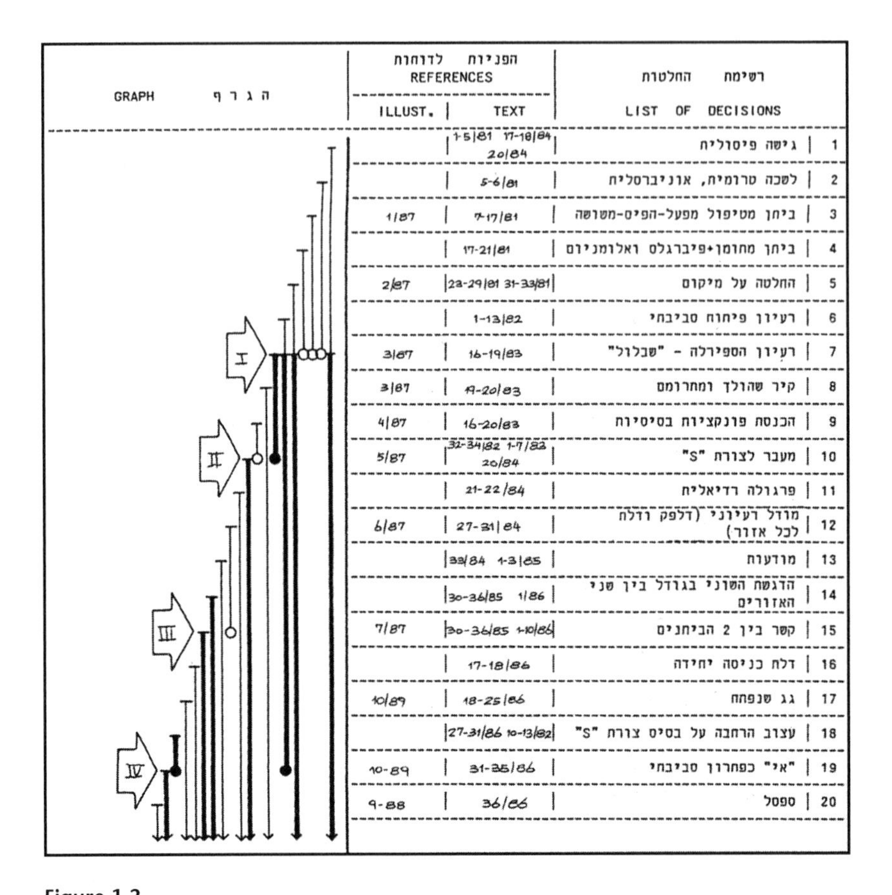

הפניות לדוחות REFERENCES ILLUST.	TEXT	רשימת החלטות LIST OF DECISIONS	
	1-5/81 17-18/84 20/84	גישה פיסולית	1
	5-6/81	לשכה טרומית, אוניברסלית	2
1/87	7-17/81	ביתן מטיפול מפעל-הפים-משושה	3
	17-21/81	ביתן מחומן+פיברגלס ואלומניום	4
2/87	23-29/81 31-33/81	החלטה על מיקום	5
	1-13/82	רעיון פיתוח סביבתי	6
3/87	16-19/83	רעיון הספירלה - "שבלול"	7
3/87	19-20/83	קיר שהולך ומתרומם	8
4/87	16-20/83	הכנסת פונקציות בסיסיות	9
5/87	32-34/82 1-7/83 20/84	מעבר לצורת "S"	10
	21-22/84	פרגולה רדיאלית	11
6/87	27-31/84	מודל רעיוני (דלפק ודלת לכל אזור)	12
	33/84 1-3/85	מודעות	13
	30-36/85 1/86	הדגשת השוני בגודל בין שני האזורים	14
7/87	30-36/85 1-10/86	קשר בין 2 הביתנים	15
	17-18/86	דלת כניסה יחידה	16
10/89	18-25/86	גג שנפתח	17
	27-31/86 10-13/82	עצוב הרחבה על בסיס צורת "S"	18
10-89	31-35/86	"אי" כפתרון סביבתי	19
9-88	36/86	ספסל	20

Figure 1.2

A representation of a student's design decisions in the course of a two-week project. Each decision is listed in the right column (in Hebrew) and represented by a vertical line in chronological order in the left column. Decision lines are trimmed (that is, the end is marked by a circle) when decisions are withdrawn. Bold lines represent major decisions. Large arrows on the left indicate points of transformation in the composition of the main design concept. Source: Naisberg 1986, 132.

to protocol analysis a short while earlier, and I found that method most appropriate and promising for the analysis of design processes at a fine granularity. I had also recently been introduced to cognitive psychology, which fascinated me and which provided a good framework for my interest in designers' thinking processes. Thus, I decided to base a notation on parsed protocols. But none of the coding systems I came up with seemed to generate any meaningful insights. At the poolside in Brighton, I decided to let go of coding, and I experienced an "Aha!" moment. On the grid paper I had brought with me, I scribbled the first hesitant linkograph-like notation. The next day, I tried desperately to reproduce my crude pencil notation on my newly acquired Macintosh SE. The first attempts were rather frustrating, and it was quite a while before I could draw anything coherent on the Mac. For a long time I continued to use large sheets of grid paper, pencils, and erasers. The concept of the linkograph evolved and acquired depth and breadth with use; each time a problem or a deficiency was discovered, the system had to be augmented with new capabilities or re-inspected altogether. To this day, our means of producing linkographs, the digital linkographer, is far from perfect, but we use it anyway.

After an initial report to the National Endowment for the Arts, I presented linkography at a cybernetics conference in Vienna (Goldschmidt 1990). A great opportunity arose in 1994, when I was invited to participate in what would eventually come to be known as the Delft protocol workshop. A number of researchers in the Faculty of Industrial Design Engineering at the Delft University of Technology, led by Nigel Cross, became interested in protocol analysis, which had become popular with researchers studying design thinking. They wanted to explore protocol analysis as a method for design research, and perhaps to plot its potential and its limitations. They invented a design task and went to Xerox's Palo Alto Research Center to experiment with it. The task was given to volunteer experienced designers, some working individually and some in teams, under similar controlled conditions. The sessions were videotaped. Two of the tapes (one representing the work of an individual and one the work of a three-person team), and the protocols that were transcribed from them, were sent to about two dozen design researchers who were experienced in protocol analysis, and they were invited to analyze the protocols by whatever method they wanted to use. When the analyses came in, the authors were invited to present them in a workshop. The fact that they all had worked from the same data made for very focused discussions. The papers that resulted were published in a special issue of *Design Studies* (volume 16, issue 2, 1995, guest edited by Kees Dorst) and in a book titled *Analysing Design Activity* (Cross et al. 1996). At the workshop, I presented a paper in which I used linkography to compare the process of the individual and that of the team (Goldschmidt 1995, 1996). On that occasion I discovered the potential of critical moves as a central feature of linkography.

Since then, progress has centered on details and further features of linkographs, but at the same time the theory behind linkography has been built up and the scope of its applicability has been extended. Somewhat unusually, the application preceded the theory to a large extent. In this specific case, research was very similar to design and was largely a bottom-up process that, by way of confirmation of experimental findings, also went back to theory in a top-down manner. That is, first there was the linkograph; its potential had to be discovered little by little. Tying it in with theory happened later. Of course, the initial reason for developing the "tool" had to do with theory, but this theory was largely implicit at first. I would claim that this hand-in-hand development of the "product" and its rationale was a typical design process. Therefore, it may be far from a chance occurrence that linkography was proposed by someone with a design background.

Chapter 2 of this book outlines the history of design thinking research in the last half-century, with an emphasis on the contribution of Christopher Alexander. Alexander published the most original, comprehensive, and well-thought-out work on design as a rational process wherein a problem is decomposed into subsets. The designer's task is to remove any misfits among responses to the subsets. The "good fit" that is to be achieved is a very important concept that has implications for linkography. Chapter 2 also presents and discusses protocol analysis as the major methodology used in research on design thinking.

Chapter 3 focuses on what is taken to be the goal of the search that occurs at the "front edge" of the design process: a design synthesis. The synthesis is an idea, a concept, or a selection of ideas or concepts that can be used to support a comprehensive, coherent design solution—something that is possible only if the design acts that implement such ideas are in congruence with one another, or (to use Alexander's term) if they display "good fit" among themselves. Generating, inspecting, and adjusting ideas is a process that evolves over a large number of small steps that I call *design moves*. From there it is a short step to a notion of a network of moves. The next step is the recognition of links among these moves as the manner in which a good fit is achieved. The notion of two modes of thinking, divergent and convergent, is also introduced in this chapter.

Chapter 4 describes the features and the notational conventions of the linkograph. It dwells on different kinds of moves and explains what aspects of the design process can be observed and measured in a linkograph. In addition to what may be referred to as the standard notation, a variant notation that has been proposed to replace or extend the standard linkograph is introduced.

Chapter 5 focuses on critical moves, arguably the most significant element in a linkograph. Critical moves are moves that are particularly rich in links. The chapter explains why this makes them important. The bulk of the chapter presents various studies in which critical moves are the key to investigations of specific topics related to design thinking.

Chapter 6 is devoted to design creativity—more specifically, to the creative process in design. Linkography is particularly well suited to the study of this important aspect of the design process. Here I return to divergent and convergent thinking and show how they are manifested in linkographs. Again, a number of cases are used to illustrate the points made.

Chapter 7 introduces thirteen linkographic studies conducted by other researchers who brought fresh insights to their investigations and reported interesting findings that extend the utility of linkography in many ways. These studies, which are quite varied, were selected in order to demonstrate the potential of linkography as a research tool in design thinking and beyond.

The book concludes with a short epilogue and an appendix that lists the main studies on which the cases discussed in the text are based.

2 Design Thinking Research

The Introduction of Design Methods

After World War II, many design disciplines throughout the industrialized world—especially architecture—experienced considerable transitions. The widespread destruction in Europe required unprecedented planning, design, and construction efforts. In North America the rapid growth of suburbs required novel approaches to design and planning. Practitioners everywhere felt unprepared for the challenges of designing large neighborhoods, entire new towns, and expansive road systems. Urban renewal projects had to respond to new welfare-state sensitivities and higher expectations in terms of building standards and performance requirements. A vast increase in higher education demanded a re-conceptualization of university and college campuses. Elementary and secondary education also required modernized facilities to suit new educational paradigms and values in largely transformed societies. Shopping malls destabilized traditional urban commercial patterns and changed the nature of towns. Accelerated technological development, partially as a result of the war, contributed to a shift from heavy industry to high-tech industry. The advent of the computer and the rapid development of computation and communication were, of course, the peaks of this revolution. Technological education followed suit, and new design disciplines were created, among them computer hardware and software engineering. Other disciplines underwent serious developmental transformations. Designers in all fields faced much greater uncertainty than they had in the past, and had to cope with many unknowns and with new needs for flexibility and change. The war effort had fostered collaborative work in which designers and scientists from different fields had joined forces to achieve specific goals. This experience created a favorable environment for interdisciplinary work, for which appropriate frameworks had to be invented (Broadbent 1973; Heims 1991). Traditional design education had not prepared designers sufficiently for the scope and nature of the new challenges, and they felt that the tools of their various trades fell short of what was required.

The tools of the trade(s) came under close scrutiny by designers and design researchers, who thought that traditional design methods had failed them and had produced unsatisfactory results. Architects experienced a particularly acute crisis, perhaps because they were in a position to evaluate and be unhappy with much that was built immediately after the war and through the 1950s in Europe and elsewhere. Direct and indirect negative feedback from users—for instance, vandalism in new housing projects—left little room for misunderstanding: people's needs were not being addressed adequately, and designers felt a pressing obligation to do something about it. Therefore, it is not surprising that architects were in the forefront and in the majority among the design researchers who sought to revolutionize the practice of designing.

The Design Methods Movement

In the early 1960s the design research community was ready to act on its members' wish to modify the practice of design. Much of the research was carried out in Britain, and it was there that an interest in what came to be called "design methods" was nurtured. In 1963 the first conference on design methods was convened at London's Imperial College of Science and Technology (Jones and Thornley 1963). It was followed by two more conferences dedicated to design methods in the same decade, one held in 1965 at the Birmingham College of Advanced Technology (Gregory 1966) and one in 1967 at the Portsmouth School of Architecture (Broadbent and Ward 1969). Proceedings were published after each of these three conferences. Across the ocean, another conference on design methods (the "First International Conference of the Design Methods Group"—as it turned out, there was no second) took place in 1968 at the Massachusetts Institute of Technology. Despite differences among these meetings, and certainly among viewpoints that were expressed in them by attendees from a wide range of disciplines, today we notice the commonalties more than the variances. Taken together, the people who were active in these initiatives and similar ones, and the work they accomplished, are now often referred to as the Design Methods movement, and that appellation is adopted here.

Members of the Design Methods movement shared the conviction that the process of designing, which was traditionally seen as being based largely on conventions, experience, and intuition (possibly "educated intuition"), should be thoroughly modified or altogether replaced by a more advanced process. Design, it was believed, should aspire to become a science, and designing should be based on systematic, scientific design methods that would draw on research and would be teachable and learnable. Herbert Simon presented a solidified view of a "science of design" in one of his 1968 Karl Taylor Compton Lectures at MIT (the text is reprinted in Simon 1982). By and large, designing was seen as problem solving, the structure of which was taken to be similar in all design disciplines. Accordingly, contributors to the conferences on design methods included, in addition to architects, representatives of other design disciplines, most of them engineers. An interest in systematic problem solving was common to all the participants, and hence there were attempts to adapt procedures that had been developed in systems analysis, in operational research, and in other fields to the solving of design problems. The then-new field of cybernetics was invoked because of its focus on the behavior of systems (Heims 1991). In a tentative science of design, designing was seen as a logical process, one controlled by rules that could be explicated and prescribed.

Many a proposed method took the form of a prescriptive model comprising operational design steps (or stages), each to be executed before the designer was supposed to move to the next step. Iterations were included to allow repetition of former steps with new information or insights resulting from feedback emanating from outcomes of earlier steps. In this view there was no difference between the design process and a design method; the method was the process. Most of the models yielded flow charts of the type shown here in figure 2.1. In some design domains—especially mechanical engineering—such models are still in use today (see, e.g., Hubka and Eder 1982, 1996; Pahl and Beitz 1984/1996; Pugh 1991; Roozenberg and Eekels 1995; Ullman 1992; Heath 1984).

Despite variations and some disagreement concerning proposed and hypothetical methods and systems, one basic model of the design process gained consensual acceptance by the entire Design Methods community.

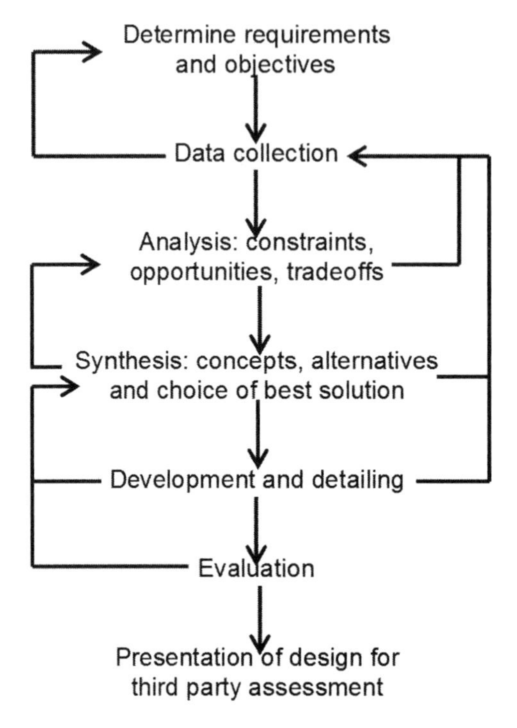

Figure 2.1
Typical flow chart of a design process or method.

According to this highly simplified model, "systematic design is a three-stage process, demanding analysis, synthesis and evaluation" (Page 1963, 205) Many of the prescriptive proposals were elaborations of the Analysis–Synthesis–Evaluation model.

The Analysis–Synthesis–Evaluation (ASE) model of the design process, first proposed by Morris Asimow (1962), quickly gained wide acceptance. R. D. Watts (1966), for example, took the ASE model very much for granted, and his adaptation of a diagram by Mihajlo Mesarović (1964) describing the design process in terms of this model has been reproduced so many times that it has become standard. Figure 2.2 is a slightly modified version of that diagram.

The depiction of the design process as a series of spiraling iterative cycles that move from the abstract to the concrete provided a powerful image, and the spiral metaphor was used by many to describe the design process. The terminology varies, but in all cases the spiral is meant to

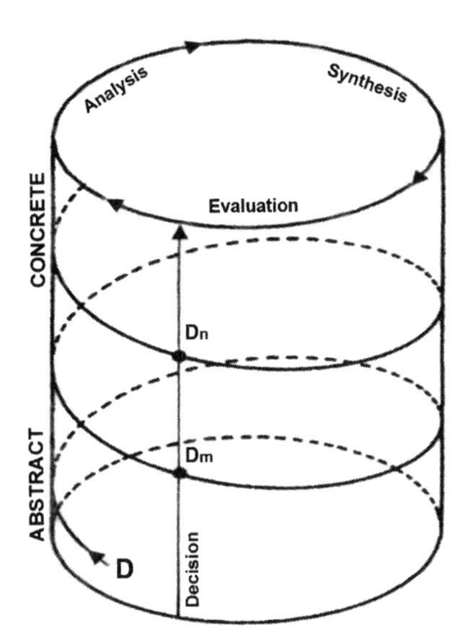

Figure 2.2
Spiral model of design process (after Watts 1966; based on Mesarović 1964).

convey the movement from a wide (abstract) problem space to a specific (concrete) solution selected for its good fit with the requirements of the task. This is achieved through the iterative use of analysis, synthesis, and evaluation as prescribed by the particular design method used (see, e.g., Zeisel 1981).

The ASE model is based on a paradigm of problem solving as information processing, a paradigm that underlay much of the period's scientific thinking and contributed to the founding of cognitive science and artificial intelligence. John Luckman (1969) defined and commented on the three stages of the model as follows:

(i) Analysis: The collection and classification of all relevant information relating to the design problem on hand.

(ii) Synthesis: The formulation of potential solutions to parts of the problem which are feasible when judged against the information contained in the Analysis stage.

(iii) Evaluation: The attempt to judge by use of some criterion or criteria which of the feasible solutions is the one most satisfactorily answering the problem.

In practice, for all but very small design problems, the whole process of design will consist of many levels, progressing from very general considerations at the start, through to specific details as the project nears completion.

> Thus, a level is synonymous with a sub-problem within the total problem where a set of interconnected decisions must be taken, and at every level to a greater or lesser degree, the stages of Analysis, Synthesis and Evaluation are used. (ibid., 129)

The premise is that designing is a combinatorial problem-solving process in which analysis of a body of available information (which must first be collected) is used to generate candidate solutions to the problem, or to subproblems. Candidate solutions are compared and assessed, and the most appropriate solution is then selected. This process is iterative, and normally the designer goes through several cycles of analysis, synthesis, and evaluation. The model assumes that, although a certain amount of flexibility is built into the process by facilitating feedback from one level to the next, on the whole the goals, constraints, and performance criteria of the design task are defined at the outset, and their transparency makes them accessible and explicable at any point in the process. John Chris Jones (1969) referred to the rational designer (i.e., one who subscribes to the use of rational design methods) as a "glass box," thus endorsing the view that performance criteria are, or should be, transparent.

Generally speaking, the Design Methods movement aspired to do away with any design tradition that was deemed "non-scientific." In sharp contrast with the past, it shied away from seeing design as an art, because art was conceived of as antithetical to science. Even freehand drawing, an age-old means of design exploration and representation, became suspect, as it leans heavily on intuition and craftsmanship and not on the logical application of a systematic method. How, then, was the form of a designed entity to be worked out? The computer was, of course, the great new hope, indeed promise. Computational drafting techniques were just beginning to be contemplated in the early 1960s, but, in line with the scientific paradigm, it was hoped and believed that computing would eventually make it possible to automate large portions of the design process, if not all of it. Replacing freehand drawing with precise machine generated drawings was an early goal of what was to develop into computer-aided design (CAD). "Experiments are being made on working out shapes on a cathode-ray tube presentation," Sydney Gregory (1966, 5) declared. "This kind of shape presentation may be readily converted into a punched tape communication." Such developments were met with great enthusiasm, as they represented a departure from craftsmanship in favor of a more trusted, more "advanced" scientific procedure. The history of CAD and CAAD (computer-aided architectural design) is well documented (see, e.g., Kalay 2004; Mark et al. 2008), as is the history of the Design Methods movement (see, e.g., Bayazit 2004).

Digital drawing was but one way in which computation was believed to be potentially useful in design. Evaluation, and therefore selection of candidate solutions, was another and possibly more important application domain. The information-processing paradigm of problem solving called for the generation of all—or most—plausible solutions (through a built-in process of optimization), and then the selection of the highest-rating solution, or the one with the best fit with the problem requirements. As has already been mentioned, design was seen as a typical problem-solving situation. According to Gordon Best (1969, 147), "designing can be usefully interpreted as a variety-reducing process." Early versions of Space Allocation or Adjacency Programs, in which criteria for adjacency of spaces (rooms) within a building were fed into a computer and assisted in creating layout diagrams that established desired adjacencies among spaces in a plan, were introduced. The most influential attempt to devise a complete system for the analysis of design problems and the synthesis of solutions was proposed by Christopher Alexander. This work anticipated the use of computational tools to assist in breaking problems into manageable subsets, in which misfits among candidate solution forms and the problem context could be sorted out. Alexander summarized that work in 1964 in *Notes on the Synthesis of Form*. That widely acclaimed book has affected design thinking profoundly for many years, and is probably the most original and significant contribution to the literature on design methods, even though Alexander later dissociated himself from the Design Methods movement.

Alexander's *Notes on the Synthesis of Form*

The introduction to *Notes on the Synthesis of Form* is titled "The Need for Rationality." In its first paragraph, Alexander states that the book is about "the process of design; the process of inventing physical things that display new physical order, organization, form, in response to function" (1964, 1). He described a problematic state of design practice that we recognize as the reality about which the Design Methods movement complained:

> Today functional problems are becoming less simple all the time. But designers rarely confess their inability to solve them. Instead, when a designer does not understand a problem clearly enough to find the order it really calls for, he falls back on some arbitrarily chosen formal order. The problem, because of its complexity, remains unsolved. (ibid., 1)

Alexander argued that the solving of a complex problem benefits from the application of a suitable method: for instance, by using paper and pencil and applying ordinary arithmetic conventions, one can easily solve, in seconds, an arithmetic problem that is very difficult to solve in one's head. But, Alexander claimed, no methods were available to simplify, and thereby help solve, complex design problems. Alexander believed that, as in arithmetic, in order to simplify a complex design problem one must have a way of decomposing it into smaller design problems, each small enough so that the designer can deal with it rationally and solve it successfully. Alexander's work was devoted to developing and explicating such a method.

For Alexander "the ultimate object of design is form" (ibid., 15), and therefore he was concerned with the generation of appropriate form in response to a given design task. A form is a successful design solution if, and only if, there is a good fit between it and its context, as specified by the givens of the task. When a good fit is not achieved, a successful design solution is not likely to be found. Because of the complexity of design tasks, potential misfits arise frequently. It is the responsibility of the designer to remove them by making the right choices and decisions throughout the design process. In other words, the task of the designer is not to create form that meets certain criteria, but to remove or neutralize all "incongruities, irritants or forces, which cause misfits" (ibid., 24). This is a heavy burden that is normally beyond the cognitive capacity of the designer, unless the scope of the problem is quite small. The question, then, is this: How does one decompose a large and complex problem into local, manageable, problems or subproblems?

Alexander distinguished between relatively simple "unselfconscious" cultures and "selfconscious" cultures, including those of contemporary modern societies, which are more complex. In unselfconscious cultures, Alexander observed, there are no explicit "design theories" and no professional designers. Everything is made according to a tradition that varies little over time and that dictates "right" ways of doing things. Of critical importance is the fact that there exist readily available accepted remedies for specific failures, should any occur. Failures, or misfits, may occur when variants of typical solutions must be produced as a result of minor changes in the context. The unselfconscious culture is seen as "self-adjusting," which implies that fitting forms persist in this culture and maintain a dynamic equilibrium with the system.

In a selfconscious culture, forms are made in a very different way. Design is a specialized activity, and its translation into actual form is indirect (that is, executed by other parties). When failures occur, adjustment is difficult because several parties are involved in reporting and describing the failures and in making decisions on the best course of action to remedy them. Because cultural changes take place rapidly, tradition is a poor guide to the making of well-fitting forms. Faced with this reality, the designer, who cannot lean on tradition, turns to "design theories" and principles that take the shape of prescriptions. Whereas the guidance provided by tradition is natural and well understood, prescriptions are rigid and often rather arbitrary because they are generalized, often quite abstract, and not well related to any local, specific condition.

Alexander recognized that we live in a selfconscious world and that no return to an unselfconscious existence is possible. However, he did not give up the aspiration to arrive at a good form from which misfits have been removed. Accordingly, he saw design as a process of error correction—a process that, he suggested, has a personal flavor and depends on commonsense-based interpretations. The design method that Alexander proposed is aimed at facilitating the process of error reduction and correction by imposing structure on the relationships among requirements and form. Alexander suggested that a comprehensive list of requirements be prepared for each subproblem. Checking requirements against other requirements reveals misfits, and requirements must then be adjusted in order to eliminate them. Needless to say, for complex problems the lists of requirements may be very long, and working through them may be laborious.

Notes on the Synthesis of Form concludes with a "worked example" concerning the reorganization of a village in rural India. The example was also presented in a paper at the first Conference on Design Method, held in London in 1963. Alexander was a major figure in the emerging Design Methods movement at the time, and within a few years of its publication *Notes on the Synthesis of Form* was one of the most influential design-theory treatises of its time. The method that Alexander propagated, however, has not fared equally well. In fact, after several attempts to implement it in practice, Alexander himself conceded that it was too laborious and cumbersome. At the same time, comparisons between design solutions that were generated using the method and schemes developed in a habitual manner without it failed to prove that the former had any visible advantages or superior quality. Alexander was the first to recognize that he was unable to resolve the problem, at least not until sufficiently advanced computational techniques would become available. He abandoned this line of work and turned to an independent exploration of the diagrams he had arrived at, later referred to as *patterns* (Alexander et al. 1977). The patterns had also been of great interest to the design community, and later they would be of interest to computer science. The unrealized hope that the method proposed in *Notes* had ignited continued to inspire researchers who refused to give up on it long after Alexander himself did. Unfortunately, no real successes were recorded.

Alexander later claimed that those who had "even made a cult of following this method" had misunderstood his intentions and should have concentrated on the ability to produce diagrams, or patterns, instead of focusing on the method that leads to their creation. In the preface to the paperback edition of *Notes on the Synthesis of Form*, Alexander wrote: "I have been hailed as one of the leading exponents of these so-called design methods. I am very sorry that this has happened, and want to state, publicly, that I reject the whole idea of design methods as a subject of study." (1971, ii)

Descriptive Design Models

To the Design Methods community, the great appeal of the method that Alexander described in *Notes* was the revelation that a productive theory of architectural design was possible (Grabow 1983). The method was seen as a demonstration of a rule-based, prescriptive system with which the entire design process could be managed. The fact that a mathematical model had been used and the fact that computation was to be employed must have added to the allure of the method. The realization that this elegant, sophisticated method delivered no practical solution to the afflictions of design practice was so disappointing that it took a long time to sink in. In fact, two decades' worth of hard work in the domain of design methods has had a negligible effect on most design domains, with the possible exception of engineering design. In architecture schools, where most of the work was done, students and faculty members alike found the implementation of various experimental methods laborious, time consuming, and unexciting. Worse, they noted that no enhancement could be perceived in the resultant design solutions.

For a long time, researchers believed that imperfections in the methods they had developed were responsible for the lack of success. The response was to try harder, and primarily to look for ways in which computation could be utilized in designing. This effort led to impressive advances in computer-aided design but had no effect on the way designers conceptualized their problems and launched searches for solutions. It was no longer possible to account for the lack of effectiveness of methods solely by pointing to imperfections in them. Clearly, other reasons had to be considered. By the mid 1970s, a small number of researchers had begun to suspect that the customary modes of thinking that designers made use of as they went about their business—practices the Design Methods movement sought to abolish or at least transform—were natural and perhaps innate ways of dealing with tasks such as designing. Designers, it was observed, appear to use steadfast modes of thinking that resist attempts to divert them from their natural course. The prescriptive nature of the various methods, which demanded that the designer follow predetermined steps in a fairly rigid order, seemed to be at odds with what was conceived of as "natural design thinking." If this view is accepted, it follows that instead of fighting natural design thinking one should go along with it, and that it could be supported if the means of support were well fitted to human design thinking.

The notion that intuitive design thinking might not be so objectionable after all required a change of paradigm. Researchers began to talk about "descriptive design models," which they contrasted with prescriptive models or methods. The argument was that good descriptions of actual design behavior were essential to progress in understanding thinking as it occurs in real-life design practice. This was understood by researchers who were interested in developing computational tools that could assist designers in the early, conceptual phases of the design process. Instead of dreaming of a computational tool that would replace the human designer, they began to talk about a partnership between the designer and the computer in which each partner would contribute what he, she, or it was best at (see, e.g., Swerdloff and Kalay 1987). It was thereby acknowledged that human designers did certain things better than computers, by which researchers usually meant that humans were better at generating new ideas. But there was a serious difficulty with the new paradigm: it turned out that, in fact, very little was known about how designers think and, in particular, about how they generate and develop ideas. Without better knowledge and understanding of design thinking, how would it be possible to ensure a good fit between it and any tools, computational or otherwise, that were to be developed?

The Impact of Cognitive Psychology

Researchers became aware of the lack of knowledge about the intricacies of design thinking when the new science of cognition had begun to illuminate various issues related to "mind," including problem solving (which was, and is, often equated with thinking). One of the research themes was domain specificity in thinking—for instance, what is specific to mathematical thinking, musical talent, or chess mastery. A handful of design researchers who believed that understanding design thinking was a prerequisite to the development of design-support tools conducted the first studies of design thinking. Not surprisingly, that work was initiated at Carnegie Mellon University, where Allen Newell, Herbert Simon, and associates had done their pioneering work on information processing and problem solving (see, e.g., Newell and Simon 1972). Young design researchers there were exposed to that work and influenced by it; a case in point is Ömer Akin, whose studies of the design process show the influence of the information processing paradigm (see Akin 1976 and, especially, Akin 1986).

The solidification of cognitive psychology as a separate area of study within psychology paralleled the establishment of cognitive science as a new and multi-disciplinary field. A major force behind these developments was the impact that computation had on researchers of thinking—an impact that led to the Computational Theory of Mind (see, e.g., Putnam 1975; Fodor 1975; Pylyshyn 1986). Essentially, the Computational Theory of Mind saw thinking as information processing that depended largely on genetically inherited neurological and mental structures rather than (as had been thought under the theory of behaviorism, the dominant paradigm in psychology up to that time) on environmental factors (on behaviorism, see Skinner 1974). Several decades earlier, Gestalt psychology had concerned itself with perception, and had taken it to be essential to problem solving. Generic principles of perception had been formulated, and empirical evidence had been used to instantiate them (Wertheimer 1923/1938). That innovative work had been rejected later by the first generation of cognitive psychologists on the ground that it lacked scientific validity. Scientific soundness was to be gained through controlled behavioral experiments with statistically sustained conclusions, which the Gestalt psychologists did not attempt to provide. However, Gestalt psychology did not die away; in later years, researchers who acknowledged its importance adopted its insights and continued to develop them under what is sometimes called "Neo Gestalt" (Robertson 1986). The principles of perception that the Gestalt psychologists set forth and their cognitive psychology successors refined and amplified were especially relevant to design thinking because they were highly connected with visual thinking. Rudolf Arnheim's influential books *Art and Visual Perception* (1954) and *Visual Thinking* (1969) are considered landmarks in research on design thinking and artistic thinking to this day.

A critical event in the history of cognitive science was the Symposium on Information Theory held at MIT in 1956, after which one of the major participants, the psychologist George Miller, remarked "It is the second day of the symposium (11 September 1956) that I take to be the moment of conception for cognitive science." (Miller 2003, 142) In this landmark symposium, linguists, communication scientists, psychologists, and others (computer scientists, philosophers, anthropologists, neuroscientists), many of whom (including Noam Chomsky, Claude Shannon, Allen Newell, Herbert Simon, and Miller) would go on to change the scientific landscape of the twentieth century, shared the theme of "mind as an information processor." The same year, 1956, saw the publication of *A Study of Thinking*, in which Jerome Bruner, Jacqueline Goodnow, and George Austin reported groundbreaking experimental work on the formation of concepts and inductive reasoning. A number of other important events—meetings and publications—also occurred during that year. It is no wonder that Steven Pinker called 1956 an "annus mirabilis."[1] With hindsight, Newell (1980) reflected on the newly founded cognitive science: "By general accord, a revolution happened in the scientific study of man in the mid 1950s, shifting the view to man as an active processor of symbolic information." (ibid., 14) "Symbolic information" was conceived as embodied in representation, external or internal. In 1960, Miller and Bruner founded the Harvard Center for Cognitive Studies. In 1967, Ulrich Neisser published *Cognitive Psychology*, which affirmed the "coming of age" of the cognitive revolution, pertaining equally to psychology and the other disciplines involved. The term "cognitive science" was first used in 1973 (Longuet-Higgins 1987).

The timing of these developments was opportune for a change of paradigm in design research. After it was recognized that design thinking would have to be understood better before it could be constructively supported by design tools and aids, a science of thinking seemed timely and inviting. Cognitive science was multi-disciplinary from its inception, and design researchers felt that it provided a framework that would allow research on design thinking. In view of the influence of Newell and Simon and their colleagues, Carnegie Mellon University was a natural breeding ground for pioneering studies on design thinking. Design thinking researchers realized that they would have to conduct empirical studies based on actual real-life evidence. They also recognized that they would have to work at a micro scale—that is, with very small units of design activity. The methodology they adopted was protocol analysis, to which the last section of this chapter is dedicated. Protocol analysis has been in wide use among design researchers for more than 30 years now, as it fits the need to explore small units of behavior in empirical settings.

In parallel to work based on protocol analysis, design thinking researchers conducted many observational studies that were particularly useful for long-term studies, for which protocol analysis is not well suited. In Britain, which took center stage in the Design Methods enterprise, the transition from "methods" to more cognition-bound research was gradual. An example is the work of Nigel Cross, whose early work (1984) is in the spirit of methods but who later (2006, 2011) accepted the descriptive design model as a research framework. Brian Lawson's *Design Thinking* (1980/2005), one of the early descriptive design research texts in Britain, was based on extensive observations, but Lawson (a psychologist as well as an architect and a design researcher) did not attempt a cognitive probing into design thinking.

Artificial Intelligence in Design

The computation enthusiasts of the Design Methods era were forced to temper their high expectations for the automation of design, but the dream did not evaporate altogether. Artificial Intelligence (AI) was born in parallel to cognitive psychology and cognitive science in the 1950s. Because cognitive science and artificial intelligence had common roots in information processing, we find some of the same names among their founders, including Herbert Simon and Allen Newell. Unlike cognitive psychology, AI looks only at formal reasoning, which, once understood, can be modeled and embedded in artificial systems (computers) and can lend them an "intelligence." The motivation behind AI research was to create problem-solving tools that would take advantage of the computer's huge storage capacity and of the possibility of running combinatorial searches that would allow a computer to "reason" on the basis of formal knowledge and rules that had been fed into the computational system earlier. An example is the chess-playing program Deep Blue, which managed to beat the grandmaster Garry Kasparov in 1997. The first commercial successes came even earlier, in the 1980s, in the form of "expert systems," which stored a large number of knowledge instances that could be matched with current problems in a domain. For example, there were expert systems for medical diagnosis that had at their disposal a huge collection of symptoms and their resolutions—the correct diagnoses. However, expert systems are limited because in a large system combinatorial explosion can easily result in counter-productive results. Robotics is currently one of the most prominent pragmatic topics in AI; another current topic of research and application is way-finding (e.g., GPS navigation systems). The researchers involved are computer scientists who collaborate with experts from other fields, including engineering design and psychology. Natural human intelligence is studied along with artificial intelligence, which attempts to model it. The common tenet is information processing, as was the case when the field was first established. Present-day AI also tries to model human intuition and judgment, which are not based on combinatorial searches; such efforts are particularly relevant to design.

As soon as AI came of age, some design researchers, especially those with strong backgrounds in computer-aided design, subscribed to this branch of research with the hope of advancing the partnership between designers and computational systems. Expert systems gave rise to *case-based reasoning* (see, e.g., Kolodner 1988), which attempted to propose solutions, mainly to architectural problems, based on libraries of precedents, or cases. The indexing system was related to a building's type, its function (e.g., a school), or other formal features, such as a building's form (e.g., a dome) or its expected performance (e.g., in energy consumption) (Coyne et al. 1990; Maher et al. 1995). The representation of knowledge is particularly important in AI in general, and in design-related AI in particular, because of the visual component of design representations. Rapid freehand sketches, which are routinely produced in the process of designing (especially in the early search phase), hardly ever comply with formal rules, and therefore they are difficult to formalize for the purpose of modeling the knowledge embedded in them. Consequently, recognition and interpretation of sketches have received a lot of attention in AI in design—see, for example, Field et al. 2010 or Gross 1994. The strong visual aspect of designing is not the only characteristic that sets it apart. Since design problems are largely ill-structured and ill-defined, it is difficult to define the knowledge that should be represented. Creative designers think analogically, and often their sources are from unexpected domains (Goel and Bhatta 2004). Combinatorial searches are, therefore, not very useful in supporting the creative idea-generation phase of design, and AI in design shifted from combinatorial searches to knowledge-based systems.

Likewise, constraint satisfaction, which had been a strong research direction in early design-related AI, gave way to attempts to optimize performance, which cannot be considered independent of form. Early work in this vein came to be referred to as "performative design" (Kolarevic and Malkawi 2005). A latter-day term used for what is essentially the same concept is "performalism" (Grobman and Neuman 2011). The ability of the computer to juggle and coordinate a large number of independent values by defining priorities and tradeoffs is exploited in such a way that the outcome is a balanced total. One of the prominent results of research along these lines is parametric design—the development of an algorithm that handles a large number of parameters, and the relationships among them, while allowing the parameters to be changed easily. Great flexibility can be achieved by simply tweaking the input values. Parametric design is used in generating form as well as in technical management of design projects, wherein changes in one parameter immediately lead to the updating of values of other, related parameters. An example of a technical application in architectural and construction design is BIM (Building Information Modeling). A BIM system takes care of necessary changes caused by alterations in specific parameters, pertaining to the form or the function of a building or part thereof. For example, if the bay size of the typical floor of an office building changes, the BIM system will update the structural plan, the widths of windows, and other components of the building.

AI has many technical applications, but they are of little interest to us in the context of design thinking at the cognitive level. The importance of AI in design in this respect lies in its ability to handle more data and more relationships among data points than a human designer can. Therefore, aside from solving routine problems and consequently saving a lot of time and other resources, AI techniques can productively generate forms and combinations of forms that may be beyond the capabilities of human designers. In design, as in other domains, AI researchers who tried to emulate human thinking based their work on imitative simulations. Another approach is constructive simulation (see, for example, Taura and Nagai 2013). Researchers who employ that approach base their work primarily on linguistic analyses and employ semantic networks. However, the system is still controlled by a human designer, who retains the power to accept or reject the offerings of the intelligent computer.

The Impact of Postmodernism

Another influence on the direction of research in design that is not often acknowledged came from a different direction. In the 1970s, postmodernism had a huge effect not only on architectural design per se (that is, buildings and their appearance) but also on a new-found interest in the process of designing (interest in the process of creation was, of course, not unique to architecture and other design fields; it was also evident in literature, in theater, in filmmaking, and in other fields). All of a sudden, early design study sketches captured the imagination of researchers and practitioners alike. Architectural magazines and books began to publish them, and galleries began to exhibit sketches by prominent architects and other designers, and also some by architects and designers who were not as well known. A case in point is Process in Architecture: A Documentation of Six Examples, an exhibition held in MIT's Hayden Gallery in 1979. In the catalog's foreword, Lawrence Anderson wrote:

> The current surge of critical admiration for architectural drawing even includes a school of thought which argues that an architect's drawings are more important indicators of creative intentions than are his buildings. . . . Here, we embrace the

notion that the profession of architecture is one of problem-solving. . . . We hope that this exhibition will shed some light on this process of design. . . . (Anderson 1979, 4–5)

The publication of James Stirling's sketches for the three German museums he designed in the 1970s (one for Düsseldorf, one for Cologne, and one for Stuttgart; only the latter was built) was quite revolutionary. Articles in *The Architectural Review* in 1976 and in *Lotus International* and *Architectural Design* in 1977 included a large number of small freehand sketches,[2] the likes of which were not usually seen on the pages of contemporary publications. Before the mid 1970s it was rare indeed to find any sketches at all in architectural publications. Michael Wilford, who was Stirling's partner at that time, explained why earlier sketches by Stirling had not been published: "Prior to the German museum projects, the early exploratory material was considered of little value and discarded once the final design had been established. More recent material is stored. . . ."[3] Two of the first studies of sketches, published by Daniel Herbert (1988, 1993), paid attention primarily to their graphic properties. In later studies (Do and Gross 1995; Goldschmidt 1991, 1994b; Suwa and Tversky 1997), sketching was investigated from a cognitive point of view in an attempt to explicate its contributions to design thinking and problem solving.

Awareness of and attention to process in practice and in general cultural contexts, especially insofar as the creative process is concerned, coincided with the research agenda of cognitive science and cognitive psychology. This set the stage for the emergence of design thinking research, which was a new field of study but also the continuation of the Design Methods movement. It takes a confluence of social, cultural, scientific, and technological developments to bring about profound paradigmatic changes in disciplines. For design research, this was the right time to move to the study of design thinking.

Protocol Analysis

According to Anders Ericsson, "protocol analysis is a rigorous methodology for eliciting verbal reports of thought sequences as a valid source of data on thinking."[4] As we have no direct access to activities of the mind, and only limited access to brain activities that can inform us of what the mind is doing, the study of thought requires a mediating agent that can convey with fidelity elements of thought and mental manipulations. Late in the nineteenth century, behaviorist psychologists who were interested mainly in consciousness (among them John B. Watson) began to collect introspective self-reports and to analyze them in an attempt to establish what the subjects had been thinking about. But introspection was soon rejected because it was claimed that people cannot accurately remember their thoughts after the fact (at least for activities lasting longer than a few seconds). To overcome this problem, the "think-aloud" method was pioneered: a subject concentrating on a well-defined task (such as solving an arithmetic problem) was asked to concurrently verbalize his or her thoughts. Real-time reports come much closer to representing thought processes than introspective reports do. Obviously, even a real-time report is not a complete representation of someone's thinking, as some of the thoughts never cross the verbalization threshold. The Gestalt psychologist Karl Duncker (1926, 1945) was an early promoter of think-aloud studies, in which verbalizations are documented in protocols and the protocols are then analyzed.

Ill-defined and ill-structured problems are more complex than well-defined and well-structured ones, and thought patterns may vary significantly among subjects. Subjects may begin by clarifying and defining a vague problem, and in all likelihood their thought processes are not reproducible in other, dissimilar cases. Ericsson and Simon (1984/1993) do not recommend the use of protocol analysis for ill-defined problems. It should be emphasized that design problems are often considered ill-defined, ill-structured, or even wicked (Buchanan 1992; Rittel and Weber 1973). Protocol analysis has, all the same, become a very popular research methodology in design—it is used to study typical (if singular) situations, and to compare processes without attempting to come up with overarching generalizations. In this respect, many protocol analysis studies of design behavior resemble the early work on thinking by Gestalt psychologists, which was essentially exploratory in nature. To distinguish protocol analysis based on real-time recordings from other varieties of protocol analysis (such as retrospective protocol analysis, discussed below), it is sometimes called "concurrent protocol analysis."

A few decades after the dispersion of the Gestalt group in Germany, the issue of accessing mental processes was again in vogue because of the interest in high-level cognitive processes spurred by the cognitive revolution of the 1960s. Capturing think-aloud verbalizations and other real-time verbalizations became much easier with the advent of the tape recorder in 1945. Not long thereafter, it became possible to transcribe recordings directly to a computer, which could then process them in various ways. In one well-known early study of thinking based on the analysis of think-aloud protocols, Adriann de Groot (1965/1978) reconstructed the "search trees" of novice and expert chess players. Subsequent studies centered on domain-specific problem solving in various disciplines, including design. The first study of such problem solving in design was done by Charles Eastman (1970). Ömer Akin, Eastman's colleague at Carnegie Mellon University, published the first study based on think-aloud recordings that was specific to architectural design (Akin 1978). As has been mentioned, Carnegie Mellon was a major center of cognition-related research in that period, and it was there that the first decisive volume on protocol analysis was written (Ericsson and Simon 1984/1993). The revised edition, published in 1993, is the most authoritative text on protocol analysis yet to have been published. Another comprehensive monograph on the topic was published by van Someren et al. in 1994.

The validity of verbalizations by individuals who are asked to "think out loud" (not a habitual behavior) was questioned. The claim was that the need to verbalize one's thoughts must affect the thinking processes. However, Ericsson and Simon (1984/1993) found that after a little training subjects' sequences of thoughts were not altered when they thought aloud. The training is meant to ensure that subjects do not focus on describing or explaining their thoughts, which requires extra (cognitive) attention to such descriptions or explanations. Instead, subjects are asked to simply give voice to their natural thoughts. The line between the two is not sharp. When subjects tend to be too self-conscious, they may engage in describing, which may well affect their design behavior (Davies 1995). Some subjects take somewhat longer to complete a task when thinking out loud, but if duration is of no relevance this is inconsequential. In rare cases participants in think-aloud experiments report that they are not comfortable verbalizing their thoughts and that having to do so affects their thinking. There are also individual differences in verbalization skills among participants, and these differences have to be taken into account in the choice of participants (van Someren et al. 1994).

Although verbal data cannot be a complete representation of thinking, they are now recognized as "second best" in that they allow access to information that cannot be obtained in any other way. Therefore, protocol analysis has become a powerful, frequently used research methodology in cognitive psychology, in cognitive science, and in other disciplines.

In design, studies of problem solving are not limited to individuals. Members of a small team often work together to produce and develop design ideas. In teamwork the concern regarding the validity of verbalizations is irrelevant, as a team's members naturally communicate verbally with one another as they work together and therefore a recording of the conversation is an authentic verbal output of real-time thinking (to the extent that talking reflects thinking). In many recent studies of design behavior and thinking, conversations of members of two-person, three-person, four-person, or five-person teams were recorded to produce analyzable protocols. Despite differences, the verbal records of individuals and teams are comparable and can be analyzed in the same way. In fact, the individual's reasoning can be compared to that of a team—"the individual designer is a unitary system that resembles a team" (Goldschmidt 1995, 209). A specific issue that arises in the case of design (and sometimes in other endeavors too) is that some of the communication, or the thinking in the case of individuals, is not verbal but graphic. Designers are in the habit of sketching as they work on design problems or as they discuss them. Informal sketches that do not use a fixed set of (formal) symbols can convey design ideas at all levels of articulation, and when designers engage in sketching they do not always accompany their sketches with words. This may make it difficult to analyze the verbal data, as they may contain "gaps" in which sketches substitute for words—especially if the researcher was not present during the design session. For this reason, video recordings rather than voice recordings are often used, as they capture sketching (as well as gestures and other non-verbal behaviors). To date there is no effective method for analyzing sketches that accompany verbal reports, but they are used to clarify verbalizations that are not sufficiently comprehensible otherwise.

Parsing protocols

Protocols are transcripts of recorded verbalizations by subjects engaged in problem solving or in some other activity the thought processes of which one wishes to capture. A complete and unedited transcript provides raw data for a study. To be analyzed, a protocol is parsed into utterances (small segments of speech). What these segments are depends on the nature of the study and the length of the protocol. Sometimes a segment is time-based—for example, three minutes of recorded speech. Often every sentence (where a sentence is understood to end with a full stop) consists of one segment. When a protocol records teamwork, the unit may be based on turn taking in speech: one member's verbalization ends when another member takes over. This may result in uneven units, since some verbalizations may be much longer than others.

Sometimes the unit of analysis departs from the direct utterances, although it is based on them. For example, a unit could be an idea, or a decision. In this case the researcher interprets the protocol and infers ideas or concepts from it. Then the consecutive ideas that are raised in the session become the units of analysis. This is particularly relevant for teamwork and for studies that center on idea generation. For studies that pertain to decision making, decisions may be inferred from the protocol. In design thinking research the most common unit of analysis is the *design move*, a small unit of verbalization lasting a few seconds.

Coding

Once a protocol has been parsed into its constituent or inferred units of analysis, protocol analysis calls for the establishment of a scheme of categories according to which the segments are to be encoded. A scheme of categories based on the theoretical model that drives the study and its specific goals is created. Categories must be well related to the particulars of the case in question (Ericsson and Simon 1984/1993). The number of categories is important, mainly because it is hard to reach meaningful conclusions with too many categories (and subcategories) but also because a large number of categories makes coding difficult and unreliable. A good way to reach the right balance between fidelity and the number of categories is to start with a larger set of categories and then use trial and error to reduce their number. Categories with very few encoded units may be discarded or merged with related categories. Ericsson and Simon (1993) report a study that benefited from a reduction of the number of categories from 30 to 15. This is an important point that many researchers overlook, which leads to fragmented results that fail to deliver a coherent picture, as there are too many categories.

The nature of categories is most important, and, like the nature of the unit of analysis (move, idea, time-based unit, etc.), it depends on the goals of the study. In design, some general and seemingly generic schemes have been suggested, among them clarifying the task, searching for concepts, and fixing the concept (Günther et al. 1996). Such schemes have also been called "process oriented." The best-known and best-developed attempt to offer a generic categorization scheme that is claimed to be valid across design domains and design tasks was proposed by John Gero (see, e.g., Gero and Kannengiesser 2011; Purcell et al. 1996). The scheme consists of three main categories: function, behavior, and structure. Together these categories are referred to as the *FBS ontology* (see chapter 7). The categories are defined as follows (Gero and Kannengiesser 2011, 370):

The *Function* (F) of an artifact is its teleology ("what the artifact is for").

The *Behavior* (B) of an artifact is the attributes that can be derived from its structure ("what the artifact does").

The *Structure* (S) of an artifact is its components and their relationships ("what the artifact consists of").

The aspired-to generic scheme of categories is meant to fill the hitherto unmet need to standardize research methods in design and to make it easier to compare and relate results obtained by different researchers across cases. However, most researchers prefer categories tailored to their goals and to the specific cases they investigate, and such categories yield context-oriented schemes. In line with Ericsson and Simon's (1984/1993) recommendations, it is also possible to analyze the same protocol using multiple schemes of categories. For example, Günther et al. (1996) devised a second scheme for a task of designing a bicycle rack to hold a backpack. Whereas the first scheme of clarifying the task, searching for concepts, and fixing the concept was rather abstract, the second scheme was content oriented and task specific. The categories of the second scheme were the bicycle, the backpack, the position of the rack, joining the pack to the rack, joining the rack to the bicycle, and the rack's structure. Obviously the two schemes are very different. They are devised for different purposes, and, since they are orthogonal to one other, no comparison is possible.

Reliability is essential in coding, especially when the number of categories is large. It is, therefore, important to employ more than one coder and to check inter-coder reliability. In addition, it may be necessary to establish a mechanism for "arbitration" in cases of disagreement. Unfortunately, many of the published protocol analysis studies in design report coding by a single coder, and therefore the reliability of the results is not guaranteed.

Analysis

In analyzing parsed and coded protocols it is possible to cut through the data in several ways, but one always obtains frequency patterns of the various types of verbalization that were recorded. Progression in time and particular sequences of categories may be deduced. Fixation, major concepts and patterns of collaboration, and role playing in teams are some of the issues that may be elucidated by analyzing protocols. Joachim Günther et al. (1996), for example, compared the processes of the individual designer and the team in the Delft protocols (which were produced for the Delft protocol workshop) on the basis of the proportion of time devoted to each activity category. They also compared the three designers in the team in terms of their contribution to the discussion per category of activity. They emphasized that what they could not do in this research was answer "why" questions, because the analysis of the data does not explain the observed design behavior.

Masaki Suwa and his associates (Suwa and Tversky 1997; Suwa et al. 1998) conducted a number of very detailed protocol studies that focused on designers' cognitive processes, especially in relation to acts of sketching. The units of analysis were design moves. In Suwa et al. 1998 the categories were types of actions; the four main categories described physical, perceptual, functional, and conceptual actions (which correspond to cognitive levels of information processing). Physical and conceptual actions were further subdivided into three subcategories each. Additional breakdowns of the categories yielded a detailed coding scheme that was subjected to macroanalysis and microanalysis. The latter was aimed at devising a taxonomy of primitives that may shed light on designers' cognitive actions. According to the authors, these studies illustrated that the primitives of cognitive design actions can be established (microanalysis) and that sketches serve as an extended external memory that the designer can use later in the design process.

Suwa et al. (ibid.) pointed out some of the predicaments they encountered, including the fact that it is difficult to encode segments (moves) that seem ambiguous and the fact that discontinuities in speech, especially while sketching, may lead to multiple interpretations of concurrent cognitive actions (that is, to uncertainty about sketching acts). The methodology used in both studies by Suwa and associates was retrospective protocol analysis. The designer was videotaped, was later shown the video recording, and was asked to comment on his or her intentions and actions.

Limitations

Alongside obvious advantages, protocol analysis has weaknesses that must be recognized:

Incomplete reflection of thinking processes Although think-aloud records come closer to reflecting actual thinking processes than introspective reports or observations, which are much more prone to interpretation (or misinterpretation) by researchers, we cannot expect concurrent verbalizations to be a perfect reflection of thinking, especially in team sessions but also in individual episodes. I adopt a Vygotskian view on the relationship between thought and speech. Lev Vygotsky (1986) distinguished between two planes of speech: inner and external. Inner speech is not a prelinguistic form of reasoning but the semantic aspect of speech, abbreviated speech, in that it centers on predication and tends to omit the subject of a sentence and words connected to it. Inner speech is a function in itself, not an aspect of external speech; inner and external speech together form a *unity* of speech. Thinking aloud can be seen as close to inner speech, whereas a conversation is certainly a sample of external speech. Both inner and external speech are, however, more than representations of thought. In Vygotsky's words: "Thought is not merely expressed in words; it comes into existence through them." (ibid., 218)

Possible interference with normal thinking patterns This is hard to demonstrate. Ericsson and Simon (1984/1993) reported no interference in the normal thought processes of individuals who were asked to think aloud after a short training session. However, some studies claim that some interference may occur, at least in some subjects.

Protocol analysis is labor intensive Parsing and encoding protocols is labor intensive, even when researchers are experienced. If the unit of analysis is about 7 seconds long, as was found in several studies, a one-hour protocol should include more than 500 units (segments; moves). Therefore, long design episodes are difficult to analyze at the cognitive level. However, it is possible to use larger or extracted units, which permits analysis of longer sessions. Of course, there are also situations (for example, dispersed teams and work in intervals in multiple locations) that make it impractical to attempt proper audio or video recording (in both of the aforementioned cases, a limited number of protocols are usually collected for any single study, and for that reason findings are hard to generalize).

Delimiting the analysis unit When people think aloud without explaining their thoughts, their verbalizations are often incomplete, repetitive, or incoherent. This can make it difficult to decide what constitutes a unit of analysis and difficult to interpret it. Because there are no standard rules of parsing, it is hard to compare studies. In addition, it is hard to decide what should be left out of a protocol—for example, verbalizations such as "oh" and "yeah," other single words, incoherent statements, and seemingly unrelated or loosely related verbalizations.

Inter-coder reliability As was mentioned earlier, reaching acceptable values of inter-coder reliability in protocol studies is no trivial matter. In better cases it is time consuming for coders to engage in deliberations meant to achieve agreement on codes; in worse cases the analysis is based on encodings by a single coder. This point is closely connected to the next one.

Ambiguity in verbalization One reason it is hard to achieve sufficient agreement among coders is that often verbalizations pertain to a number of topics in an intertwined manner and it is hard to decide how to categorize them. In addition, as was pointed out earlier, coders encounter verbalizations that are difficult to make sense of, and they have to rely on their own interpretations (which are sometimes quite speculative); this leads to differences among codings and even among the codes used by the same coder in different instances.

These limitations are not as severe as they may sound. If one accepts the fact that protocol analysis has limitations, and uses it only for what it is useful for, then the most important thing to do is maintain inter-analysis and intra-analysis consistency. This ensures that, even though the studies are not without shortcomings and limitations, they can arrive at reliable findings and solid conclusions.

Related Research Methods

Although I have suggested that concurrent protocol analysis is the best methodology available today for the study of design thinking at the cognitive level, a number of other methodologies that are in use in design thinking research should be acknowledged.

Retrospective protocol analysis In retrospective protocol analysis, subjects are asked to solve a problem as they normally would but are not necessarily asked to think aloud. Later (but as close as possible to the session in question) the video recording is shown to the subject, who is asked to comment on his or her thinking. Usually most of the comments refer to important events in the process, so researchers are able to track the important decisions (including those that were later abandoned). Often a researcher gets good documentation of the final solution and how it was achieved, but this method is less valid if one is interested in the moment-to-moment evolution of the subject's thinking. A version of retrospective protocol analysis that emphasizes explicit explanations of design acts that designers are required to provide in the viewing session was used by Taura and Nagai (2013), who called their method "extended protocol analysis." Their aim was to use semantic network techniques to calculate the expansion of the designer's "thought space." Sometimes retrospective protocol analysis is chosen because it is less labor intensive and can therefore be used to analyze somewhat longer sessions. Per Galle and László Kovács (1996) devised "replication protocol analysis," a method for the analysis of real-world design events. Their deliberate purpose was to capture not what transpired on the fly, but the "post hoc rationalization" of the design. Their method called for the reconstruction of a design process, from the given program to the final solution, by a trained designer who was not involved in the case. The result of such a reconstruction is a series of arguments that lead from the requirements to the solution. This may be repeated with more "replicators" to provide the most credible course of reasoning. Galle and Kovács applied replication protocol analysis to an entry in an architectural competition and claimed that the analysis yielded many insights into design reasoning. They concluded that the method is particularly handy for lengthy processes wherein it is impractical to apply protocol analysis. I accept the claims but continue to argue that the major problem of fidelity to real thought processes, if those are the object of inquiry, is not solved in retrospective protocol analysis of any kind.

Interviews Another method that yields deliberate post hoc information about design processes and design reasoning is interviewing designers (see, e.g., Lawson 1994). It is, of course, useful to learn how designers regard their own processes, but the fidelity problem looms heavily in the case of interviews: even the most conscientious of designers is likely to tell a story of how he or she wished to have designed. Interviews are useful in biographical accounts. The short and focused interviews that are sometimes conducted right after a think-aloud exercise, known as "debriefings," are useful for elucidating protocol passages that otherwise would be unclear.

Observation Where the interpretation of behavior is the major goal of a study, observing problem solvers at work is an appropriate method. In design research, observation is a useful method—particularly in real-life situations such as design teams in industry and when the goal is to describe meta-behavior, sequences of activities, or allocation of roles. In a well-known study in this category, Eckart Frankenberger and Petra Badke-Schaub (1998) observed an engineering team as it performed a design task.

Gestures Studying gestures is a recent addition to research methods in design. A major motivation is that gestures accompany and augment verbalizations in design, and sometimes substitute for speech or sketching. If we could interpret them accurately, we might gain access to thinking that is not externalized, or to inner speech. Gestures may be most relevant to the study of social aspects of team interactions in design sessions, where body-language may turn out to be quite revealing. Willemien Visser and Mary Lou Maher (2011, 219) predicted that a good understanding of the role of gestures in design thinking would affect "how we support and augment designers using computational systems."

Eye tracking Eye tracking, a long-established research methodology in psychology, is used mainly to study attention and perception. One motivation for employing it is a desire to study the psychology and pedagogy of reading and practical issues of human factors—for example, how to optimize the design of an airplane's dashboard. There are also many commercial implications, from developing guidelines for the arrangement of products on the shelf in the supermarket to designing Web pages. The latter has become a proliferous research topic in Web usability (Jacob and Karn 2003). Other than in Web usability, however, eye tracking is not a commonly used methodology in design research.

The Suitability of Protocol Analysis

Far more than any other methodology, concurrent protocol analysis has established itself as a major research methodology in design thinking. If carried out meticulously, protocol analysis is reliable and useful. It entails subjects verbalizing their thoughts with no attempt to provide superfluous explanations, and parsing and coding "by the book" (optimally by three parsers and three coders, with high inter-coder agreement). Under these conditions we gain high-fidelity access to thought processes and sequences that are not otherwise accessible. The methodology is especially suited for investigating the solving of well-defined problems. In the case of ill-defined problems, such as design tasks, it is not as easy to arrive at generalizable results. All the same, protocol analysis has been recognized as sufficiently promising to warrant a special workshop (see chapter 1). The workshop was convened in the Faculty of Industrial Design Engineering at the Delft University of Technology in 1994 (see appendix), and the papers presented were turned into an influential book (Cross et al. 1996).

Among the most important lessons learned from this concentrated effort was that protocol analysis is not well suited for long episodes. The Delft task lasted two hours (already quite long), but most design tasks take much longer, and it is not practical to attempt to record think-aloud sessions or even team sessions in the whole course of a design task. Therefore, it must be clearly understood that protocol analysis as a research methodology is limited to short stretches of time—not more than a few hours (unless one uses sizable segments or derived entities such as ideas or decisions as the units of analysis). Luckily, no long stretches are required for the study of cognitive processes, and a sufficient number of data points can be obtained in a relatively short time since the unit of analysis is small. Therefore, if the goal is to explore design thinking from the cognitive viewpoint, protocol analysis is a suitable methodology.

3 Design Synthesis

The Front End of the Design Process

From the cognitive perspective, the design phase of the greatest interest is the early, preliminary phase—the "front edge." Because most design problems are ill-structured and ill-defined (Simon 1973), the early phase of designing is when designers have to come to terms with the task—that is, interpret it, frame it, and reframe it (Schön 1984) until it is sufficiently coherent to generate solution ideas. The process of clarification and framing and the process of searching for a solution are not sequential; rather, they occur in parallel (Dorst and Cross 2001). We talk about a search for a solution that takes place within a space: problem solving in general has been described as occurring within a problem space and a solution space (e.g., Reitman 1964; Simon 1973), with a difference between well-structured and ill-structured problems (Goel 1995). Dorst and Cross (2001) proposed, for design, the co-evolution of problems and solutions in what may be seen as a unified problem/solution space. Specific to design, the term "design space" has been adapted from artificial intelligence (see, e.g., Woodbury and Burrow 2006), and Coyne et al. (1990) have claimed that "spaces of designs" can be defined by abduction. In its current interpretation it is less formal and akin to what Schön (1983) called a "design world." A design world or space encompasses, among other things, prevailing cultural and professional norms, the designer's personal values, his or her repertoire of solutions and professional skills, and the context in which the task is set. The search at the front end of designing is seen as taking place within a design space in which the designer experiments, makes propositions, tests, evaluates, compares alternatives, asks questions, and raises doubts—all with the aim of achieving a coherent construal of the problem and a satisficing (to use Simon's term) solution that is explainable and justifiable. It has to be justifiable because the proposed solution is always one of at least several possible design solutions. When presenting a design proposal (solution), one always has to explain why this is the best possible choice under the circumstances. That is, a design always comes with a rationale for its particular features.

The importance of the front edge of designing is in the idea-generating process that takes place in it, usually in an intensive manner, in either a highly structured process or with designers having free rein. At the end of this phase a solution-in-principle is achieved (sometimes called a "parti," especially in architectural design), which is then further developed and articulated, until ultimately the designed entity can be fully specified and thereby ready for implementation (construction, production, manufacturing, assembly). Good ideas at the front edge will lead to a successful result, whereas ideas of lesser quality may well result in less successful outcomes. In terms of resource investment (time, money) the conceptual front edge, which is relatively short and often involves a small number of designers (and others), incurs only a small fraction of the overall design costs, while subsequent phases are much costlier, irrespective of the quality of the initial ideas. Therefore it is of crucial importance that the search at the front edge should yield the best possible ideas. What are good, leave alone best, ideas? This is a philosophical question of some magnitude that I shall not endeavor to treat here in depth. All the same, based on common practice, it is possible to assert that a work of design is usually considered successful if it is novel (in industrial products, this is often a technologically oriented criterion), even surprising; meets requirements and needs, whether or not such needs were pre-specified (certain innovative designs even create needs, such as the first iPhone); comes with a reasonable price tag; is easy to create, use and safely dispose of; and last but not least, is attractive and appealing to potential users.

Now that the importance of the early stage of the design process is evident, it is clear why we are interested in researching it, and in particular the thinking that is discernible at this stage. As we saw in the previous chapter, a relatively recent yet keen interest in what may be termed design thinking or design cognition has led researchers to concentrate less on methods and more on an attempt to comprehend modes of design thinking, sometimes referred to as design behavior (although thinking is only part of behavior). Indeed, the principal themes in the major journal *Design Studies* between 1996 and 2010 were found to be "design process" and "design cognition" (Chai and Xiao 2012; Cross 2010). The purpose of such research is to find out how designers think, how they learn to think in "designerly" ways (Cross 2006) and acquire design expertise, and what distinguishes the thinking of good designers from that of less accomplished or proficient designers. In other words, which traits of thinking are likely to yield better design outcomes, and can they be taught, enhanced, and supported? A lot of questions may be posed such as: how does a design stage in which a breakthrough is achieved compare to a stage wherein no breakthrough or even no progress is attained? What thought patterns distinguish an expert from a novice designer? How does visual thinking and the making of sketches aid thinking processes? Are certain design thinking patterns indicative of creativity? Obviously, this is a non-exhaustive list of research issues. The research methodology of protocol analysis comes in handy in answering such questions. As has already been mentioned, despite limitations it provides better access to thought processes than other methods at our disposal and this is why protocol analysis has become the principle methodology of design thinking research (Chai and Xiao 2012).

Design Moves

Cognitive psychology and the research traditions in the behavioral sciences teach us that in order to understand design thinking, like any thinking, we should concentrate on small increments of thought. This means abandoning sweeping "comprehensive" models such as the "spiral model" of design (see figure 2.2). The models advanced by earlier "design methods" were linear, even if the linear progression was curved into a spiral and included iterations and repetitions of certain stages. The deep underlying premise of those models was that the design process comprises separate phases and designers progress from one phase to another, with backtracking where it is necessary. Our new understanding of the process leaves behind the linear model. Regardless of design phases, which no doubt exist but which teach us little about thinking, the premise now is that one must look at small segments of the process in order to understand thinking characteristics. For most researchers protocol analysis is a most suitable method to explore these small segments.[1]

Design protocols are generated and parsed into segments like any other protocols. Unlike some other protocols, they are often accompanied by sketches that are used primarily to interpret verbalizations. As we have seen, parsing may be time-based (e.g., three minutes of verbal output), or semantically based (e.g., one sentence), or they may be based on units of content that comprise one sentence, part of a sentence, or more than one sentence; in teamwork, turn taking is also a common parsing principle. In the content-based category we find definitions of analysis units such as step, action, movement, or move. What "move" connotes is akin to its meaning in chess: a step in the process that changes the situation. There is some agreement on the use of this term (e.g., Dillon 2010; Goldschmidt 1995; Suwa et al. 1998), although this definition does not match Schön's use of the term "design move" (Schön 1992). In his interpretation a move is an act, rather close to a decision, made between acts of seeing; in this view the design process is composed of cycles of seeing, moving, and seeing. Here a more general view of a design move is upheld, whereby a design move is a step, an act, an operation, that transforms the design situation somewhat relative to the state it was in before that move (Goldschmidt 1995). Seeing can therefore be a design move, if we can capture it through the designer's verbalization in think-aloud documentation. Moves are normally small steps, discernible from their contents, and with some training it is not difficult to reach agreement and consistency in parsing a protocol into moves and deciding which utterances are meaningless and should not be designated as moves ("yeah," "OK," "emm," and so on); such utterances are removed from the analysis. David Botta and Robert Woodbury (2013) point out that the term "conversational move," coined by Paul Grice (1975), carries an evocative similarity to the term design move, as a design protocol can be seen as a record of a conversation among designers or of a designer with himself or herself.

Several studies concluded that the average duration of a move in a design session is about 7 seconds (Baya 1996; Baya and Leifer 1966; Goldschmidt 2012; Kan and Gero 2008; Andrew Milne, personal communications[2]). Moves generated in teamwork are shorter. However, if we use the concept of move as the basic unit of analysis and not a time-based unit, we should bear in mind that moves vary in length and duration.

The following example is a short vignette from a protocol derived from a recording of an architect named Martin, who was thinking aloud while working on the design of a small library (see the appendix). It is parsed into three moves, which in this case correspond to sentences:

> We start creating a hierarchy: the large trees, the parking lots, the pedestrians, an entry axis.
>
> I would then look for a direct relationship between entrance and exterior, because here, the real edge is not this [edge of building], for me it's that [edge of site].
>
> I would try to have an important element; would therefore make the axis I mentioned before, this one [points to sketch].

Moves are not the smallest possible units of analysis. A move may be parsed into its constituent arguments, which are the smallest semantic units that hold a comprehensible concept. For example, the third move in Martin's utterance above is composed of two arguments. The first argument states that the designer would like to introduce an important element, without specifying what kind of element that could be; the second argument specifies the important element in terms of an architectural feature, in this case an axis:

> I would try to have an important element.
>
> I would therefore make the axis I mentioned before, this one.

For certain purposes it is of interest to analyze protocols using arguments as the basic units. This was done to investigate the relationship between embodiment and rationale in design thinking (Goldschmidt 2001, 2012), where embodiment denotes physical properties of a design element or component and rationale the reason for selecting or desiring certain properties. These two modes of reasoning are the scheme of categories by which the arguments are encoded. However, more often we want to concentrate on larger units: the move, or, in some cases, derived units such as ideas or decisions that are more complete and are stand-alone units.

The difficulty in establishing appropriate universal schemes of categories for protocol analysis in design, which was discussed in chapter 2, is not surprising. Design tasks differ greatly in nature and scope, resulting in diverse foci, and accordingly designers must attend to changing aspects of the design task. As a result, attention may be directed to form or to function, to the whole or the details, to technological issues, to ergonomic considerations or aesthetic values, and so on. Within a single task, too, different phases may require different approaches. Personal dispositions of designers also affect what they choose to tend to and determine their priorities. In addition, the purpose of each study of the process of design is different. Consequently, it is hardly possible to develop a single scheme of analysis categories that would be useful across the board for protocol studies in design. When I first began to use protocol analysis, I experimented with schemes of categories but was disappointed with the results. Not only did no assurance surface that the categories were appropriate, but the significance of the findings (which indicated what kind of design activities were carried out, what the relationships among them were, and when they occurred) was not satisfactory. Findings of this sort are, of course, important for some purposes, especially when they are used to compare performances of different populations—for example, experts vs. novices—on the same task. Comparisons are of the essence in protocol analysis of any kind. However, categorizing design activities was not helpful when the goal was to fathom thinking processes.

The feeling that coding-based protocol analysis was too case specific, and the uncertainty about what could be learned from these analyses that would have some general validity, led to the question whether design protocols could not be analyzed in a different way. Our interest was clearly in design cognition and not in kinds of design acts, which were taken to be contingent on the task, the phase, and the designer's priorities. Experience as a designer and as a teacher in dozens of design studios of varying standing led to the conclusion that the most crucial thing in a design process is the solidification of a major idea, or combination of ideas, that could bring together all the major aspects the design had to respond to. In other words, synthesis, or integration, was the major goal of conceptual design. As Christopher Alexander pointed out so eloquently, even the simplest of design tasks is complex and necessitates an integration of responses to many requirements and desires, which may even be conflicting (for example, advanced technology and high-quality materials versus low cost). Alexander (1964) talked about a "good fit" that must be achieved among design components by resolving "misfits." John Archea (1987) used the metaphor of "puzzle making" to describe how architects achieve a unified whole by fitting discrete pieces together. Arriving at a state of good fit is no trivial matter; indeed, it has long been considered a mystery, magic, a manifestation of creativity that cannot (and some thought should not) be explained. Alexander, Archea, and some other researchers thought otherwise, of course; so did some of the psychologists who began to unveil creative processes.

On the view that design processes are not a matter of magic and that the thought processes that underlie them must be explicable in terms of thinking in general, a way was sought to analyze design protocols that would reveal something about the thinking involved, regardless of the specific design domain or task. It was clear that the analysis would have to be based on very small segments that mapped well onto design moves. This happened at precisely the time when the design research community began to direct its attention to design thinking, and psychological concepts gained a foothold in the explorations that researchers began to undertake. The concomitance of two modes of thinking and reasoning is one of these concepts.

Two Modes of Thought

Several psychologists subscribe to the view that we use two systems of reasoning—indeed two modes of thought—in everyday life, and that the balance between them is particularly pertinent to the understanding of creative thought. Different authors have used different terms to describe the two systems. Steven Sloman (1996) described an associative, similarity-based system versus a symbolic, rule-based one. The associative system makes use of visual representations when they are relevant, and design is a case in point; the rule-based system specifies a rationale. In chess, for example, there is evidence that pattern recognition and rational "forward search" are deeply entangled (Linhares et al. 2012); this may suggest a similar entanglement of systems in other instances of problem-solving thinking, such as designing. Liane Gabora (2010, 2) talked about associative thought and analytic thought; the former tends to be intuitive and "conducive to unearthing remote or subtle associations between items that share features or are correlated but not necessarily causally related." "This," Gabora continued, "may lead to a promising idea or solution, although perhaps in a vague, unpolished form." In contrast, analytic thought is rule based and convergent, and is "conducive to analyzing relationships of cause and effect between items already believed to be related" (ibid., 3). Recently Daniel Kahneman, whose interest in decision making is well known, published a book (*Thinking, Fast and Slow*) in which he argued that fast thinking is mostly intuitive and based on memory and emotion, whereas slow thinking is rational and entails calculating consequences. All these descriptions may be seen as roughly corresponding to *divergent thought* and *convergent thought*. These terms have been used by creativity researchers, with a pronounced emphasis on divergent thought, which was seen as the hallmark of creative thinking (see, e.g., Finke et al. 1992; Mednick 1962). Divergent thinking is defined as "thinking that moves away in diverging directions so as to involve a variety of aspects and which sometimes leads to novel ideas and solutions; associated with creativity." Convergent thinking is demarcated as "thinking that brings together information focused on solving a problem (especially solving problems that have a single correct solution)."[3] There is much more literature on divergent thinking than on convergent thinking.

Today there is evidence that creative thinking involves both divergent and convergent thought. Gabora (2010), who gave a neurological account of creative thought in terms of memory activation, suggested that divergent thought is associated with defocused attention and convergent thought is related to focused attention, and that these two types of attention give rise to different memory activation patterns (that is, different patterns of connections among neurons in the brain). Gabora asserted that creative thinking requires the flexibility to shift between the two modes of thinking. In her words, "creativity involves the ability to either shrink or expand the field of attention, and thereby match where one's mode of thought lies on the spectrum from associative to analytic according to the situation one is in" (ibid., 3). Min Basadur (1995) used the words "ideation" and "evaluation" to describe the scope of the spectrum to which Gabora referred, and related them to divergent and convergent thinking. These researchers emphasized that the two modes of thought complement one another, and that shifts between them are frequent. According to Paul Howard-Jones and Steve Murray (2003), in creative thought these modes of thought serve to ensure originality (divergent thought) and appropriateness (convergent thought).

Design must perforce be seen as a creative activity, in that one brings into being a representation of an entity that does not yet exist. Design thinking and reasoning is therefore a typical case of creative thinking, and we can now talk about the synthesis that is to be achieved during the early phase of the design process as a series of cycles of divergent and convergent thinking (or any of the related terms used in the relevant literature) in which ideation and evaluation follow each other in frequent proximity, pertaining to embodiment and rationale. This notion is in line with the agreement that design is not a linear process, which may in itself imply more than one mode of thinking. We shall revisit the important concept of divergent and convergent thinking and reasoning in chapter 6, which focuses on design creativity.

We can now go back to design moves, which are obviously not generated in isolation but which relate to one another in various ways. It is proposed that revealing the links among design moves is the key to understanding the dual modes of design thinking and arrival at a design synthesis. This is the case because "effective reasoning in a creative endeavor must perforce aim at first mining and then relating to one another the many items of data that are relevant to the task" (Goldschmidt and Tatsa 2005, 595).

Design Synthesis as Backlinks and Forelinks among Moves

Design moves are brief acts of thinking, lasting around seven seconds. They are generated sequentially in time. Taken together, they express the design thinking process. Since moves are not generated as autonomous entities, they form continuums of various lengths in which they are interrelated, or linked. The pattern of links is neither known in advance nor fixed in any way, but it can be established empirically for each sequence of moves. How can we determine links among moves?

Links are based on the contents of moves. Deciding whether two moves are linked is done by using common sense under the condition of good acquaintance with the discipline and with the design episode in question. Acquaintance is essential to ensure that the person who judges whether or not a link exists understands precisely what the designer was doing, or thinking, despite difficulties that can arise in deciphering think-aloud documentation, for example, repetitions, jargon, incomplete sentences, unclear speech, and use of "this," "that," "here," "there," and similar words when referring to representations such as sketches or other objects that were present in the work environment. Video recordings and copies of sketches help in interpreting such utterances but do not always aid in making sense of incomplete or unclear sentences. However, a sufficiently experienced observer in the relevant field of design who followed the design session carefully can, upon reading the (parsed) protocol several times, use what

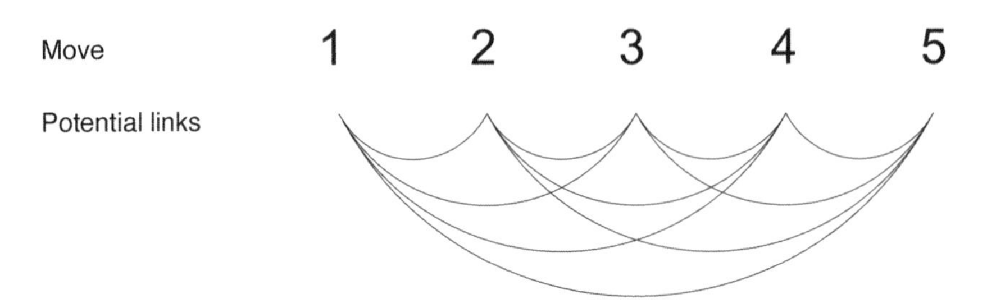

Figure 3.1
Testing for links among five moves. The test is performed ten times.

may be called "educated common sense" to determine whether a link exists between two moves. In a perfect study, three judges are employed and the decision "link" or "no link" is determined by the majority: consensus or two votes for one of the two options.[4] No encoding of moves is required; we want only to establish the existence of links, or the lack thereof.

How is a parsed protocol analyzed for links among moves? It is done systematically, by asking "Is there a link?" for every pair of moves in a sequence. First we number the moves sequentially. Then, starting with move 2, we test whether it has a link to move 1. Next we go to move 3 and test whether it has a link to move 2 and whether it has a link to move 1. For move n, we have to ask this question $n - 1$ times for possible links between move n and all preceding moves, namely 1, 2, 3, . . . , $n - 1$. For n moves, we must perform this test $n(n - 1)/2$ times in order to include every pair of moves in the sequence. Figure 3.1 illustrates the process of testing for links in a sequence of five moves; the number of tests is $5(5 - 1)/2 = 10$.

The tests described above were performed directionally—that is, we tested for links between every move and each of the preceding moves. The direction is backward in terms of a linear sequence in time. Any links we establish this way are therefore called *backlinks*. The symbol < denotes backlinking. However, once we have established a backlink, say between move 2 and move 1, we may also refer to a forward-bound link, or a *forelink*, between move 1 and move 2. Forelinking is denoted by the symbol >. We say "forward" because this is a link between a move (move 1) and an anterior move (move 2). Forelinks are therefore virtual and can be established only after the fact. Every link is one move's backlink and the other move's forelink. Therefore, the number of backlinks and forelinks is equal, and if

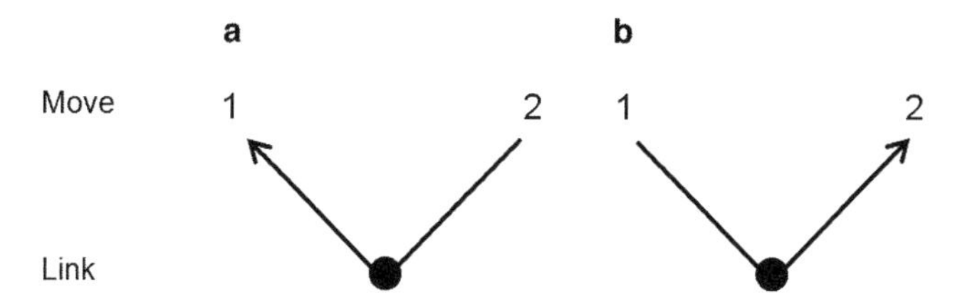

Figure 3.2
Link between moves 1 and 2. (a) Move 2 has a backlink to move 1. (b) Move 1 has a forelink to move 2.

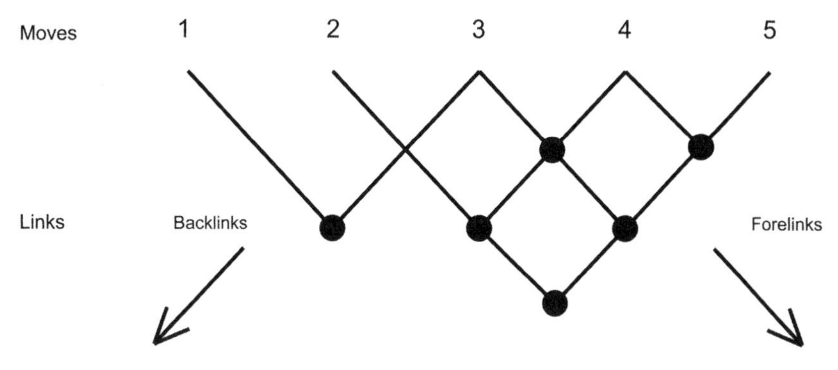

Figure 3.3
Linkograph with five moves and six links. Nodes are links; lines are network grid lines only.

we add up all backlinks and forelinks we obtain twice the total number of actual links. Figure 3.2 shows a link between moves 1 and 2; the same link is move 2's backlink and move 1's forelink.

In a sequence that contains more than two moves (as practically all design episodes do), we get a network of links that are represented as nodes. Most network depictions or graphs of processes represent the entities (moves, in this case) as nodes and the links as connecting lines. Here we wish to concentrate on links; they are our variable, and therefore they have become nodes in a graph that portrays the network of links among moves. The representation is therefore called a *linkograph*. Figure 3.3 shows a linkograph in which five moves are interconnected through six links. In this linkograph, move 1 has one forelink (to move 3). Move 2 has no backlink but has two forelinks (to moves 4 and 5). Move 3 has one backlink (to move 1) and two forelinks (to moves 4 and 5). Move 4 has two backlinks (to moves 2 and 3) and one forelink (to move 5). Move 5 has three backlinks (to moves 2, 3, and 4). A move's backlinks are "strung" along grid lines that originate at the moves and turn diagonally leftward to meet the linked move. Respectively, forelinks are lined along grid lines that originate at the moves and turn diagonally rightward, again to meet the linked move. Obviously, the first move can never have backlinks and the last move can never have forelinks.

Why do we stipulate forelinks, and why is it logical and beneficial to distinguish between backlinks and forelinks? Let us remember that design synthesis at the micro (cognitive) level is understood as emanating from a search that consists of cycles of acts of ideation and evaluation. These acts gradually shape an original design proposal, or solution, until it can be deemed appropriate. The design acts in question are defined as moves, and we posit that links among them enable an integrated end result, or a "good fit" of the synthesis. Are originality and appropriateness achieved in the same way? They cannot possibly be achieved in the same way. To achieve originality, the designer must propose something. To ensure appropriateness, it is necessary to evaluate a proposal by ensuring that it is consistent with previous steps taken to accommodate requirements; if it is not, there may be contradictions (misfits), which are likely to cause difficulties or even to lead to the failure of a proposed solution that does not meet the requirements. Since moves are very small steps, it is never enough to propose something; further steps must build on it (or challenge it) and develop it in order to arrive at a complete synthesis. Likewise, when we evaluate, we often match a proposal with several previously raised issues. When we propose, we look forward, and the move we make will probably link to further subsequent moves, which follow immediately thereafter or occur later in the process. When we evaluate or assess, we look backward to what has already been done to make sure that a good fit exists between the current move and previous work, and that no apparent contradictions, mismatches, or other negative consequences are evident in the design process. Looking backward creates backlinks. Looking forward creates forelinks. The two types of links have very different meanings, and therefore we distinguish between them. Such a distinction can be expressed in quantitative terms, and expressing them quantitatively is significant when we analyze and when we compare protocols of design sessions.

To demonstrate this notion, let us return to the brief vignette from Martin's process of designing a small library that was presented earlier in this chapter. Here is the vignette again, parsed into three moves:

Move 1 We start creating a hierarchy: the large trees, the parking lots, the pedestrians, an entry axis.

Move 2 I would then look for a direct relationship between entrance and exterior, because here, the real edge is not this [edge of building], for me it's that [edge of site].

Move 3 I would try to have an important element; would therefore make the axis I mentioned before, this one [points to sketch].

Martin had been given a shape representing a library's "footprint" in the middle of a rectangular site. In move 1 he referred to the site, in which there were large trees and on which he had placed parking lots and determined where the entry to the library would be. Martin is an architect who often uses axes in his designs (Wrede 1986), an axis being an imaginary line that visually connects design elements. In this vignette, as a matter of habit or routine, he talked about creating an "entry axis." Move 2 expanded on the relationship between the entrance and the exterior, and, since this move referred to the entry and its axis mentioned in move 1, a backlink is established between move 2 and move 1. In move 3 Martin returned to the entry axis of move 1 and asserted that it was an "important element." Move 3 therefore has a backlink to move 1, but it does not relate to the relationship to the exterior and therefore it is not linked to move 2. After the fact we see that, whereas move 2 has no forelink to move 3, move 1 has forelinks to both move 2 and move 3. Move 2 asserts the position of the entry as part of a hierarchical arrangement of elements connected by an axis. Move 3 provides an explanation for the axis: it is an important element. Move 1 also connects building elements with outdoor elements, and move 2 explains that this is done because, for Martin, the extent of the design is the building together with its surroundings, ending only at the edges of the site. A linkograph depicting the network of moves and links in this short vignette is shown in figure 3.4. This example demonstrates that a good fit between a proposal and its rationale is not pulled out of the designer's sleeve as a "fait accompli" but is built up small step by small step. Proposals are made and then assessed, or a rationale is put forth and a suitable embodiment is then proposed; the order in which

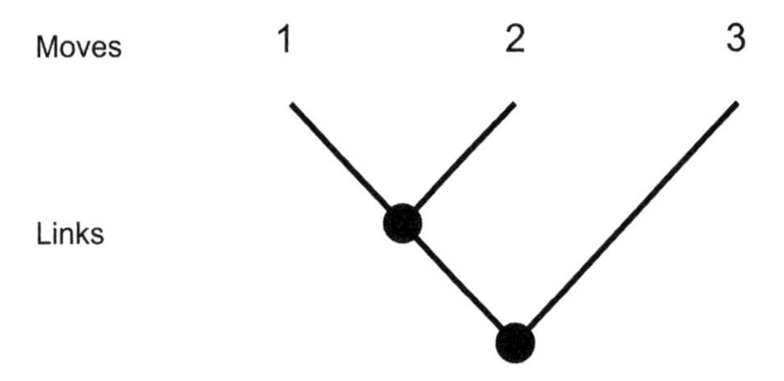

Figure 3.4
Linkograph derived from a short vignette of Martin's protocol.

these types of moves succeed one another makes no difference (Goldschmidt 2012).

As was claimed earlier, good design boasts a well-integrated solution that takes care of the many issues that must be addressed. Good and creative design also manifests a coherent, novel, comprehensive "leading idea" that elevates the design from a mere solution to a problem to a social, artistic, technological, or generally cultural statement that is appreciated by the public at large. A leading idea is not a "thing apart"; rather, all design decisions must be compatible with it. This is precisely what a design synthesis denotes. If this is indeed the case, then understanding the properties of the network of links among design moves should shed light on the thinking that brings into being well-integrated works of design—both good, creative ones and lesser ones.

Linkography thus concerns itself with links among design moves, as it is believed that this is the best way to capture the essence of design cognition and behavior. Although links are associated with the achievement of synthesis, it must be emphasized that linkography does not explain causality, as the actual contents of design moves is disregarded after links are established (contents may, of course, be visited in complimentary analyses). Linkography is flexible, since base lines for variables to be measured can be calibrated to suit the needs of a study. However, we must insist on consistency in handling the data and in performing the analyses.

4 The Linkograph: A Network of Links

Chapter 3 introduced the origin of the linkograph as a way to notate design moves and the links among them. The first linkographs were drawn by hand, usually on grid paper. Figure 4.1 is an example from circa 1993. In the early 1990s the first little piece of software for the production of linkographs was created by Shahar Dumai. Called MacLinkograph, it was meant for Macintosh computers. Unfortunately it was not upgraded when new operating systems replaced the one we had been working with, and eventually MacLinkograph became obsolete. By using a Java platform, Linkographer, developed in 2004–05, avoided the fate of its predecessor.

A linkograph is basically a modified representation of a matrix; indeed, some researchers prefer to stick to a matrix representation (see, e.g., van der Lugt 2001). The graphic notation used here for linkographs is a directed graph, although no arrows are used. It was chosen because it emphasizes the arrangement of the links in a network. The grid lines make the visualization of the network and its structure particularly compelling, and this representation is superior if we wish to emphasize the idea of links as nodes rather than connecting lines. Matrix representations are, however, perfectly legitimate, and for certain purposes (coding, for example) they may have advantages, especially for a long linkograph that contains more than 100 moves.

Either way, a linkograph may be seen as an enlarged depiction of a very small design space within which the designer is working at a specific moment. Links alone do not give a complete description of the design space of course, and the depiction is therefore partial. Nonetheless, it allows access to the designer's thinking process at that point. If we also encode the moves (and we could even encode the links), the picture becomes quite

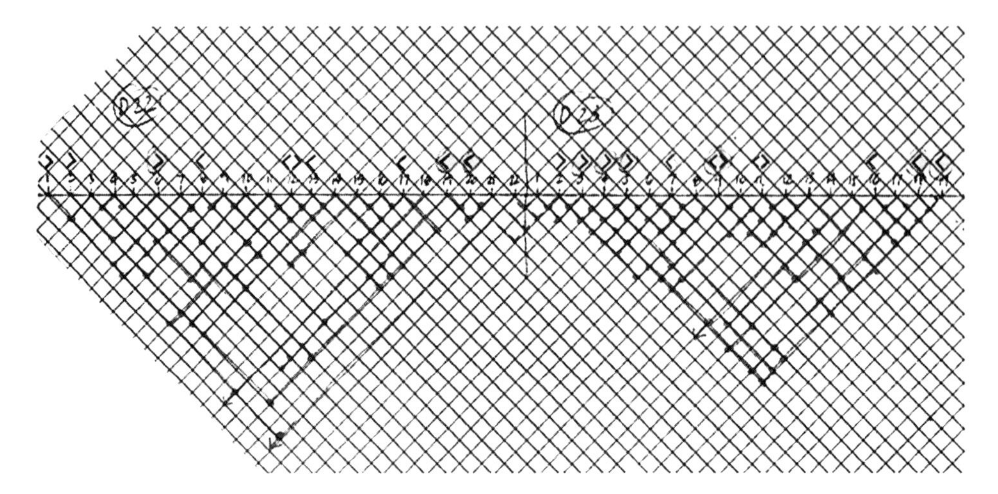

Figure 4.1
Portions of two adjacent linkographs (D22 and D23) drawn by hand on grid paper.

comprehensive. No other representation of the design space yields the kind of information that can be inferred from a linkograph. In our studies, a complete picture of the design space was not the main concern. Wanting to look at the "how" of the design process, we left out the "what." The linkograph serves this purpose very well.

Linkographer displays a network that, in addition to space for nodes that are the links, has the following:

- a line for sequential move numbers (the number of moves is flexible)[1]
- background grid lines wherein the portions that are activated when a link is notated are highlighted
- horizontal lines to indicate the span of links (discussed later in this chapter)
- a line to identify designers (useful for team design sessions)

In addition, there are three lines for the indication of critical moves, to which chapter 5 is devoted. Figure 4.2 shows the Linkographer template ready to be used.

The next few sections describe the different types of moves according to the links they generate, and the structure of the design session as portrayed in a linkograph in terms of link distribution and patterns in the network. Also featured is the span of linked moves—that is, how far apart linked

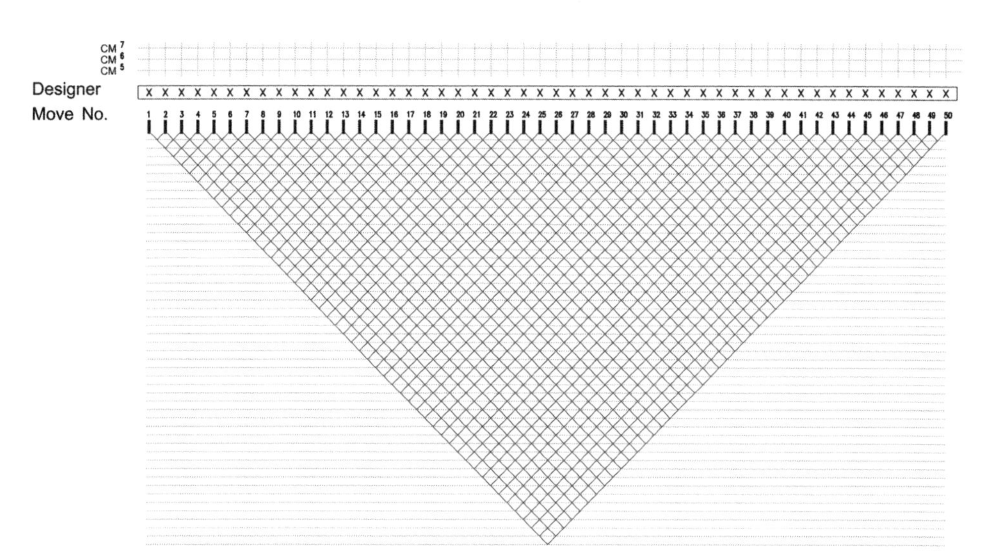

Figure 4.2
A blank linkograph network in Linkographer.

moves are. A general measure of the density of links in a linkograph or part thereof is also introduced, and a glimpse of one other linkograph representation is presented.

Types of Moves and Their Linking Patterns

The rate of link generation is not fixed. Some moves generate more links than others, and generated links may be mainly backlinks or mainly forelinks. We identify three types of moves: orphan moves, unidirectional moves, and bidirectional moves. In addition, we distinguish a class of richly linked moves called *critical moves*.

An example will illustrate the different kinds of moves. The protocol in question records a team of three undergraduate industrial design students (A, B, and C) working on the design of a movable ashtray for use by large numbers of smokers in an outdoor location such as a park or a beach. In this part of the design process, the designers discuss a proposal that envisages an "ashtray" (or rather a device that fulfills the same purpose) in the form of a big sticky surface onto which smokers can toss their cigarette butts. The discussion lasted a few minutes, during which 27 moves were made. At

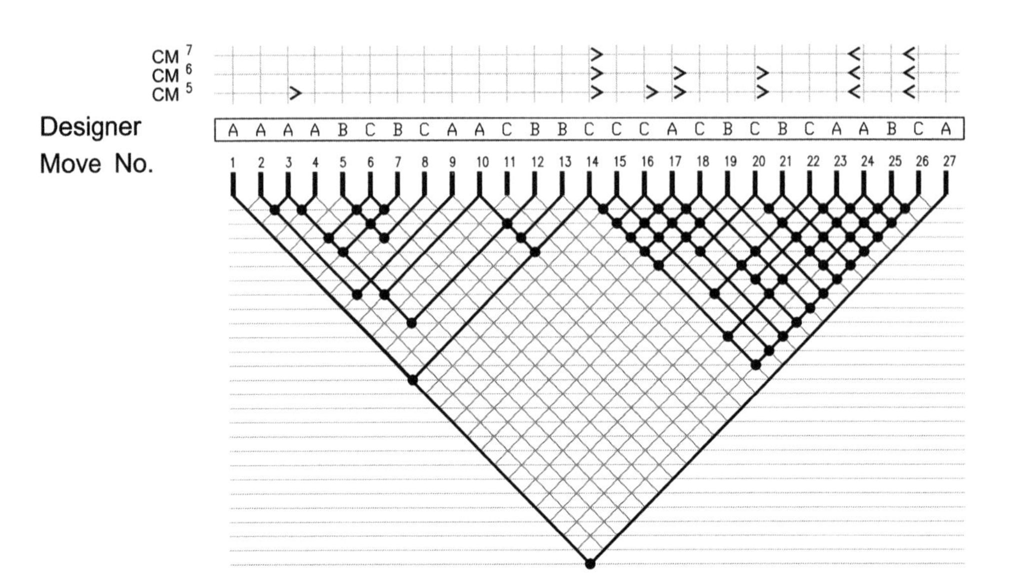

Figure 4.3
Linkograph of ashtray design vignette.

the 27th move the discussion switched to another alternative solution.[2] A linkograph notating the links among the 27 moves in this short vignette is shown in figure 4.3.

A few features of the link pattern are immediately apparent. The process can be seen as having two parts: from move 1 to move 14 few links are generated, and from move 14 to move 26 many links are generated. I shall comment on this difference a little later; here, the difference between moves in terms of links they generate, or do not generate, is discussed.

Orphan moves

There is one move in the ashtray linkograph above that has no links at all: move 11, which reads "What happens if it starts raining?" In evaluating the emerging design, it occurred to designer C, who made this move, that the solution would have to be effective in all kinds of weather. She asked how rain might affect the ashtray. The question of dry or wet conditions had not come up earlier in the discussion, and the teammates paid no attention to it, perhaps because they did not consider it relevant and perhaps because they thought it should be addressed later. Therefore, this move has no link to any previous move, nor does any subsequent move in the present sequence link to it. Hence, move 11 has no links. Such a move is referred to as an *orphan move*. Small numbers of orphan moves can be found in many linkographs, but we observe more of them when the designers are novices than when they are experienced and expert. A possible reason for this is that experts are able to anticipate the implications of their moves for longer stretches of future probable moves. In chess, for example, masters spin longer chains of planned future moves than novices (Chase and Simon 1973). In chess as in design, this makes it easier for experts to avoid orphan moves.

Unidirectional and bidirectional moves

The following moves have only backlinks: move 4, move 7, move 8, move 9, move 12, move 13, move 26, and, of course, the last move, 27, which by definition can have no forelinks. In contrast, other moves have only forelinks—in this case, the first move 1 (by definition) and moves 2 and 5. Moves that link only backward or only forward are called *unidirectional*, whereas the others are bidirectional, as they have links both backward and forward. Unidirectionality is, of course, the only possibility for the first and the last move. Other unidirectional moves suggest that at the instant of their generation the designer was concentrating either on what had transpired up to that point (in the case of backlinks only), or on new thoughts that left behind what had been done thus far, but to which later moves form links.

All other moves in this sequence, with the exception of the orphan move 11, are bidirectional. If we count out the two extreme moves, we have seven unidirectional moves with backlinks only (<Udir), or 28 percent; two unidirectional moves with forelinks only (Udir>), or 8 percent; and a majority of fifteen bidirectional moves, or 60 percent. The proportion of bidirectional moves, close to two-thirds, is typical, although on average the proportion tends to be a little higher for experienced designers. The ratio of <Udir to Udir> moves is 3.5:1, which is on the high side; the average in some other cases is around 2:1. In our sample, nearly all of the unidirectional moves are concentrated in the first half of the sequence we are looking at, whereas the second half, from move 14 onward, is characterized by an overwhelming dominance of bidirectional moves. This may suggest a sequence that is not very well integrated. The balance between bidirectional and unidirectional moves, and the proportion of both in the overall number of moves, may teach us something about the nature of the work done in this particular sequence of moves. More important, bidirectional moves suggest a rapid shift between the two modes of reasoning that are associated with divergent and convergent thinking. As was mentioned in chapter 3, the flexibility to shift between divergent and convergent thinking is typical of creative thinking. In this vignette, the first part is "weak" in that little progress was made, whereas in the "strong" second half more creativity was evident (this topic is elaborated further in chapter 6).

Critical moves

We have distinguished between moves with and without links and between moves that form links solely forward or backward and those with links in both directions. We now want to concern ourselves with special, and arguably the most important moves, those forming a particularly large number of links. They are called *critical moves* (CMs). Moves vary in the number of links they generate. If our basic premise that links are a primary indicator of the quality of the process is correct, it follows that critical moves are of special significance.

How many links must a move have in order to qualify as critical? The answer is that the number depends on the "grain" of the analysis, or the overall number of links. "Grain" pertains to the propensity of the researcher to establish links when analyzing a design episode. If the inclination is toward stringency in judging whether links exist, the overall number of links will not be very high and therefore a relatively low number of links will suffice in order for a move to be considered critical. If more leeway is allowed in establishing links, the number of links will be high and more links will be necessary in order for a move to be seen as critical. The threshold number for qualifying links as critical is therefore flexible, and it is established in each study in accordance with the analysis granularity and the goals of the study. Sometimes more than one threshold is used in the same study, for the purpose of comparison between parameters under the different thresholds. We therefore have to indicate the threshold when we talk of critical moves. We do so by adding it in superscript: CM^t, where t is the chosen threshold. Linkographer can indicate critical moves at three different thresholds, as shown in figure 4.2. It is good practice to choose a threshold that yields about 10–12 percent CMs of the total number of moves in a sequence.[3]

It is important to clarify how the designated number of links is counted. We could look at the overall number of links a move generates, or at the number of links in one of the two directions (backward or forward). Because it allows richer insights into the process, the second option was chosen so that criticality indicates links in one direction, either backward or forward. In other words, it is sufficient that a move generate a designated number of links in one direction to be labeled critical, regardless of the number of links it generates in the opposite direction. This is also indicated in the notation: <CM^t designates a critical move due to t or more links backward, whereas CM^t> notates a critical move due to t or more links forward. Only in rare cases does a move have as many as the threshold number of links (or more), both backward and forward—that is, at least 2t links in all. For a threshold t, the notation in this case is <CM^t>. The notation of CMs in Linkographer distinguishes between <CMs and CMs> at each threshold level.

In the ashtray linkograph shown in figure 4.3, critical moves are specified at three thresholds: 5, 6, and 7. At the highest threshold we have three CMs as follows: moves 24 and 26 are <CM^7s; move 14 is a CM^7>. As we lower the threshold, more moves "pass" the criticality test; in this case, only CMs> are added to the count of critical moves: moves 14, 17 and 20 qualify as CM^6s>; at the level of CM^5> we find moves 3, 14, 16, 17, and 20. There are no <CMs> in this sequence at any of the designated thresholds. Of all moves, 11 percent are CM^7s, 19 percent are CM^6s, and 26 percent are CM^5s. For most purposes we would choose a threshold of seven links for this sequence in the various calculations concerning critical moves. Critical moves are of great importance in linkography; their significance is explained and demonstrated in the next chapter. Here, however, let us look at the linkograph's structure, which is determined by patterns of link distribution in the network.

Distribution of Links

Figure 4.3 shows clearly that moves vary in the numbers of links they generate. This is not surprising in a spontaneous exploratory process of thinking wherein a large number of issues are examined. How are links distributed in relation to the moves that generate them?

Whereas orphan moves have no links at all, critical moves generate, by definition, a large number of links. As we have seen, the criticality threshold is adjustable and is optimally set for the proportion of CMs to be around 10–12 percent. Because the links form a network, it would be interesting to find out whether the percentage of links generated by critical moves is constant, and if so what this percentage is. We set out to find how the networks behave in this respect. Because of a possible incompatibility due to different thresholds for criticality, we did not calculate the percentage of links associated with critical moves in various studies. Instead, the contribution of links by the top 10 percent of moves was recorded—that is, the 10 percent that had the largest number of links. This was done for several studies of experienced and student designers (see appendix). The results are reported in table 4.1.

The results confirm that critical moves contribute more than their share in the move "population." Their contribution appears to be quite constant across sequences of varying lengths (numbers of moves), ranging from twice the average contribution of all moves in the case of experienced designers

Table 4.1
Contribution of the top 10 percent moves across cases.

Study	No. of participants	Total no. of moves	Link contribution by top 10% moves
Experienced designers			
Wang-Habraken	1	35	18.8%
Daum-Cohen (architect)	1	30	20.7%
Delft individual	1	191	19.0%
Delft team[a]	3	624	23.0%
MIT library footprint[b,c]	7	304	23.2%
Average			**21.0%**
Student designers			
van der Lugt[a]	5	72	25.3%
Daum-Cohen[b] (first year)	8	336	26.4%
Daum-Cohen[b] (fourth and fifth year)	8	403	25.3%
Neumann[a] (ashtray, long version)	3	47	25.7%
Average			**25.7%**

a. Team protocol.
b. In multi-participant studies not involving teams, the result is an average of values obtained for individual designers.
c. Excludes a first-year student who participated in the experiment.

to a factor of two and a half in the case of novices (design students).[4] These ratios are not very high, but they are still significant. If we remember that the percentage of critical moves is sometimes 12 or even higher, we may expect an even larger contribution of critical moves to the general network of links.

In sequences of up to 100 moves we find that moves can have any number of links between zero and more than a dozen. Interestingly, for sequences no shorter than about 20 moves, the average number of links per move (the link index; see later in this chapter) is fairly stable. Regardless of sequence length and experience of the participants, it is around 2.0. This means two backlinks and two forelinks per move, because each link is one move's backlink and another move's forelink. Therefore, if links are not to be counted twice, the number of links in a sequence refers to the total number of backlinks only, or forelinks only, or the sum of half of each.

The frequency of link generation—that is, how many moves generate a certain number of links (backward + forward)—tends to be a normal distribution, as figure 4.4 shows. Orphan moves on one end and critical moves on the other end cause the frequency graph to be asymmetrical, as all orphan moves generate 0 links but critical moves vary in the number of links they generate, thus we get a tail that represents a small number of moves that generate a large number of links. If we disregard the right-hand tail of the graph (that is, a small number of extreme critical moves, in this case those with more than eleven links), we get a normal distribution. The peak of the distribution, at four links per move, is created by 15.4 percent of all moves. Each of these moves generates four links (in both directions), and together they contribute 12.3 percent of all links. This is the largest group of moves with the same number of links. Moves that generate up to three links, and moves that generate five or more links, form smaller groups. Obviously, as can also be concluded from table 4.1, the higher the number of links per move, the higher is the proportional contribution of a certain group to all links. In this study, 29 moves (only 4.6 percent of all moves) have eleven or more links each, and contribute 12.5 percent of all links. We see that the contribution of a small group of link-intensive moves is roughly equal to that of the much larger group of moves having an average number of links.

Figure 4.4 represents a single study, but it is based on a fairly large sample: 624 moves. We cannot expect a similarly normal distribution in small samples, or single linkographs, especially short ones. However, the dominance of a relatively small number of moves that generate a large number

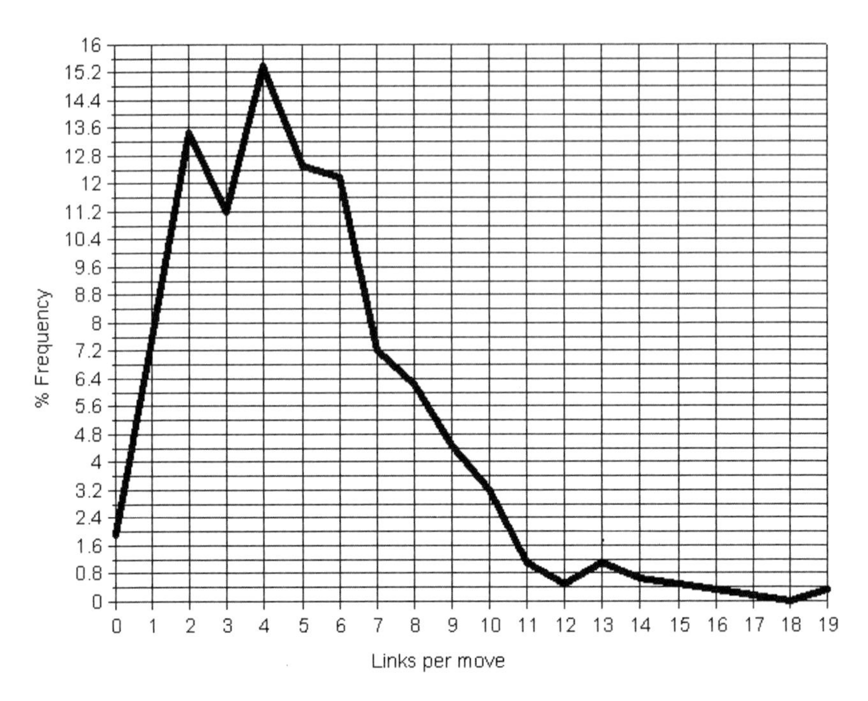

Figure 4.4
Frequencies of moves by number of links per move, Delft team protocol. $N_{moves} = 624$.

of links is clear in all cases, and we should therefore pay special attention to these moves and their role in the process of designing.

Link Patterns

The ashtray linkograph, which is repeated with additional information in figure 4.5, presents three different linking patterns that are visibly discernible in linkographs: chunk, web, and sawtooth track.

Chunk

As has already been pointed out, this linkograph is visibly divided into two halves, the first half comprising moves 1–14 and the second moves 14–26. Move 27 links back to the first move, but at the same time it breaks away and turns to a different potential solution. Move 14 is a pivot move that connects the two halves. Each of the halves is graphically distinct as a discernible triangle called a *chunk*. This case is extreme in that the two chunks of the linkograph are connected by a single move. Sometimes there

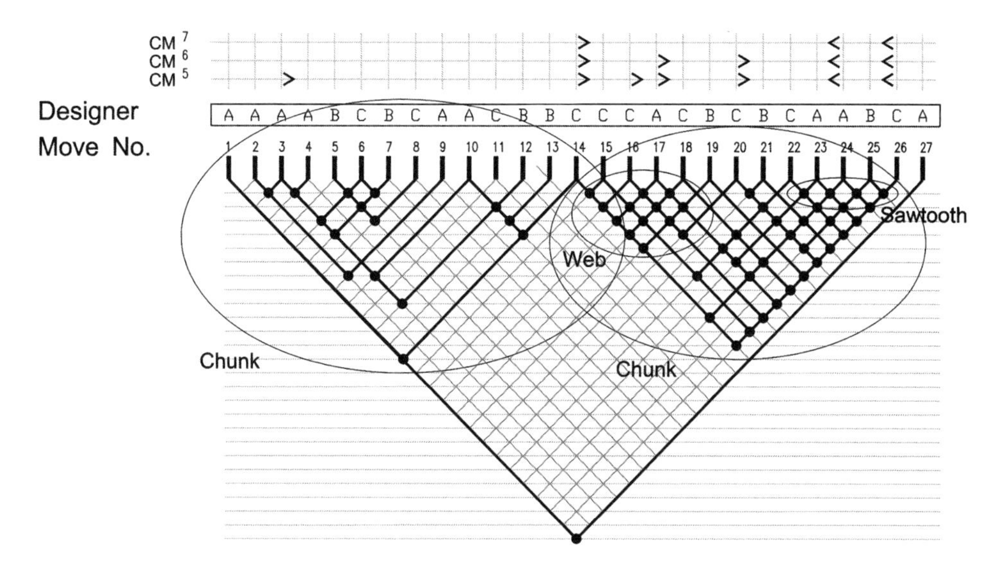

Figure 4.5
Link patterns in ashtray linkograph.

is no pivot move, but in most cases we find a few links between adjacent chunks, through moves that are not necessarily pivots but create an overlap between chunks. Chunks may also be entirely separate, with no links at all to connect them. A chunk is a block of links among successive moves that form links almost exclusively among themselves and are loosely or not at all interconnected with other moves. Typically, chunks are created by a sequence of between a dozen and two dozen moves, but sometimes they are longer and reach three dozen moves. More substantial chunks were not found, even in long linkographs. This may be related to the finding that the maximum number of symbols retrievable from short-term memory is constant (Ericsson and Simon 1984/1993).

What is the significance of chunks in the design process? The interlinked moves within a chunk stand for a cross-examination of relevant properties, related questions, and possible implications of a design issue. When this examination is exhausted, at least for the time being, or when it is interrupted, a new cycle of thought begins in which another issue comes under scrutiny. While inspecting one issue, a designer (or a team) focuses on that issue and directs almost all of his or her (or its) attention to it; only occasionally is the issue related to a previous topic, and this is where we find links to previous chunks. This mode of thinking reinforces our understanding of design problem solving as a sequence of examinations of subproblems that are limited in scope. There comes a point of course in which subproblems are consolidated and solutions are integrated, or synthesized, into a single design proposal. Chunks reflect the structure of the thinking process, which is easily captured in a linkograph thanks to its graphic properties.

In some linkographs it is difficult to define chunks. We can assume that the processes they represent are less structured than processes with clear chunking, as there is no sequential treatment of clearly outlined issues. Figure 4.6 is an example of such a linkograph. Linkographs with no chunks represent poorly structured processes and are an indication of inefficient design thinking and reasoning.

Web

A *web* is formed when a large number of links are generated among a relatively small number of moves. As in the case of a chunk, the geometry of the linkograph dictates a triangular enclosure of the web. In the ashtray linkograph we see a clear web of links between moves 14 and 19 (see figure 4.5). The links that interconnect moves 20–26 may also be considered as

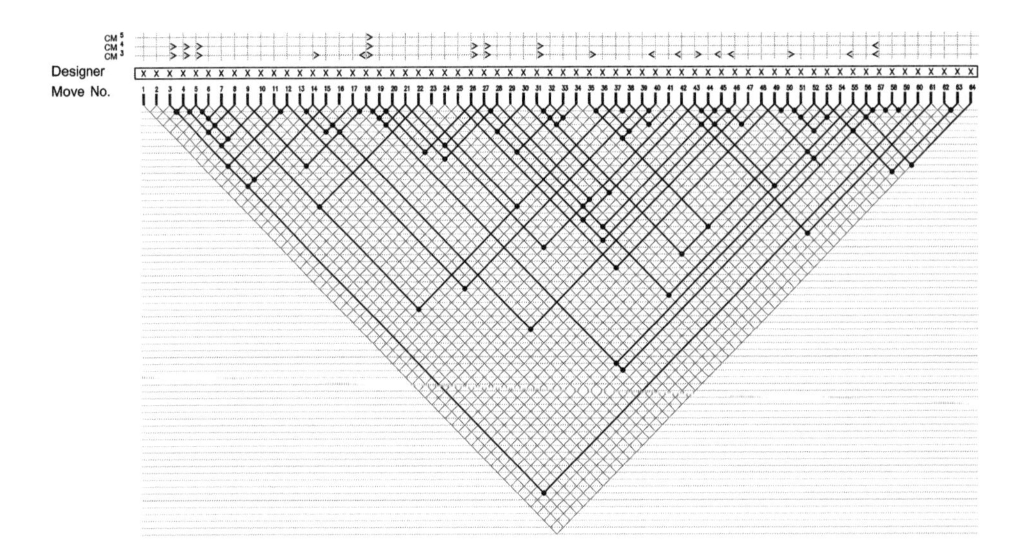

Figure 4.6
A poorly structured design process: a linkograph with no chunks (MIT library study, Gideon).

a web. The web is a portion of the network in which the density of links is especially high. Webs are smaller than chunks and are not found in all linkographs.

What does a web signify? It records a brief and intensive passage of a few moves in which a certain issue is very thoroughly inspected and its aspects are woven together to make sure they are in agreement with one another. For example, in moves 14–19 in the ashtray vignette the team discussed the prospect of having to deal with heavy smokers who smoke 40 cigarettes a day. In move 20 they went on to talk about average smokers and their habits. Webs are found when something needs particular clarification or when an idea is being built up by bringing up several of its aspects almost concurrently. Miller's (1956) finding that we can entertain 7 ± 2 items in short-term memory when processing information explains the fact that most webs pertain to a sequence of no more than seven densely interlinked moves. The web in figure 4.5, for example, comprises six moves (moves 14–19), and the sequence 20–26 is seven moves long.

Sawtooth track

In some instances a sequence of moves link each to the preceding move. The link lines in such a case describe a zigzag pattern reminiscent of a sawtooth. When this occurs, we conclude that the thinking at that point is very linear—one thing leads to the next, and each move reacts to what was just said or done, without a more holistic view. In the ashtray vignette we have an example of a very short sawtooth track between moves 22 and 26. To qualify as a sawtooth track, at least four moves must be involved; however, most sawtooth tracks are much longer. Sawtooth tracks are found especially in vignettes wherein the number of issues discussed is very small and in situations such as question-and-answer sequences in teams or teacher-student interactions in the studio during a "desk crit." When sawtooth tracks are not integral parts of a larger network but rather stand alone, we may conclude that at that point the designer is not engaged in a synthesis process but rather builds one observation or proposition upon another in a linear string, with no attempt to widen or deepen the investigation.

Link Span

The distance between two linked moves is called a *link span* (L.S.).[5] In the case of sawtooth tracks, moves link to immediately adjacent moves, and

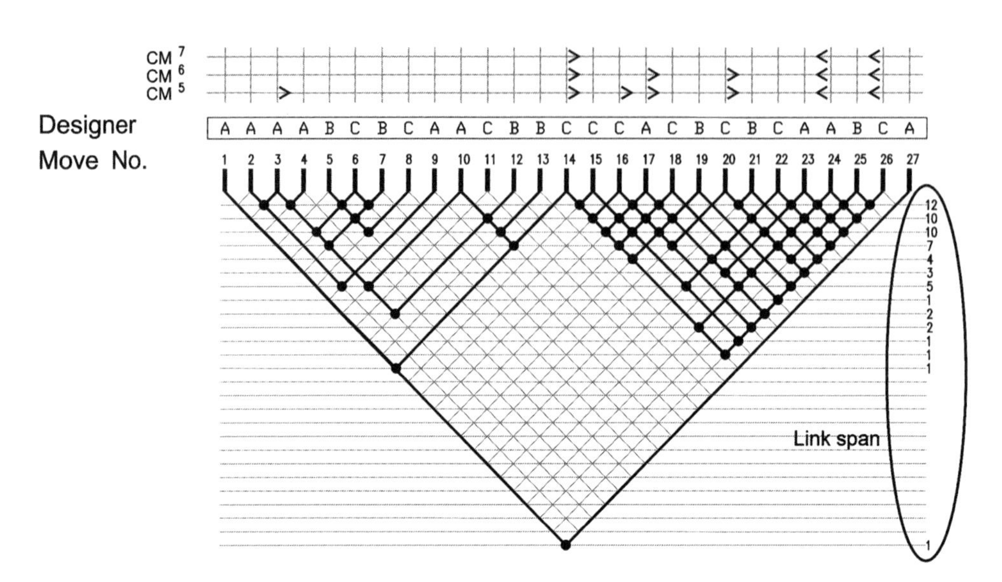

Figure 4.7
Ashtray linkograph with counts of link spans.

the link span is therefore L.S. = 1. Move 6 in the ashtray linkograph has backlinks to moves 3 and 5 and a forelink to move 7. For the links of move 6 to moves 5 and 7, L.S. = 1. For the link to move 3, however, L.S. = 3. In the same linkograph, the farthest-apart linked moves are moves 1 and 27; in this case, L.S. = 26 (see figure 4.7).

Because of the geometry of the linkograph, all links with the same L.S. are horizontally aligned, and the horizontal grid lines on which they are strung are visible. Linkographer can count the number of links on each of these lines (that is, for each L.S. value). This count is (optionally) displayed to the right of the linkograph. Figure 4.7 shows the L.S. count for the ashtray linkograph.

Link span values are worthy of a more detailed study; they are correlated here with what we know about cognition in general and design cognition in particular. Because of memory limitations, it is not easy to refer to a thought one had a long time ago, unless the earlier thought was particularly important and meaningful. At the micro-scale we are talking about, "a long time" means minutes, or hours in extreme cases. Since moves represent brief instances of thought, we do not expect them to generate many backlinks to moves that were made much earlier, because such moves may have already faded away from working memory (with the exception of very significant moves, which are also likely to have been reinforced by repetition). Rather, we would expect most links to connect moves with relatively recently generated moves that are still fresh in working memory. George Miller's 7 ± 2 dictum is remembered here, which specifies that the processing of information in short-term memory is limited to about seven items. Accordingly, we would expect most links to be formed between moves up to L.S. = 7. Of course, what "most" means here has not been specified. Does it mean any percentage over 50, or a very elevated percentage (say, 90 or higher)? To find out, we plotted the link percentage at L.S. values up to 7 for several sample design vignettes. This also allows us to see the buildup to that point. The results are shown in figure 4.8. At L.S. = 7, the designers whose processes were linkographed achieved, on average, 78.2 percent of the total number of links in the given sequence.[6] At L.S. = 3, the percentage was 56.6.

Some qualifications to these findings must be offered immediately. First, a distinction should be drawn between short and long sequences. We cannot expect similar results for sequences of fewer than 30 moves and

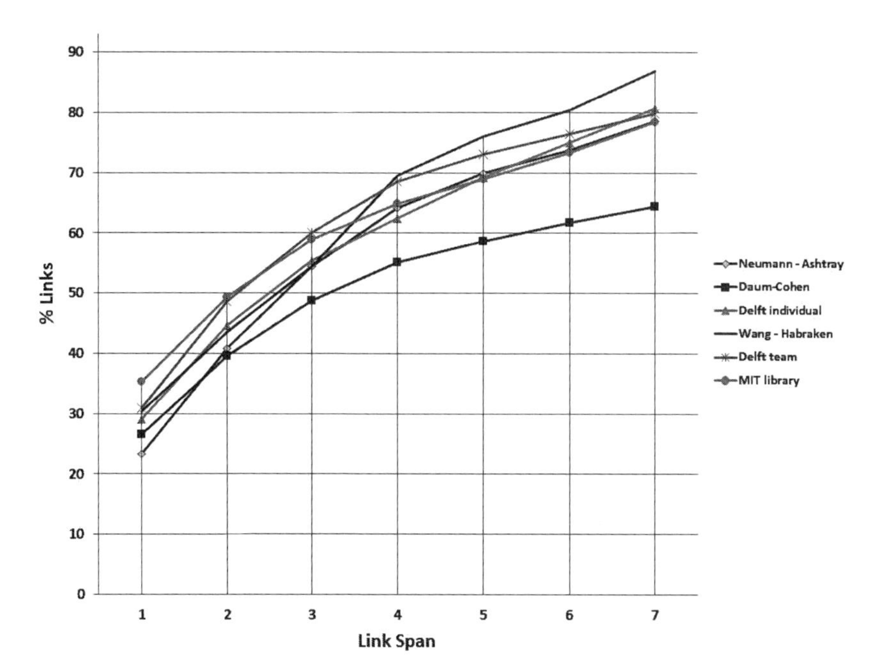

Figure 4.8
Percentage of links per L.S. value.

sequences of more than 70 moves. Indeed, we find considerable differences between short and long sequences. For example, the level at which 75 percent of the links are achieved in the Delft linkographs varies between L.S. = 4.7 for short vignettes and L.S. = 7.1 for long ones. Likewise, for the MIT vignettes the values are L.S. = 6.0 for short and L.S. = 8.6 for long linkographs. Short vignettes comprise about two dozen moves, generated in a little under three minutes. Long vignettes comprise about 60 moves, produced in about seven minutes. Obviously, the chances of linking back to previous moves over a long span may be greater in a seven-minute process than in a three-minute process. However, we can clearly see that, for the most part, across shorter and longer sequences, the achievement of links is within the bounds of Miller's dictum[7]: nearly all designers and design teams achieved 75–80 percent of links among moves at L.S. = 6 or 7 (see figure 4.8).

We must bear in mind, though, that we have found the link spans at which 75–80 percent of links are achieved to be up to six or seven moves apart. But the remaining 20–25 percent of links occur at longer spans, beyond Miller's dictum. How do we explain such linking? For example, in the ashtray linkograph (figures 4.5 and 4.7), Move 14 links back to move 1 and forward to move 26, and the respective link spans are L.S. = 13 and L.S. = 12. Let us look at the three moves in question:

Move 1 So there we have to make some choice

Move 14 Maybe we should write down some criteria because I think that this [points] maybe . . . but if people have 40 cigarettes a night

Move 26 Yeah, but if you go two or three times and you smoke 15 then this thing is not useful. Because you will not proceed. . . .

The first half of move 14 "closed" a cycle dedicated to the clarification of the problem and a short, brainstorming-like session in which some preliminary solution concepts were suggested. By the time move 14 was made, the designer who made the move felt that, in order to continue the work, evaluation criteria would have to be established, and this marked the end of the cycle (chunk) that started with move 1, to which move 14 linked. The second half of move 14 raised a new issue—that of heavy smokers. This started an intensive discussion on the implications of heavy smoking behavior that ended in move 26, which linked back to each and every move in this cycle, or chunk. In both cases the link spans are quite long (although occasionally we encounter linkographs with longer spans). Two hypothetical explanations come to mind. First, in teamwork longer link spans are more frequent because each team member may relate to his or her previous moves, regardless of moves by other team members that were made in between this designer's moves. Second, if sketching takes place by an individual or by team members, the sketches serve as an external memory extension that is available to the designer(s) during the session, thus circumventing memory limitations such as those expressed in Miller's dictum. Since sketching is very common in design sessions, it comes as no surprise that in 20–25 percent of cases link spans are longer than L.S. = 7.

Link Index

The number of links in linkographs varies greatly among cases. There are individual differences of course, but the most influential factor is the length of the linkograph. In a network comprising a large number of moves, there is a larger potential for links. Let us remember that in a saturated network the number of potential links is $n(n-1)/2$, where n is the number of moves (a saturated network is entirely hypothetical; no such networks occur in reality). Let us calculate this number for a network with 50 moves. The number of potential links is 50(50–1)/2 = 1,225. If we add just one move, the number of potential links becomes 51(51–1)/2 = 1,275. In other words, the addition of one move adds 50 new potential opportunities for links (links of the 51st move to all previous 50 moves). Therefore, it is not possible to compare processes and their linkographs on the basis of the nominal number of links. Consequently, we talk about the proportion of links in a network, and the term we use is *link index* (L.I.). A link index is the ratio between the number of links and the number of moves that generate them in a linkograph or part thereof, expressed as a proportion. The highest L.I.s are found in webs, which are defined *a priori* as high-link-density groups of moves. The same session may display different L.I. values for different phases. For example, in the ashtray linkograph the number of moves is 27 and the number of links is 60. Therefore, $L.I._{1\text{–}27} = 2.2$. If we calculate L.I.s for the two halves of the linkograph separately (in which case the link between move 27 and move 1 is not included), we get $L.I._{1\text{–}14} = 1.1$ and $L.I._{14\text{–}27} = 3.1$. This is in line with the visible difference in linking activity between the two halves of the process, as captured in the linkograph.

A link index is a fast indication of the amount of linking activity in a design episode, which in turn hints at the designer's effort to achieve a synthesis. However, we must be careful not to conclude that a high L.I is necessarily a hallmark of good or creative design. A high L.I. may be the result of many repetitions or many attempts to explore alternative ideas with little continuity among them. Indeed, we found no correlation between L.I. values and design quality (Goldschmidt and Tatsa 2005). The link index is thus a value that must be used cautiously and only where appropriate.

Matrix Linkographs

As was noted at the outset of this chapter, a linkograph is based on a simple matrix, and the notation used here is preferred because of its visualization power. However, a matrix is also a possible choice. For an example, see figure 4.9, in which the units of analysis are ideas generated by a team of four designers in an idea-generating session. Among the criteria Remko van der Lugt (2001; also see appendix) used to determine the session's success was the building of ideas on ideas previously expressed by teammates. To that

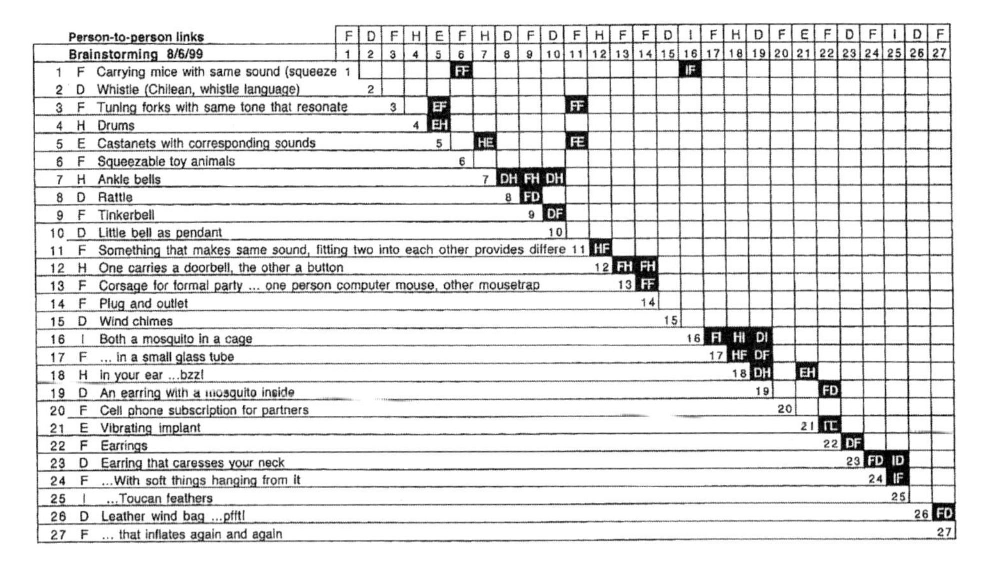

Figure 4.9

Matrix linkograph (van der Lugt 2001). Ideas generated by team members are listed chronologically. Reprinted with permission.

end, van der Lugt inferred ideas that were raised in the session and listed them in a matrix-type linkograph. Next he marked links among them as black squares in the matrix. For each link, the initials of the participants whose ideas were linked were marked in the appropriate black link square: first the originator of an idea, then the participant whose idea built on it. This facilitated identifying the links between members of the team and, conversely, the links wherein a participant built on his or her own earlier idea. The results were compared across teams and across methods of idea generation.

Another feature of van der Lugt's work that is worth noting, irrespective of the chosen modality of representation, is his distinction among different types of links. Since in his study links are transformations of ideas, van der Lugt, building on work done by Stanley Gryskiewicz (1980), proposed three types of transformations:

Supplementary Small change results in minor improvements.

Modification Structural changes in an idea result in a major change while preserving core aspects of the original idea.

Tangential There is a major "leap" to a new concept, based on a remote association with the original idea.

Coding the links can be useful, and one should keep in mind the possibility of executing such coding, along with the possibility of coding moves, as in conventional protocol analysis. Such coding does not contradict linkography, but rather is capable of augmenting it.

5 Critical Moves

Let us reiterate the fundamental premise underlying the linkography theory, which is that the quality and the creativity of a design process depend on the designer's ability to synthesize a solution that exhibits a good fit among all its components. The solution must respond to a large number of requirements and desires; beyond that, a creative solution is expected to be novel and exciting. The claim is that at the micro scale such synthesis is achieved by interlinking the very small design steps called *moves* that are made in the process of designing. A logical consequence of this assertion is the hypothesis that critical moves (moves with a particularly high number of links) are especially significant in the design process. A distinction is made between critical moves due to backlinks (<CMs) and those due to forelinks (CMs>); on rare occasions moves have a large number of links in both directions (<CMs>). It was also stipulated that "criticality" is established on the basis of a threshold number of links (in either direction), and that this threshold is determined case by case according to the granularity of the study. It is also possible to set more than one threshold in the same study for the purpose of examining a process at multiple levels. To check the hypothesis that critical moves are indeed the most significant moves in a sequence, the next sections look at several studies that establish the relevance of critical moves as indicators of important properties of thinking in the design process.

The Critical-Path Test

Ming-Hung Wang and John Habraken (1982) studied the design process from the point of view of the necessary and sufficient constituent operations involved, and their sequence. In their view, there are six such operations (see appendix).[1] They used a think-aloud protocol of a design session to demonstrate that. A designer was asked to arrange furniture and other items (referred to as *variants*) in an apartment, the plan of which was provided. The task was deliberately made very simple so that the study could focus on essentials. The protocol was broken into design steps in which decisions were made. Next the operations that were carried out at about the same time were consolidated into one step. In a total of 12 steps, 35 decisions were made. Wang and Habraken then drew a network graph that represented the process according to their analysis, wherein nodes stand for decisions and connecting arrows stand for operations. Figure 5.1 shows the final network graph.

Wang and Habraken proceeded to determine a critical path that included eight major decisions made in the course of the process, identified by their

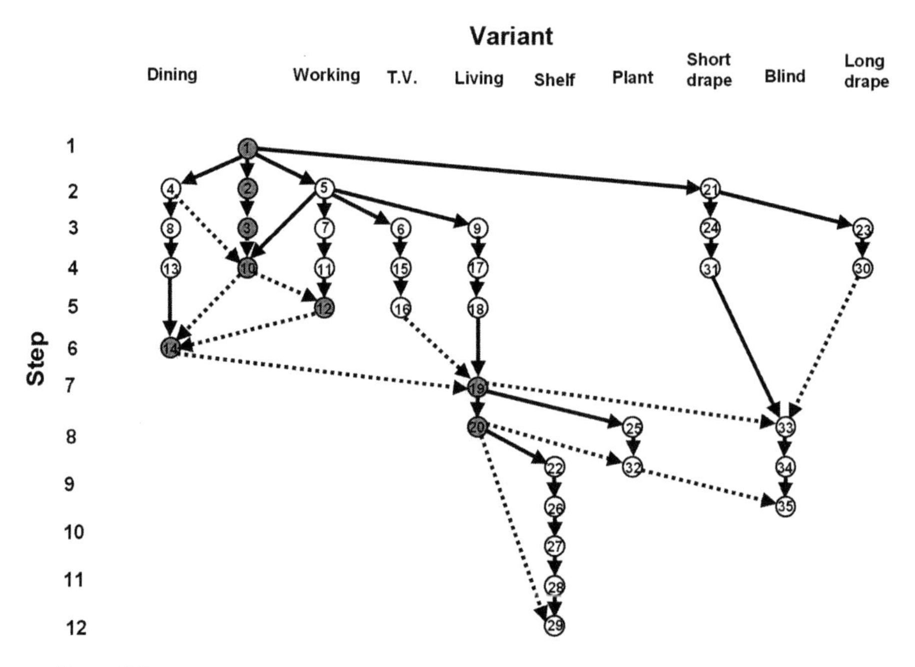

Figure 5.1
Network graph, adapted from Wang and Habraken 1982. At each step, the designer made decisions (represented by nodes) concerning one or more variants. To reach decisions, the designer carried out operations (represented by arrows). Dotted arrows represent "dummies" that refer to "information flow between nodes, without time and labor costs." Because Wang and Habraken emphasized the importance of these dummies, they are treated here as full-fledged equivalents of operations.

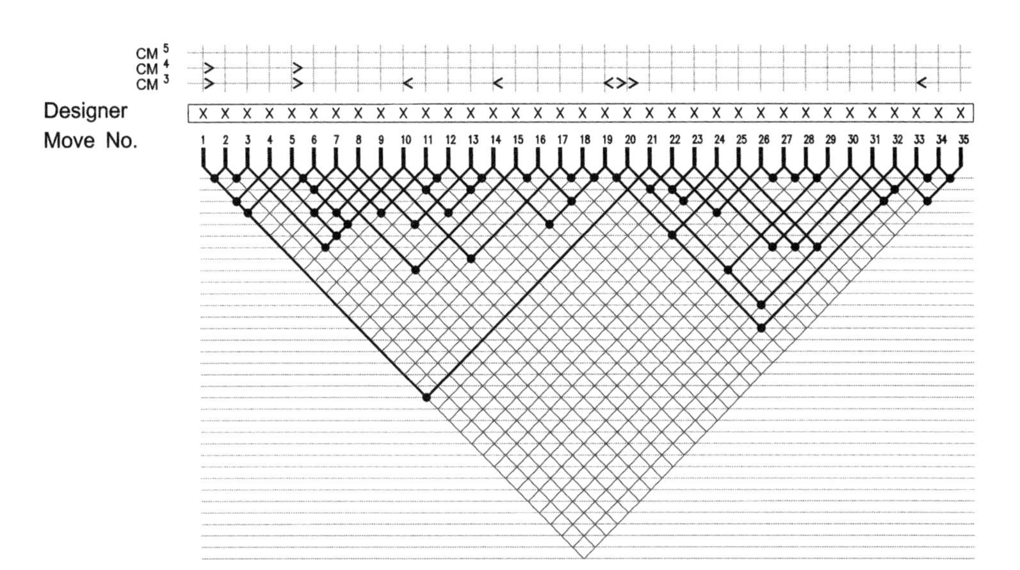

Figure 5.2
Linkograph based on Wang and Habraken's network graph (figure 5.1). In this graph the nodes represent links among design decisions, here shown as moves. Diagonal lines connecting decisions with links are grid lines that have no operational significance, as opposed to Wang and Habraken's network graph. Here they facilitate the count of links associated with each decision, and they help perceive the structure of the process.

sequential numbers: 1, 2, 3, 10, 12, 14, 19, 20. This critical path was based on their expert assessment of the evidence in the protocol (the contents of the decisions are not relevant to the present discussion).

The linkograph shown in figure 5.2 is based on information in figure 5.1. However, in this linkograph nodes are links, and Wang and Habraken's nodes—design decisions—are constants. Decisions are equated with moves, and links are Wang and Habraken's operations.

Using the linkograph, we can single out the decisions that have the highest number of links. Here we borrow Wang and Habraken's use of the term "critical path," but we establish an independent critical path. This critical path is not based on an educated assessment of the process as in Wang and Habraken; it is based on a count of decisions with at least three backlinks or forelinks (a threshold that was established for this case[2]).

We obtain the following critical path at the level of CM^3: 1, 5, 10, 14, 19, 20, 33. Although this critical path and Wang and Habraken's critical path

Table 5.1
Critical paths in Wang and Habraken's expert assessment, and in linkograph.

Decision no. (Wang and Habraken)	1	2	3	5	10	12	14	19	20	33
Critical Path Expert assessment (Wang and Habraken)	x	x	x		x	x	x	x	x	
Critical Path Linkograph, CM^3	x			x	x		x	x	x	x

are not identical, they are reasonably similar (five identical decisions out of eight and seven in the two critical paths, respectively)—see table 5.1. Decision 5 is the implementation of decisions 2 and 3, which brings the two critical paths even closer.

We were able to verify a positive relationship between criticality of decisions, as determined by the intensity of interlinking, and criticality as determined independently by other, unrelated criteria, in this case expert assessment. This result supports the notion that important instances of designing and design reasoning are indeed detectable by the high number of links they form, backward or forward, relative to other moves in the same sequence. To further fortify this conclusion, let us now look at another study that inspects the change in the number of links with the self-assessment of the importance of ideas in students' projects.

Self-Assessment of Ideas

Dan Tatsa, who was interested in what transpires in the design studio, conducted a study that involved close scrutiny of students' development of their semester-long projects (Goldschmidt and Tatsa 2005; see appendix). He made lists of all design ideas that were raised in each of the projects of the eight students who participated in the study. The number of ideas was in the hundreds in every case. After the end of the semester, each student was presented with the list corresponding to his or her project and was asked to mark which of the ideas made a positive contribution or a *major* positive contribution to the project. Later, Tatsa called the contributions the students had rated major "very critical" and the other positive contributions simply "critical" (other ideas were not marked as positive contributions).

Next, Tatsa set out to generate linkographs with ideas as the unit of analysis, a procedure that was repeated three times. First, a linkograph was plotted for each student's project in order to get an overview of the pattern of links among all ideas. (This was extremely labor intensive—for the project with the highest count of ideas, 275, it was necessary to consider 37,812 links. Tatsa did all the work.) Second, linkographs were generated that looked only at links among the ideas the students had rated as critical. This was done for four projects. Further linkographs were drawn for a smaller number of ideas—those the students rated as having made a major (very critical) contribution to the project. Links for the latter two sets of linkographs were produced by three judges (the experimenter and two naive judges, both expert designers), and were arbitrated by agreement between at least two judges. Table 5.2 shows the number of links in all three sets of linkographs for the projects by the students Meirav and Ronen. We should look at proportions, of course, and therefore the values we are interested in are expressed as the link index in each case.

The results are impressive. We see an incremental increase in the number of links generated by an idea with a rise in its self-assessed criticality.[3] In

Table 5.2
Incremental growth of link index with idea criticality, Tatsa's study.

		Meirav		**Ronen**	
		Experimenter	**3 judges**	**Experimenter**	**3 judges**
All ideas	Ideas	158		177	
	Links	156		118	
	L.I.	**0.99**		**0.67**	
Critical ideas	Ideas	95	95	39	39
	Links	128	101	35	36
	L.I.	**1.35**	**1.06**	**0.90**	**0.92**
Very critical ideas	Ideas	23	23	10	10
	Links	56	41	13	13
	L.I.	**2.46**	**1.78**	**1.3**	**1.3**

Meirav's case the link index grew from 0.99 to 1.35 to 2.46 in the shift from all ideas to critical ideas to very critical ideas (experimenter's judgment). Ronen achieved overall lower L.I. values, but they too grew with criticality: from 0.67 for all ideas to 0.90 for critical ideas to 1.3 for the ideas he deemed very critical (note that the percentage of critical and very critical ideas is considerably lower in Ronen's case than in Meirav's). Since these are self-assessments it is difficult to calibrate valuations across participating students. All the same, the unequivocal conclusion is that the more meaningful and helpful the idea is according to the student-designer, the denser the network of links it is involved in according to the external judges. This tendency is noticeable both in the analysis performed by the three judges and in the analysis undertaken by the experimenter alone, and it holds despite some differences between the experimenter and the three judges (which is more pronounced in the case of Meirav).

As in the study by Wang and Habraken, the value of this investigation resides in the fact that the determination of criticality is entirely independent of, and therefore orthogonal to, the link analysis. Our results also corroborate Remko van der Lugt's (2003) findings that the ideas considered most meaningful by the designers themselves in his experiments had a significantly higher number of links than other ideas.

It is therefore encouraging to reiterate the claim that links among ideas (decisions, moves) are of great importance in the cognitive processes involved in searching for successful solutions to design problems. This is by no means obvious or trivial. Whereas designers are said to be synthesizers of ideas almost by definition, we have hitherto had little evidence that this is true at the cognitive scale of very small steps (we should remember that the duration of design moves is no longer than a few seconds). In particular, critical ideas, defined merely by a high number of links they generate to other ideas, are also the most important concepts in the eyes of the designers themselves, although they are not involved in determining links.

Armed with this affirmation, let us proceed to explore critical moves and what they tell us about reasoning in designing.

Critical Moves as Structure Anchors

In chapter 4 we saw that linkographs reflect the structure of design thinking and reasoning in a sequence under scrutiny. In particular, the presence of chunks tells us that the designer thinks systematically about successions of subproblems or issues (see figure 4.5). The lack of chunks is evidence of the opposite: that the designer is engaged in thinking about a single issue, or is "jumping" back and forth among several issues (see figure 4.6). Now we want to find out whether the position of critical moves adds to our understanding of the structure of the thinking process. To do so, let us examine several design episodes from various studies.

The Wang-Habraken linkograph revisited

Let us take another look at the linkograph of Wang and Habraken's 1982 study (figure 5.2). It contains two clear and slightly overlapping chunks, the first stretching from decision 1 to decision 21 and the second from decision 19 to decision 33. Decisions 19, 20, and 21 connect the two chunks; decisions 34 and 35 can be seen as "add-ons" to the second chunk. Here the terms "move" and "critical move" (abbreviated CM) will be used to refer to decisions.

There are seven CM[3]s, most of them in the first chunk. The critical moves, by sequential number and dominant direction, are as follows: in the first chunk, 1>, 5>, <10, <14, and <19>, and in the second chunk <19> (overlap with the first chunk), 20>, and <33. Here and in many other linkographs, the positioning of the critical moves is not random.

The first thing we observe regarding the critical moves is that the sequence begins with a CM> (here it is the first move; elsewhere it could be a somewhat later move). In a symmetrical manner, it ends with a <CM (here not the last move, but nearly the last). What does that signify? The designer started by making a proposition, to be explored in subsequent moves. When the sequence achieved a clear ending, there was a conclusive move—not necessarily one that pertains to the entire process, but possibly one that pertains to the last issue inspected. Indeed, in this linkograph the CM> at the beginning and the <CM at the end are not linked to each other but are linked to other moves in between. They can be seen as initial and final moves of chunks rather than as critical moves that begin and end the sequence. The first chunk of our linkograph does not have a final <CM; move 1 links to move 21, which is not a CM. In the second chunk, however, the first move, 19, is a CM> (as well as a <CM). Therefore the second chunk begins with a CM> and ends with a <CM that is linked to it. This makes a lot of sense: if a chunk is a block of moves that treat defined issues, often

in order to ascertain that a proposition is viable, then the chunk begins with the proposition and ends with a conclusion of some sort. Of course, an issue may be left unresolved, or the exploration is short and limited and within the same chunk related issues come up, in which case there might not be a final <CM, as in the case of the first chunk in this linkograph. In some cases the opposite is also true—that is, a chunk may not have an initial CM> but may have a final <CM.

Chunks are relatively large structures. Within them we may find smaller structures, such as webs (in the Wang-Habraken linkograph there are no webs), or less clear-cut clusters that are visually discernible by the triangles that outline them. For example, a loosely defined structure can be discerned between move 3 and move 10. Such structures have no name, since they are not sufficiently defined, but they may be noticeable. In the small structure, the final move, 10, is a <CM, and it also includes a CM>, move 5, that seems to move the process forward with a number of subsequent moves that respond to it with backlinks, up to move 10. Another <CM is found in move 14, but its links are "local"—that is, its backlinks have short spans (it backlinks to moves 10, 12, and 13) and it probably has no structural significance in the sequence. Likewise, the backlinks of move 19 are "local" (it backlinks to moves 14, 16, and 18), and it is not the closure of a longer exploration at the magnitude of a chunk, or even an otherwise loosely defined structure.

On the other hand, the forelinks of move 19 embrace the entire second chunk. Together with the next move, 20, which is also a CM>, they set the scene for the design activity in this chunk that ends with the final <CM. Technically move 20 is also part of the first chunk, but its significant links, which make it a critical move, pertain to the activity of the second chunk. There are no smaller cycles in this chunk; in this it differs from the first chunk. <CMs> are quite rare, and when they occur they are usually pivot moves, as in this case. In the two-way critical move in this vignette, the designer summed up what he had done thus far (which concerned the lining up of several "place variants") and got ready to deal with "unoccupied" space, which he assigned to plants.

The positions of CMs (most of them, at least) help us to understand the structure of the thinking process of the designer. Another detailed example will help to further instantiate the role of critical moves as "structure anchors."

The Delft team protocol

The Wang-Habraken study draws attention to structural properties of the process of design reasoning, which are discernible in both graphic representations of the process (figures 5.1 and 5.2). The linkograph is particularly revealing in this respect. Despite the simplicity of this case and the lack of breakthroughs (for which there was no need in this episode), the analysis establishes a hierarchy of more important and less important decisions.

A detailed example from the Delft team protocol will illustrate how CMs are related to the structure of cognitive activity, or reasoning, during a design search. A team of three experienced designers (John, Ivan, and Kerry—see the appendix) worked for two hours to design a rack to hold a given backpack, with a bedroll strapped to its bottom, which was to be attached to a given mountain bike. Linkographs of units 37, 38, and 39 of the team protocol (out of 45 units into which the protocol was divided) are used; the total duration of which is close to 10 minutes.

Unit 37 Figure 5.3 is a linkograph of unit 37, a relatively long episode, comprising 62 moves (duration: five minutes). The subject matter of the team's deliberations in this episode was the complete rack and its joints to the bicycle, with an emphasis on the rack's structure. In the 15 minutes preceding this episode, the team had discussed features of the rack, the backpack that was to be fastened to it, and mounting points on the bicycle to which the rack could be attached. In unit 37 they took a more holistic view at the design components; at the end of this unit, they felt that the design was "under control" and it was time to finalize details. The linkograph shows that the recorded episode is divided into three main phases: (1) moves 3–15 (preceded by two "extracurricular" moves, 1 and 2, in which the team checked its schedule), (2) moves 15–45, which describe a large chunk, and (3) from move 45 to the end. The linkograph shows graphically that moves 15 and 45 are "pivots" that end one phase and start another. The third phase is a compendium of three very small chunks (moves 45–52, moves 53–57, and moves 57–60) and two final moves (61 and 62). Move 62, which links back all the way to move 4, "closed" this unit before the team moved on to different subject matters in the next unit. Within the first and second phases we also distinguish smaller cohesive parts and webs of especially densely interlinked moves (e.g., moves 15–20 and moves 30–35).

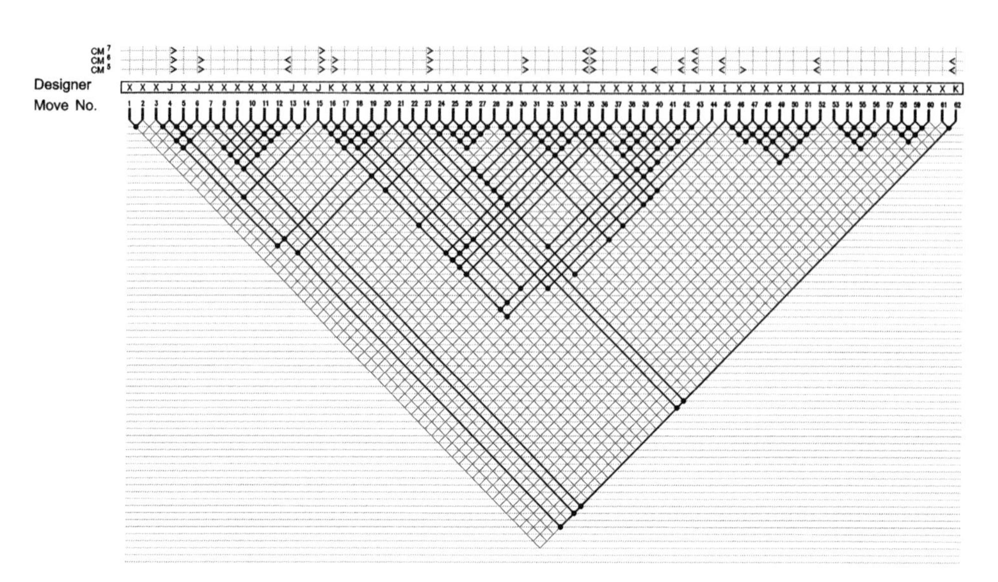

Figure 5.3
Linkograph of unit 37, Delft team protocol.

Let us look at critical moves at a threshold of seven links. There are five such moves, one of them double-speared: 4>, 15>, 23>, <35>, and <43. All the CM^{7}s are located in the first two phases; there are none in the third phase. We should now like to take a close look at the positions these moves occupy in the sequence of moves. Move 4, which is near the beginning, brings up points related to the bedroll that is strapped to the backpack and how the rack's frame is to accommodate it, to which other moves, in phases 1 and 2, backlink later:

Move 4 (John) and and I guess if I had to express that someway, I would I would see it as being something like er [sketches] here's the front of the frame and there's the backpack sitting like this; oops I guess I've got that backwards, sorry, the frame went backwards now because we're gonna have the bedroll off the back, so it's probably open at the rear

The bedroll is not picked up in further moves of this phase, and the issue reaches no conclusion (however, there seems to be an implicit agreement on the point advanced in this move). Move 15, the last in this phase, refers to the frame, going back to an earlier proposal that describes it as being made of metal tubes:

Move 15 (John) and then Kerry's got the, OK, we'll assume Kerry's tubes; or can it be a single tube now, can it just be like a tube that does this, that's folded one time like this

The proposal to replace several thin tubes with one heavier and stronger tube elicited a discussion of the best structural solution. Eventually the next critical move was made. In that move, the issue of tubes was put aside temporarily and the properties of the rack to be placed on top of the tube frame (which the team had come to call the "tray") were discussed:

Move 23 (John) and this could just have little snaps to the er er, to these rails, so that to these tubes; so we have this folding down spec; so that if this junc[tion] point here had a pivot at it and and then it's kinda like you're folding TV trays; you just unclip this guy from here and you unclip, well you probably don't need to unclip the back one, you just unclip one of these and then you can swing the legs flat

The ensuing discussion addressed the foldability requirement, which the team's members had overlooked thus far and to which they now had to find a solution. In move 35 the discussion returned to the tubes, and a single-tube solution that appeared to be optimal was chosen:

Move 35 (Ivan) or look, they went with the [looking at existing designs that were provided to the team]; if you go with the big fat tube instead of that little skinny stuff you could probably get away with one tube and then you just do the same concept that they've done there

The design of the tube structure remained a major issue, as it determined possible geometries of the solution as well as the weight of the entire device – an important consideration. Move 43 finalized the tube deliberations and confirmed that the best solution was one "beefy" tube:

Move 43 (John) by just making that [tube] beefy enough

Having come up with a satisfactory solution to the structural issue, the team went on to discuss joints among components of the system, easy mounting and release of the rack, and the possibility of locking the rack to guard against theft. These were simpler and easier issues for the team; decisions were made quickly, and the discussion did not yield any critical moves.

Upon inspecting the linkograph, we discover that the positions of the critical moves are not random. They occur primarily around the beginnings and endings of bigger and smaller chunks of interrelated moves, with CMs> at beginnings and <CMs at endings. Indeed, with the exception of move 43 and move 35 (which is critical in both directions), all CMs have a forelinking orientation and reside at beginnings of chunks, or even entire phases of the design. This is a little harder to discern in the case of moves 23 and 35, which occur in a larger structural unit spanning the whole of phase 2 (moves 15–45). However, on careful examination we see that this stretch of moves can be broken down into smaller groups (moves 15–20 and moves 30–35 were already singled out as discernible groups). We cannot fail to see that move 23 is one of only two moves connecting phase 2 to phase 1. The other is move 21, which also connects phase 2 to phase 3. But move 21 addresses the manufacturing of the "tray," a theme that was taken up in depth elsewhere in the process and received almost no attention in this unit.[4]

Move 43 occurs near the end of a small chunk (moves 35–43) that is not very independent structurally, and which is close to the end of phase 2. The other backlinking CM, move 35 (which is double-speared), is likewise at the end of a smaller and not easily distinguishable chunk, but it also introduces the next chunk (to which it has forelinks).

This pattern is logically explainable. The moves in every group of densely interlinked moves (the density varies, of course) have some content in common; otherwise there would not be a significant number of links among them. Therefore it is logical that many subsequent moves link back to one of the first moves that introduce the thematic content in that particular group of moves. Likewise, by the same logic, the last move to deal with that content before the design process turns to other issues links back to the largest number of former moves that partook in the discussions in a particular chunk or phase. Because design processes are not entirely "pure" or logical, we do not always observe the pattern we are describing here, and sometimes the pattern is discernible but incomplete and weak. However, in linkographs of well-structured episodes we can often observe the CM positioning at beginnings and endings of webs, chunks, phases, and entire units, with double-headed CMs occupying a special place in the resultant pattern (also see decision 19 in the Wang-Habraken process, illustrated in figure 5.2).

When we lower the CM threshold, we get more CMs. This allows for a finer analysis. For example, if we choose CM^{6} for Unit 37, the number of

CMs goes up from five at CM^7 to thirteen, distributed throughout all three phases: 4>, 6>, <13, 15>, 16>, 23>, 30>, <35>, <42, <43, <45, <52, <62. At this level the number of <CMs and the number of CMs> are equal; with one exception, we find only CMs> up to the double-speared move 35, after which all critical moves are <CMs. The exception is move 13, a <CM that, together with moves 4 and 5 (both CMs>), "frames" phase 1. Thus, we see that the structure of reasoning is captured by the location of critical moves at this level too. In this highly ordered unit, the correspondence between structure and the location of CMs is visibly perceivable in the linkograph.

Linkographs of episodes in which we find no or very few CMs (at a reasonable threshold) can be assumed to have a poor structure, in addition to possibly being non-conclusive and devoid of important decisions. Sometimes we find CMs at locations for which there is no logical account; in such cases the reason may be many repetitions that contribute little to the process but produce CMs at "non-strategic" locations. The linkographs of units 38 and 39 of the same Delft team protocol, directly following unit 37, are shown in figures 5.4 and 5.5 respectively. Comparable in length and in number of links, they will serve to illustrate the difference between a poorly structured pattern of reasoning and a relatively well-structured one.

Unit 38 After the tray concept had been well established, in unit 38 the team was looking at how the backpack was to be fastened to the tray and what implications this might have for the tray's properties (figure 5.4). The team members compared the joining options of snaps, straps, and drawstrings; these devices were very familiar to the team, and there was no need for lengthy discussions. However, no agreement was reached, and the unit ended with the following two moves:

Move 28 (John) are we designing three different things [three different fastening devices]

Move 29 (Kerry) no we're designing one thing

The unit can be divided into two phases: from the beginning to move 22, and from move 21 to the end, subdivided into two small groups of moves (21–25 and 26–29). Move 21 is a pivot move that connects the two phases. Moves 26–29, which interlink only among themselves, are a kind of add-on to this unit's deliberations. No immediately discernible structure is revealed, but less well-defined structures may include the groups of

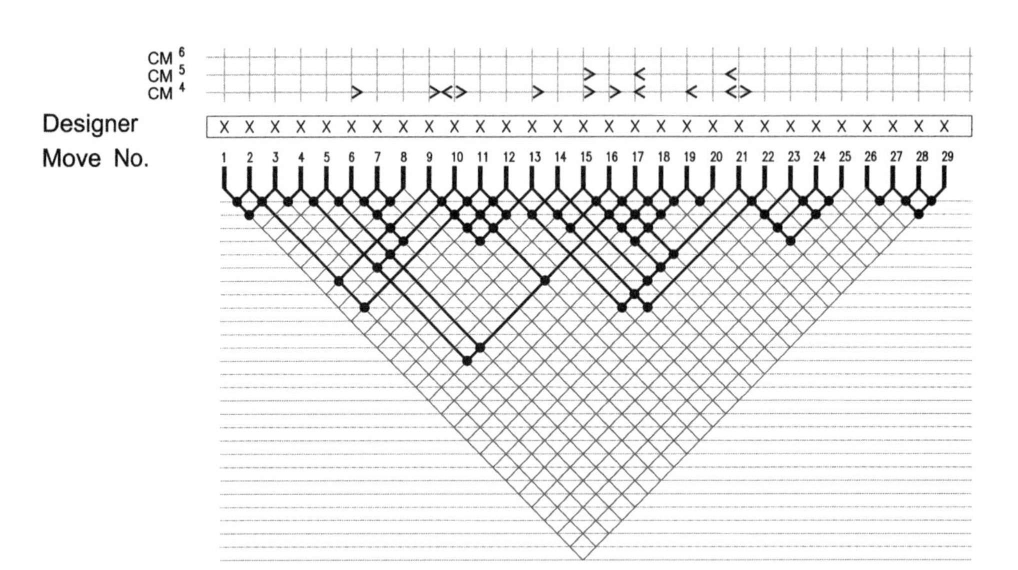

Figure 5.4
Linkograph of unit 38, Delft team protocol.

moves 2–11, moves 4–17, and moves 12–21. Two small webs exist, between moves 9–13 and moves 15–19. Critical moves can be established only up to the threshold of five (in a short sequence such as this one, especially if we deduct moves 26–29, this is a reasonable threshold), at which we have three CMs: 15>, <17, and <21. Move 15 is at the head of a web, move 17 is at the tail of a group, and moves 21 and 22 close the first phase. All of these are strategic points, albeit weak ones. If we lower the threshold to 4, we get many more critical moves. The most noticeable feature at this level is the double criticality of move 21, which is now critical owing to its links in both directions, a feature that is found almost exclusively in pivot moves. However, move 10 is also double-speared, although it does not have a similar distinguished pivot position in the sequence of moves. Move 9 is at the head of one of the webs, and move 19 is at the tail of the other web. The rest of the CM^{4}s in this sequence do not occupy strategic positions. The lack of clear grouping and the inconclusive positioning of several CMs in this sequence lead to the conclusion that this unit is poorly structured.

Unit 39 By contrast with unit 38, we can read structure into unit 39 (figure 5.5), which is dedicated to establishing the tray's dimensions. The unit is

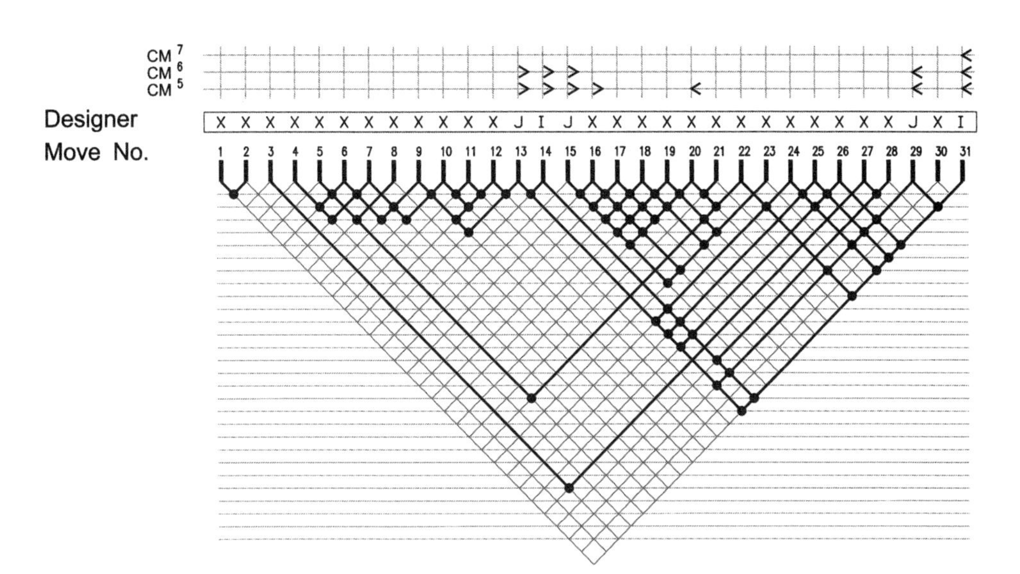

Figure 5.5
Linkograph of unit 39, Delft team protocol.

divided into poorly structured activity during moves 1–13 and adequately structured activity from move 13 to the end, with a web embedded in this phase (moves 15–20). Although the unit is short, there are five CM^{6}s, of which three are CMs> at the beginning of phase 2, and two are <CMs at its end. The discussion in the second phase was highly focused, and decisions regarding the tray's dimensions were reached. The discourse is well captured by the CMs—for example, the first and the last (a CM> and a <CM respectively):

Move 13 (John) OK let's draw fifteen inches OK, and it's probably, what, two inches deep

Move 31 (Ivan) I think you're two inches over the [tray length]

Units 38 and 39, despite their similarity in terms of number of moves and links, are very different in terms of structure, and this is revealed in the existence or lack thereof of critical moves at an elevated threshold and the positioning of critical moves in the string of moves. For an overview of link statistics pertaining to units 37–39, and for averages for a larger sample (14 units totaling 624 moves), see table 5.3.

We see that unit 37 has the highest values of all variables among the three units surveyed (although they are lower than the average of the

Table 5.3
Link statistics, units 37, 38, and 39. Delft team protocols.

Unit	No. moves	L.I.	% CM^5	% CM^6	% CM^7
37	62	2.7	24.2	21.0	8.1
38	29	2.0	10.3	0	0
39	31	2.1	22.6	16.1	3.2
Average across 14 units	624	2.4	26.4	17.3	9.8

larger sample in some of the parameters). The link index and notably the percentage of CM^6s are higher than the average, which appears to be positively correlated with the structured reasoning in unit 37.

Next let us consider two bolder hypotheses: that critical moves are indicative of the quality of design processes and that they can help us understand the dynamics of a design team. To do so, we shall look at critical moves differentially, as it is claimed that <CMs and CMs> have different roles. We shall begin by looking at the number of links generated by these two types of critical moves.

Process Productivity and Balance between <CMs and CMs>

Gestalt psychologists distinguished between reproductive and productive problem solving (Wertheimer 1945/1971). The former refers to processes for which problem solvers can reproduce routines that are familiar to them from successful solutions to earlier problems. If the current problem is not novel and resembles problems encountered in the past, reproduction is sufficient to yield a solution to the current problem. However, if the present problem is novel and does not resemble previously solved problems in any substantial manner, and a novel solution is sought, reproductive processes are not sufficient. The problem solver must then engage in a productive problem-solving process that entails restructuring the problem so that he or she can get a handle on it. Max Wertheimer coined the term "productive thinking," by which he meant the kind of thinking that people demonstrate when coming up with novel solutions to problems. Following in Wertheimer's footsteps, the term *productive designing* is introduced. Since most design problems are ill-defined and ill-structured, and therefore novel, designers have to engage in productive processes in order to arrive at solutions. It is maintained that design productivity is reflected in the structure that can be observed in a linkograph. The balance between <CMs and CMs> is also very telling.

Three design episodes, involving the architects Gilbert, Gideon, and Glenda, are used to qualitatively investigate the productivity of their processes in a design task. They are taken from the MIT "branch library" experiment, in which architects were given an outline of a small library building (referred to as a "footprint") and were asked to comment on how different entry options affected the building's design (see the appendix). These episodes were chosen because of the considerable differences in the extent to which they achieved design solutions.

Gilbert

Gilbert had difficulty with the very ambiguous task, and contented himself with offering lengthy commentary on its various aspects. (The problem he tackled was "branch library II," a variation on the original "branch library" task. See the appendix.) Preoccupied with what were described as existing walls in the library site, he studied every aspect of them in order to decide whether, and how, they could be incorporated into the library's design. Not considering it necessary to arrive at a decisive solution, he opted for an analytic approach that he took to be more appropriate.

The linkograph drawn for Gilbert (figure 5.6) spans 63 moves, with 53 links interconnecting them. Although two overlapping phases are discernible (moves 1–35 and moves 28–63), the linkograph does not suggest a very clear structure—and achieving a clear structure would be difficult with so low a number of links. Note, too, that there is only one critical move at the level chosen for this study, namely a threshold of at least four links; this is move 3, a lengthy move in which Gilbert first considered pros and cons of using the existing walls:

Move 3 My sense would be that we could build on top of the walls. You could say that you have so much of the wall started, let's build on top of it and go with that. My sense would be that would not be a good decision to make for several reasons. One, you don't know about the actual structural integrity of the walls. So let's not do that. Two, no matter what we do, it's never going to match. If the wall has been built for some period of time, when we come in and stack new stuff on it, it isn't going to match even if we had the exact same builder. Plus, when you take a wall that's 2′6″ high and 20 feet long, it's like "Why bother?"

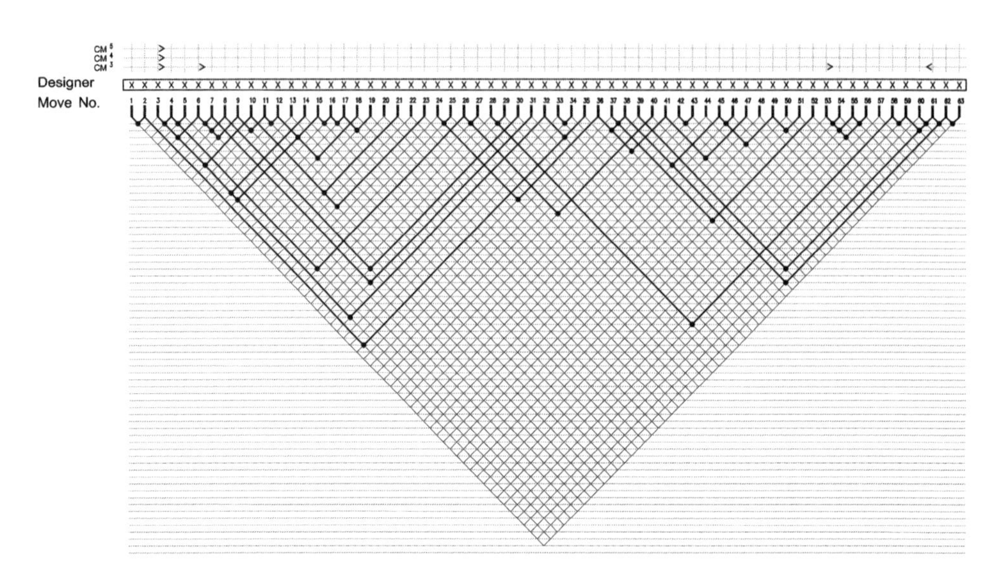

Figure 5.6
Linkograph of episode from Gilbert's design process, branch library design exercise.

Later the walls led to the establishment of a grid that was to become the foundation of the library design, but Gilbert was satisfied with a lengthy analysis and did not actively engage is arriving at a design solution.

The low performance indicators appear to reflect Gilbert's interpretation of his role, which yielded loosely interlinked bits of commentary that were not integrated into a whole.

Gideon

Gideon, a practicing architect, was oriented toward solutions, probably as a result of his daily experience in practice. Like Gilbert, Gideon was presented with the "Library II" task. The library he imagined was a simple wooden structure with a hearth and a prominent chimney. The space within the library would be flooded with light coming through a glass wall and through windows in the roof (skylights).

The linkograph of an episode from his process, shown here in figure 5.7, includes 64 moves—one more move than Gilbert's episode. However, Gideon's moves are interconnected with a much larger number of links: 80. There is also a fair number of critical moves, eight of them at the level of CM^4. Structurally, however, Gideon's linkograph does not offer more

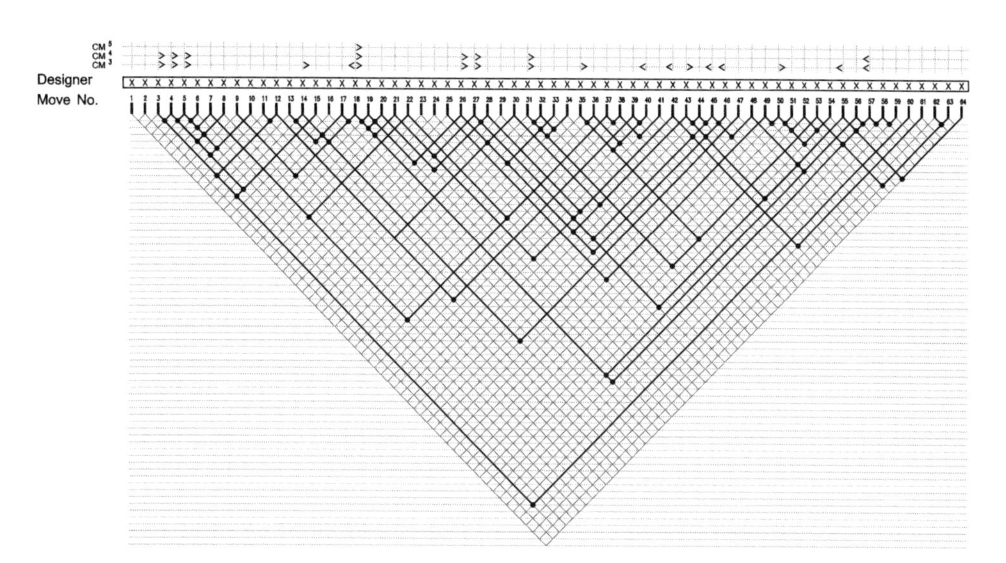

Figure 5.7
Linkograph of episode from Gideon's design process, branch library design exercise.

clarity than Gilbert's, and well-defined groupings of highly interlinked moves cannot be discerned.[5] The fact that all the critical moves other than the last are CMs> tells us that Gideon kept advancing new ideas, but there is no evidence that they resulted in firm decisions before the process moved on to new concerns. An exception is move 18, to which the sole <CM in the linkograph (move 57) backlinks. Move 18 is interesting because at a lower level (CM^3) it is critical in both directions, thus having a bit more of a structural role in the process:

Move 18 We don't know which direction the building is going yet, but I would place the hearth first as way of organizing the rest of the idea and the plan.

Gideon repeated the main ideas several times, and reworked them; as a result, quite a number of links in his linkograph stem from repetitions of similar thoughts. This may explain the relatively poor structure of the process as revealed by the linkograph, despite the many links and critical moves.

Glenda

In the episode analyzed, Glenda's process was highly structured. It comprised 50 moves with 80 links among them—the same number of links as

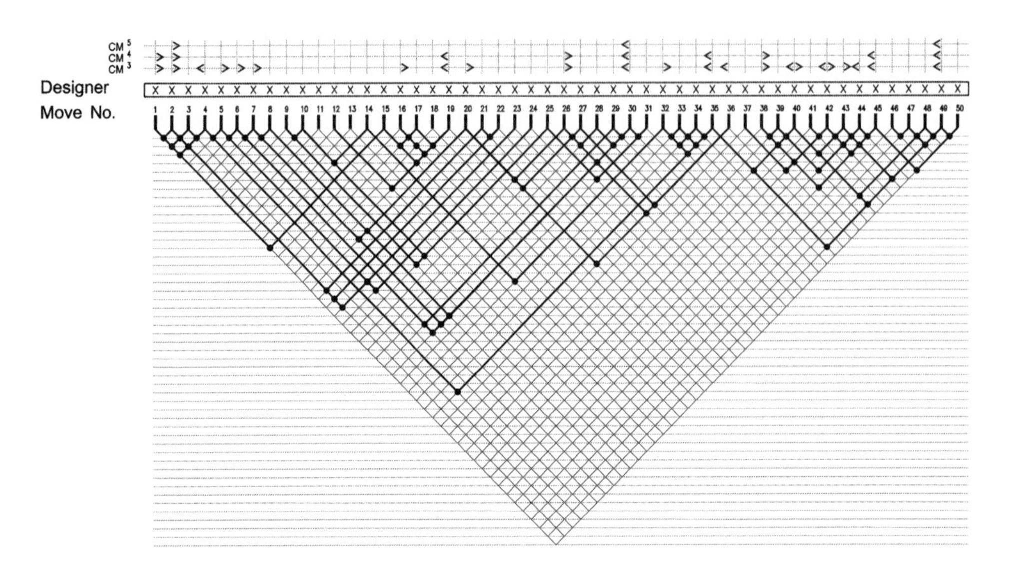

Figure 5.8

Linkograph of episode from Glenda's design process, branch library design exercise.

in Gideon's case, but in a shorter stretch of moves. The linkograph (figure 5.8) shows a clear division into two phases: moves 1–36 and moves 35–60. There are a number of small, dense hunks of links that fail to qualify as webs because they are too small (1–4, 15–19, 32–35, 42–45). There are nine CM^4s that are almost equally divided between CMs> (four moves) and <CMs (five moves).

In this episode, Glenda took a very solution-oriented approach to the task and advanced an idea that emerged after she had imagined a slightly different setting for the library—an urban rather than a suburban one. She assumed that the library would be enclosed by two party walls in a row of contiguous structures. Having drawn the library's footprint between these walls, she made the following move:

Move 38 and my first inclination is to divide it [the given layout] into nine squares. The nine-square configuration is classic

She provided some explanation to the nine-square (3×3) choice, talking about its prominence in classical urban design. Then she made the following three consecutive moves:

Move 40 So now these are what I'll call solids, that's built area, and these are voids [open space]

Move 41 No, that's not [a 3 × 3 square shape]; I'll extend this [by] one [row of 3 squares]

Move 42 It doesn't quite work with nine, it has to be twelve. I'll extend it to twelve . . . a variation on the nine squares

Ideas in this episode referred to various planning and architectural precedents, including the traditional North African Kasbah structure and the well-known prototypical house plans suggested by Serge Chermayeff and Christopher Alexander (1965). Glenda's moves in this brief vignette were very "designerly" (to use Nigel Cross' word; see Cross 2006): she reframed the problem (from a suburban to an urban context) and made transformations in her emerging conceptual solution as needed. Because the classic nine squares did not work, she accepted a twelve-square variation on the theme as satisfactory. The episode is productive in that a solution is in fact created and put forth and in that the process conforms to the Gestalt definition of productive thinking.

Table 5.4 summarizes a few parameters related to moves and links for the three episodes we have looked at. Clearly, Glenda emerges as the designer with the highest scores for these parameters: her link index is nearly twice that of Gilbert, and the percentage of CMs in her episode is more than tenfold compared to the percentage of CMs in Gilbert's episode. She also has a good balance between critical moves in the two directions, which will be addressed in the next section. Gideon's scores are somewhere between Gilbert's and Glenda's.

Balance between <CMs and CMs>

The balance between <CMs and CMs> is of particular importance. Gideon and Gilbert generate only, or almost only, CMs>, which suggests that they come up with ideas but do not bring them to fruition, in the sense that they

Table 5.4
Statistics on links and critical moves, branch library design exercise.

	No. moves	L.I.	% CM^4	% <CM^4 of CM^4	% CM^4> of CM^4
Gilbert	63	0.8	1.6	0	100
Gideon	64	1.3	12.5	12.5	87.5
Glenda	50	1.6	18.0	55.6	44.4

Table 5.5
Statistics on links and critical moves, team and individual designer, Delft protocols.

	Team	Individual
Link index	2.75	2.67
% CM^7 of all moves	12.42	10.14
% <CM^7s : % CM^7s>	43 : 57	43 : 57

are not developed, evaluated, or summarized. In Glenda's case the proportion of the two types of CMs is almost equal, suggesting balanced cycles of idea generation and assessment toward a solution. The quantitative results, although pertaining to partial episodes only, confirm an expert's unbiased observation and assessment of the productivity of the three designers throughout the design sessions.

We return now to the highly productive Delft workshop designers – the individual as well as the team. Like Glenda, they have been shown to reach balanced proportions of <CMs and CMs>, as shown in table 5.5. It so happens that the proportion of 43 percent <CMs versus 57 percent CMs> is identical for both the individual designer and the team. They have also attained almost similar link indices, with no statistically significant difference between the two processes (five units each, 21 and 25 minutes respectively).

A balanced proportion of critical moves in both directions suggests that ideas that are brought up are pursued and inspected, and conclusions (positive or negative) regarding their appropriateness and utility are drawn before the designer moves on. This is a hallmark of expertise: no time or effort is wasted on ideas that cannot be followed. At the same time, no ideas that are brought up are abandoned without undergoing at least some exploration.

The link index can tell us at least something about design productivity, but records of the critical moves in both directions can tell us more.

Backlinks and Forelinks of Critical Moves

As has been demonstrated, critical moves are of great significance in design thinking, and <CMs and CMs> occupy fairly well-defined positions in linkographs, which in turn represent the process of design thinking and reasoning. It is time now to return to the claim (made in chapter 3) that the design process aims at synthesizing a large number of issues into subsolutions and ultimately into one comprehensive solution.

In chapter 3, attention was called to two modes of thinking that synthesizing entails—modes that can be equated to divergent thinking and convergent thinking. At the cognitive level at which we examine design processes, the two types of thinking must more or less co-exist if a fruitful process is to be maintained. To see what this means in linkography, let us look at the link patterns of critical moves.

The way to explore this question is to look at all the links generated by critical moves—not only links in the direction that won them criticality (that is, either backward or forward), but also links in the opposite direction. A CM> may also have backlinks, and a <CM may also have forelinks. What is the proportion of a CM's links in each direction? A preliminary analysis that included five units from the Delft team protocol (32–37; units 34 and 35 are grouped together) was carried out; the results are summarized in table 5.6. These units comprise 298 moves, of which 76 are CM^{6}s—that is, each has at least six links backward, forward, or (in rare cases) in both directions.[6]

We see that in this sample, for both CMs> and <CMs, nearly three-fourths of the links are in the direction in which criticality was designated, but another one-fourth are in the opposite direction. As table 5.7 (which

Table 5.6
Backlinks and forelinks formed by <CMs and CMs>, Delft team protocols.

	<CM^6			CM^6>		
Unit	No.	< links	links >	No.	< links	links >
32	8	69	16	11	27	102
33	0	0	0	2	1	13
34/5	10	68	31	12	34	81
36	10	69	32	9	32	57
37	7	47	12	7	23	61
Total[a]	35	253	91	41	117	314
%		**73.5%**	26.5%		27.2%	**72.8%**

a. <CMs> are counted twice.

Table 5.7
Backlinks and forelinks formed by CMs across studies.

	CM[a]	<CM			CM>		
Study		No.	< links	>	No.	<	links >
MIT	CM^{4}	12	58 (76.3%)	18	24	34	109 (76.2%)
Delft Individual (sample)	CM^{7}	8	61 (80.3%)	15	11	25	88 (77.9%)
Delft team (sample)	CM^{7}	28	229 (80.4%)	56	33	88	302 (77.4%)
Daum-Cohen novices	CM^{6}	16	126 (78.8%)	34	28	48	206 (81.1%)
Daum-Cohen advanced	CM^{6}	26	184 (81.8%)	41	34	57	276 (82.9%)
Ashtray (long)	CM^{7}	2	19 (82.6%)	4	3	8	23 (74.2%)
Total		92	677 (**80.1%**)	168	133	260	1004 (**79.4%**)

a. Mixed CM thresholds are used, chosen to be relevant for particular studies.

represents a wider sample of cases extracted from various studies) shows, a stable proportion of links is maintained in the designated criticality direction across cases, although this proportion reaches 80 percent rather than the 73 percent of the previous, more limited study.

These results suggest that the intricate process of design reasoning is non-linear, in the sense that at least as far as significant (critical) design moves are concerned, every step is in fact double speared: it moves forward, but it also makes sure that it is congruent with what has already been achieved, and it validates what has been done thus far with an eye on ways to proceed from that point. Eighty percent of the effort is devoted to the "major" immediate goal; the remaining 20 percent is reserved for the "minor" companion goal.[7] It is proposed that this pattern represents a cognitive strategy that ensures the efficiency and effectiveness of reasoning in designing: it safeguards continuity while also guaranteeing that progress is made, and it serves the need of sustaining a solid and comprehensive design rationale for the entity that is being designed. We take this to demonstrate the divergent-convergent thinking pattern that is a must in creative thinking (see, e.g., Gabora 2010). The success of this cognitive strategy depends on an equilibrium between structure and content.

Structure-Content Relationship in Design Thinking

In all the investigations that have been presented thus far, design moves were looked at only in terms of the links generated. Moves' contents served only to illustrate the kind of deliberations designers are engaged in while designing. Coding of moves was avoided for the most part. However, design moves differ, and if we wish to relate structure and content in design reasoning, moves must be coded. A variety of coding schemes may be used for this purpose. The present study, which attempts to examine this relationship, pertains to a subset of the Delft team protocols (units 32–37, 298 moves, 21 minutes), and the moves under scrutiny are only those identified as CM^6s. At the outset the links that serve to establish critical moves are determined on the basis of the moves' contents, but no coding is involved in establishing CMs (for a detailed presentation of this study, see Goldschmidt and Weil 1998).

First a coding scheme should be established, and the moves must be encoded accordingly regardless of any links they may have. If this scheme pertains to structural properties of design reasoning, linkography should make it possible to correlate data regarding structure with data regarding content. For the purpose of analyzing structure, a coding scheme pertaining to categories of designer activities was developed. The scheme is context independent and problem independent; it is akin to one of the classification schemes of Purcell et al. (1996).

The coding scheme (CS) called *designer activity* comprises three major categories, A, B, and C, the first of which is subdivided into five subcategories, as follows. (Subcategories A_2–A_4 were grouped together for the sake of a clearer analysis.)

A—*Search and development*

- A_1—*Proposal* dealing with function or performance
- A_2—*Clarification* of functional aspects
- A_3—*Analysis* (of function or performance)
- A_4—*Explanation* (of function or performance)
- A_5—*Assessment* or *evaluation* (of function or performance)

B—*Support* of/*reference* to previously expressed idea(s)

C—*Remarks* (agenda; jokes; miscellaneous)

These categories are considered to be structural because they are independent of variables pertaining to subject matter, task definition and scope, and working style. In this design episode the functional performance of the entity that is being designed (a bicycle rack) is predominant in the design process, but the categories also hold for cases in which other factors might be of greater importance. For example, appearance and aesthetic considerations may be overriding in graphic design assignments. It may be argued that in such cases it is the *function* of the designed product (say, a poster) to attract attention. Therefore, the above categories are seen as a generic *structural* coding system for design moves.

Using these structural categories, the critical moves in units 32–37 of the Delft team protocol were coded. Each CM was coded once or twice, according to the categories it reflects (because some moves received a double coding, on the average each move was coded into 1.06 categories). Table 5.8 presents the category distribution for CM^6s as derived from the linkographic analysis.

Hypotheses

The following hypotheses are based on the assumption that there is a relationship, indeed a correlation, between properties of structure and properties of content in design reasoning and these properties are reflected in the protocol. Two hypotheses relate to <CMs and CMs>, respectively.

Table 5.8
Category distribution per CM, coding scheme: designer activity.

Unit	32		33		34/35		36		37		Total	
No. CM^6	<8	11>	<0	2>	<10	12>	<10	9>	<7	7>	<35	41>
A_1	2	7	0	0	1	2	4	5	1	6	8	20
A_2–A_4	5	3	0	0	6	5	4	2	4	1	19	11
A_5	1	0	0	0	0	1	0	0	1	0	2	1
B	1	5	0	1	2	1	2	1	1	3	6	11
C	0	0	0	1	0	4	1	2	0	0	1	7
Total[a]	9	15	0	2	9	13	11	10	7	10	36	50

a. The discrepancy between the number of nominal CMs and the total number of coded CMs is due to the fact that some moves have a double coding and are therefore counted twice. Likewise, <CMs> are counted twice.

Hypothesis 1 (<CMs)

The coding of <CMs tends to pertain to one or more of the categories A_2–A_5, B, and C. <CMs do not tend to pertain to category A_1.

Hypothesis 2 (CMs>)

The coding of CMs> tends to pertain to one or more of the categories A_1–A_4 and C. CMs> do not tend to pertain to categories A_5 and B.

It follows from these hypotheses that CMs> and <CMs have equal tendencies to pertain to categories A_2–A_4 and C. For each hypothesis, every CM was marked [+] if it confirmed the hypothesis and [–] if it did not. A <CM> received two marks, once as a <CM and once as a CM>. CMs with a double coding were marked [+] or [–] if both instances either confirmed or disconfirmed the hypothesis; if one coding confirmed the hypothesis and the other did not, it was marked [+/–]. In a final count, all [+/–] marks were discarded. The final count is given in table 5.9. The counting method explains the differences between the values in table 5.8 and those in table 5.9.

Next it was necessary to test whether the coding of each CM tends to pertain to specified categories and does not tend to pertain to others. If the overall tendency reaches a percentage above chance level (50 percent), the tendency is confirmed; otherwise it is not confirmed. For each hypothesis we calculated the percentage by dividing the total number of <CMs and CMs> that support or do not support the hypothesis (and therefore have received a [+] or a [–]) by the total number of <CMs or CMs>, as given in

Table 5.9
Hypotheses testing. Coding scheme: designer activity.

	32	33	34/35	36	37	Total[a]
Hyp. $1_{c.s.1}$ +	5	0	8	7	6	26
Hyp. $1_{c.s.1}$ –	2	0	2	3	1	8
Hyp. $2_{c.s.1}$ +	7	1	10	7	4	28
Hyp. $2_{c.s.1}$ –	4	1	1	1	1	8

a. The discrepancy between the number of nominal CMs and the number of coded CMs is due to the fact that some moves have a double coding and are therefore counted twice. Likewise, <CMs> are counted twice. The differences between values in this table and in table 5.8 are related to the actions associated with the assignment of +, –, and +/– marks.

tables 5.8 and 5.9. Thirty-five <CMs and 41 CMs> were thus tested, yielding the following results (note that this is the nominal number of CMs; see the notes to the tables):

Hypothesis 1 (<CMs)

Hypothesis supported: (26/35) x 100 percent = 74.3 percent. Hypothesis not supported: (8/35) x 100 percent = 22.9 percent

Hypothesis 2 (CMs>)

Hypothesis supported: (28/41) x 100 percent = 68.3 percent.

Hypothesis not supported: (8/41) x 100 percent = 19.5 percent

The conclusion is that hypothesis 1 and hypothesis 2 are supported beyond the chance level ($p < 0.05$). The confirmation of the hypotheses suggests that in design reasoning structure and content are indeed correlated. One might argue that this is a trivial finding, since we obviously expect an evaluative move to deal with previous moves, not with future ones. Similarly, a new proposal has less to do with past moves and would, in all likelihood, be dealt with in subsequent design acts. However, as linkographic studies show, design reasoning is not that simple. We should remember that the definition of "move" pertains to a very small design output unit that, on the basis of content, can potentially generate a large number of links. Every CM generates an average of ten links (in this example), but only some of them are in the "designated" direction (see the preceding section). Because "content" is determined by common sense, intricate backlinks and forelinks may be expected at what may be called a "semantic level": it is sufficient for any common element to be present in two moves to potentially establish a link between them. Therefore, a move's category/link-direction relationship is by no means obvious. In addition, the correlation that was established results from analyses of content and structure that are perpendicular to one another (that is, entirely independent), and therefore no circular or causal relationships exist between structure and content as defined here.

The same experiment was repeated with a different coding scheme (Goldschmidt and Weil 1998) wherein the categories were only partially structural, meaning that they were not entirely context independent. The categories were related to the level at which design actions were undertaken: the level of a holistic view of the entire entity being designed (in this case bicycle and rack), or the level of subsystems (bicycle only, rack only), or the level of details. The reason this scheme is not context independent has to do with the fact that in different design phases designers are likely to focus on different levels and therefore a study of an episode early in the design process would yield different results than a study of a much later episode. Indeed, a hypothesis that related CMs> to a holistic treatment of the entire system was not confirmed, probably because the protocol was taken from the middle of the second hour of a two-hour session.

Jean Piaget (1971) and other structuralists who were dedicated to the discovery and explication of structure in thought and matter were highly aware of the complex relationship between structure, often equated with form in their writings, and content. Structuralism endeavored to reintegrate content with form, and Piaget's version of this proposed integration theorizes that content and form (structure) are nested hierarchically in a system, "each element being 'content' relative to some prior element and 'form' for some posterior element" (ibid., 29). This notion assumes a transformational relationship between structure and content. I believe that in reasoning the relationship between the two does not have to be hierarchical; rather, content and structure concurrently describe the state of a system at any given point and in effective reasoning they are apparently extremely well coordinated. I hope to have demonstrated that, at least in design reasoning, this is indeed the case, and the proof rests with the properties of critical moves.

Studio Ideas Revisited

Dan Tatsa (see appendix and earlier in this chapter) found a correlation between independent linkographic counts of critical ideas and ideas that students assessed as important to their own designs. Let us return to the design studio and look at students' ideas from a slightly different perspective. Hagay Hochman and Itay Dafni (see appendix and Goldschmidt et al. 2010) were interested in "desk crits" (critiques) in the studio and the "ownership" of issues and ideas that emerge in this setting. The desk crit is the most prevalent practical instructional setting in schools of all design disciplines; this particular case looks at an architectural design studio. Students meet with their teachers in the studio regularly (two or three times a week) to present the progress they have made on their projects and receive feedback from the teacher. The communication between the teacher and the student is a conversation based on the student's materials (drawings, models, etc.) that is often accompanied by sketching. The duration of a crit ranges from 10 minutes to nearly an hour. Hochman and Dafni recorded three desk crits in three different studios of second-year students. The names of the students were Mani, Alona, and Yoav.

After producing protocols of the three crits, Hochman and Dafni generated linkographs. They did so in two stages. In stage 1 they produced full linkographs in which they notated links between all verbalizations of the two parties (student and teacher). In stage 2 they erased from the linkographs all links between verbalizations by the same party—that is, a student's link to his or her own former verbalization, and a teacher's link to his or her own previous verbalization. The new partial linkographs (particularly the one for Yoav's crit) were much less dense. Figures 5.9–5.11 show the two linkographs—one full, one partial—for each of the three crits.

Next, Hochman and Dafni singled out critical moves (verbalizations) at the level of three links. They chose a low threshold in order to have a sufficiently large number of moves to point to actual trends. They focused on CMs>, because they were interested in moves that raise new issues that elicit subsequent discussion. Because they knew who had generated each move, they could count the number of CM^3s> by each of the parties for each crit. Table 5.10 shows these counts, expressed as nominal numbers and proportions, after discarding a few moves at the outset of each crit; these moves occurred during the students' introductory presentations, before the conversation had actually begun. The rightmost column shows the results without those introductory moves discarded. Regardless of the number of verbalizations, in all cases the teachers emerge as having made a higher proportion of CMs>, with the exception of Alona's crit before the deduction of introductory moves, wherein the proportion is almost equal. This confirms that critical verbalizations in which new issues or ideas are raised are more often made by teachers than by students. The participants in this experiment, students and teachers alike, were not aware of this analysis. Hochman and Dafni wanted to know what their perception was of who raises issues in crits: Did they know that issues were raised mostly by the teachers? To find out, they used a brief questionnaire in which one of the questions was "Who normally brings up issues in crits?" The students and the teachers were asked to rate, on a scale of 1–5, the frequency with

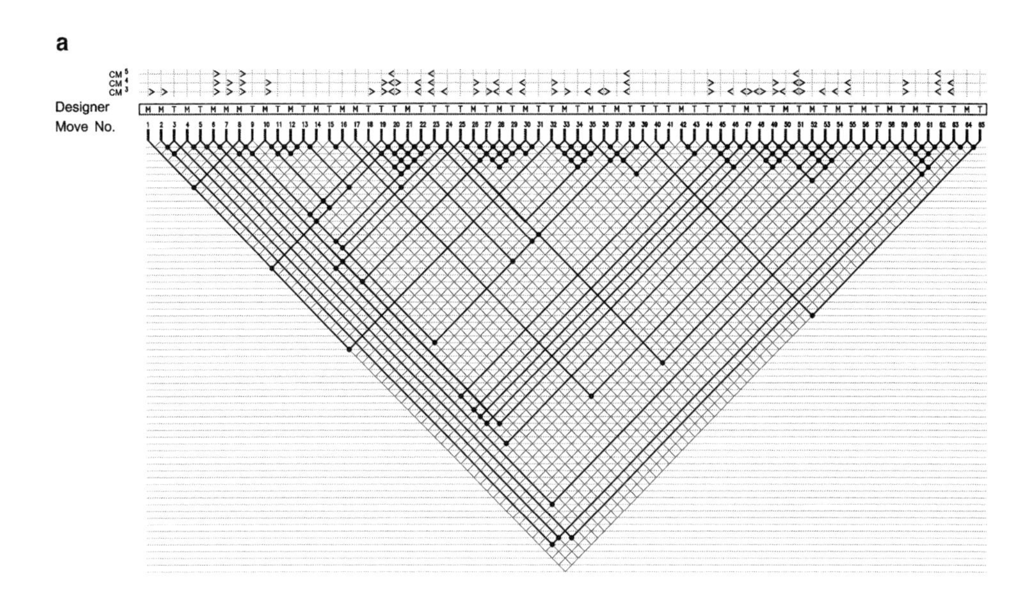

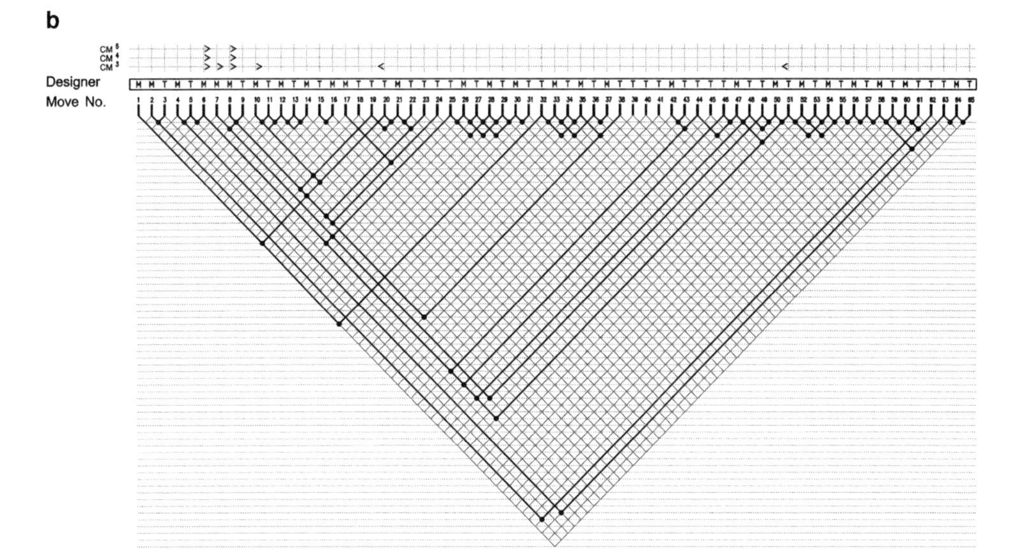

Figure 5.9

Mani's crit. (a) Full linkograph. (b) Partial linkograph.

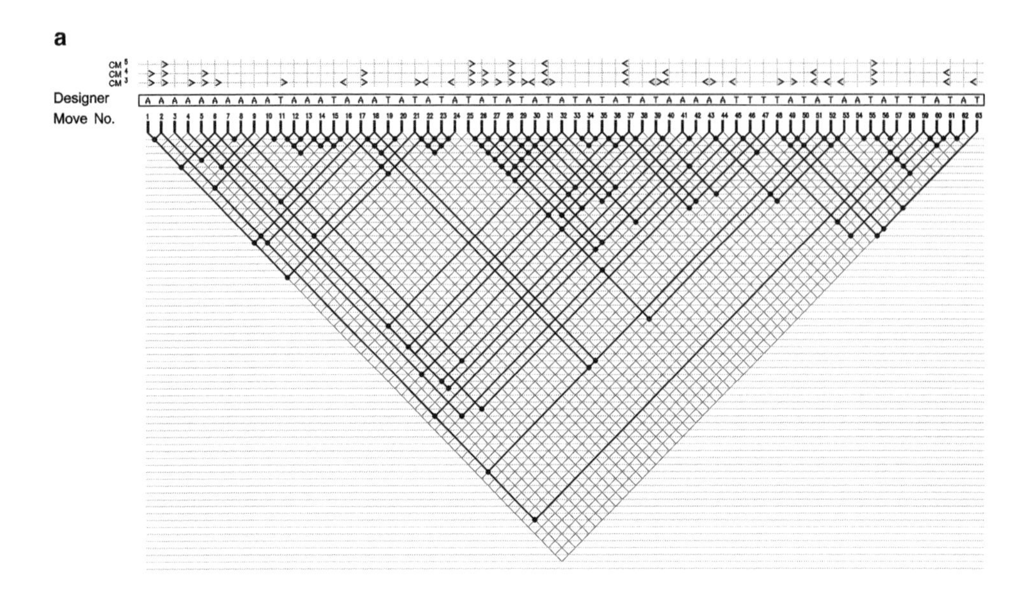

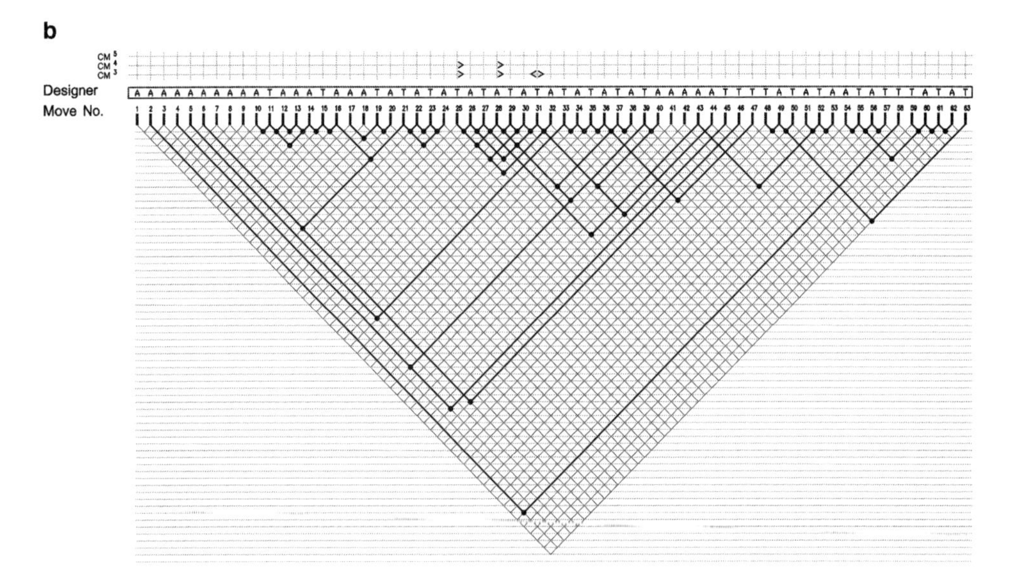

Figure 5.10

Alona's crit. (a) Full linkograph. (b) Partial linkograph.

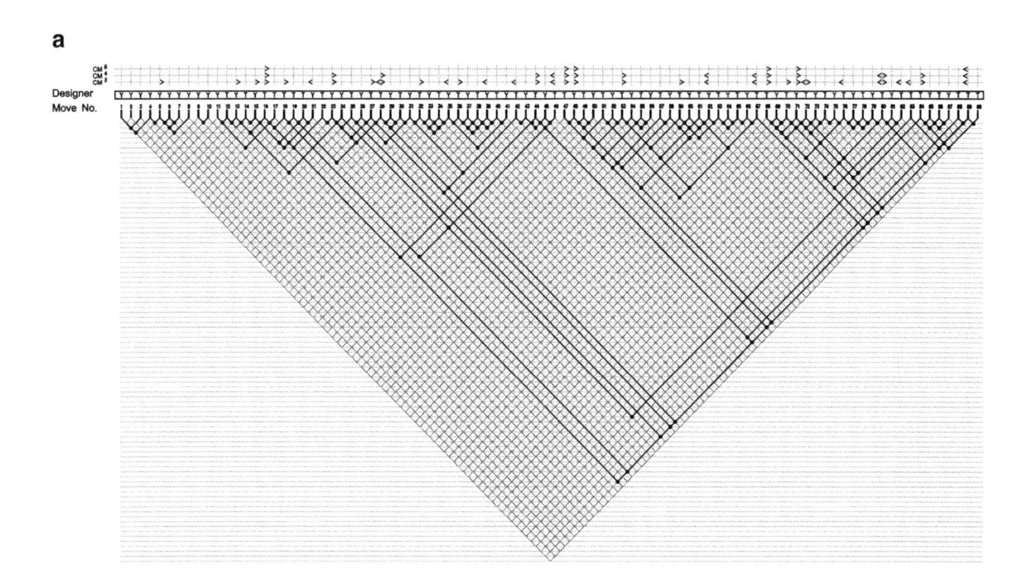

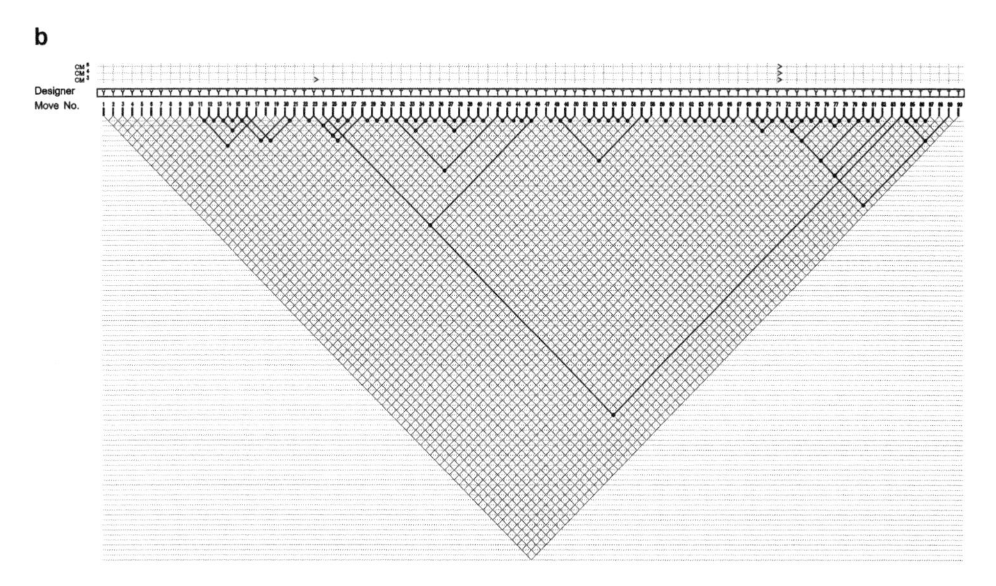

Figure 5.11
Yoav's crit. (a) Full linkograph. (b) Partial linkograph.

Table 5.10
CM^3s> across crits.

	Verbalizations	CM^3s	CM^3s>	CM^3s> (incl. introductory moves)
Mani	27 (41.5%)	15 (37.5%)	3 (21.4%)	9 (45.0%)
Mani's teacher	38 (58.5%)	25 (62.5%)	11 (78.6%)	11 (55%)
Total	65	40	14	20 (6 introductory)
Alona	37 (58.7%)	18 (52.9%)	5 (35.7%)	10 (52.6%)
Alona's teacher	26 (41.3%)	16 (47.1%)	9 (64.3%)	9 (47.4%)
Total	63	34	14	19 (5 introductory)
Yoav	45 (50%)	11 (31.4%)	3 (16.7%)	6 (28.6%)
Yoav's teacher	45 (50%)	24 (68.6%)	15 (83.3%)	15 (71.4%)
Total	90	35	18	21 (3 introductory)

Table 5.11
Self-assessment of issue-raising during the crit (scale of 1–5).

	Who brings up issues in crit	
Participant's perception	**Student**	**Teacher**
Mani	5	2
Mani's teacher	3	4
Alona	4	2
Alona's teacher	3	3
Yoav	3	3
Yoav's teacher	2	4

which issues were raised by students and by teachers. Table 5.11 shows the responses.

Mani and Alona thought that they raised most new issues in their crits, but their teachers did not think so. Mani's teacher thought that he raised most issues, a perception that is corroborated by the findings in table 5.10. Alona's teacher felt that he and the student raised an equal number of issues; that is true if we count Alona's introductory moves in the analyzed session, but if we deduct those moves the teacher raised almost twice as many issues as Alona. Yoav thought that he and the teacher were even in raising issues, whereas his teacher correctly estimated that it was he who raised more issues, which is also what the empirical results in table 5.10 tell us. These results suggest that teachers are better than students at assessing their respective contributions to raising issues and ideas in crits. A study of CMs> gives us an accurate picture, whereas a self-assessment can be biased and misleading. Students tend to appropriate ideas proposed by teachers and to think of them as their own.

In a study of eight students, Tatsa—using records based on his observations of the party that generated ideas for each project, and the students' assessments of who had generated them—found similar tendencies (Goldschmidt and Tatsa 2005). Many of the students thought the teacher's ideas were their own. These interesting findings suggest that the teachers in question were good pedagogues, in that they allowed the students to appropriate ideas without insisting on their ownership. They also suggest that the students were learners: it is much easier to learn if one can relate to ideas as one's own, especially in creative disciplines in which students are very sensitive to the ownership of ideas. Many students resent using the ideas of others (especially teachers), although most of them know that there are advantages in adopting ideas and relating to issues raised by a teacher. It is therefore an indication of good teaching skills that a teacher is able to raise issues in such a way that a student is able to appropriate them and to experiment with them in his or her design work. However, if we want to know what has really occurred, linkography and especially critical moves give us an unbiased picture.

Critical Moves and Team Dynamics

We now return to the Delft team protocols (units 32–37, 21 minutes, 298 moves), but this time we shall look at the individual designers who are the team's members: Kerry, Ivan, and John, three experienced industrial designers who work together in real life.

Teamwork has been studied from many perspectives. Here the modest goal is to look at the contributions of the three members to the "move economy" of the process. We should keep in mind that this team is unidisciplinary, as the members are designers of equal standing who are working together to design a backpack carrier for a bicycle. Their relative

Table 5.12
Percentage of critical moves contributed by team members, Delft team protocol.

		% CM^6			% CM^7		
	% of all moves	of total	of <	of >	of total	of <	of >
Kerry	29.9	27.4	34.3	22.0	32.4	35.3	28.6
Ivan	31.9	**37.0**	28.6	**43.9**	24.4	17.6	33.3
John	**38.2**	35.6	**37.1**	34.1	**43.2**	**47.1**	**38.1**

contributions were examined by looking at the critical moves they achieved at two levels, CM^6 and CM^7, while distinguishing between <CMs and CMs>. Table 5.12 summarizes the count of these moves, expressed as proportions.

The first thing we notice is that the three designers were not equally active. They made different numbers of moves, John leading the way with 38 percent of all moves. This suggests that we have no reason to expect a uniform contribution of critical moves by the team's members, either. There can be many reasons for uneven performance—expertise and interest in the subject matter, personality traits and dispositions, social circumstances, distractions, and so on. In this case, Kerry, the only woman on the team, appeared at times to be uneasy. At one point, after being teased by her teammates, she even said (jokingly) "Help! I want out of this exercise." Nigel Cross and Anita Clayburn Cross (1995), who analyzed the same protocol from the point of view of social dynamics, went as far as to suggest that Kerry had been intimidated by the two male designers. This may have been the reason for her somewhat lower performance in this session, but of course there could have been other reasons. Needless to say, it is normal to find differences among the contributions of a team's members. Contributions may change from phase to phase of a process and, of course, from one project to another. Therefore, we chose to look at contributions only to the critical moves that were generated in this vignette, and a comparison of contributions at two threshold levels is very telling of the team's dynamics.

At the level of CM^7, John was clearly the chief contributor. He generated more CM^7s than his share in the general move count—43 percent, versus 38 percent in the general move count. Many of his CM^7s had a backlinking orientation—he generated nearly half of the <CM^7s. Kerry was responsible for only one-third of the CM^7s, still slightly higher than her share in the general move count. She generated more <CM^7s than CM^7s>. Ivan, who generated 32 percent of the moves, contributed only one-fourth of the CM^{7}s, mostly CM^{7}s>. What do these numbers reveal?

John and Kerry, who generated mostly <CM^{7}s, albeit in different proportions, seemed to be assessing and reinforcing previous moves, perhaps solidifying design decisions after discussion. In Kerry's case, this happened especially in one of the protocol units in which technical details of joinery of the rack to the bicycle frame were discussed. Kerry is an experienced cyclist, and in that unit John said "we can assume Kerry has expert knowledge." Ivan, on the other hand, made many more CM^{7}s> than <CM^{7}s—almost twice as many, and the proportion is not far from John's CM^{7}s>. We interpret this to mean that Ivan was less inclined than the others to look back at what had already been thoroughly discussed in order to declare, and perhaps repeat, a decision or an assertion. He was more preoccupied with raising new ideas and questions, and this was reflected in his high proportion of CM^{7}s>. This manner of performance in the team, or design behavior, may be a result of personality traits or a perception of his role on the team. Ivan was the appointed "timekeeper" in this design process; he adhered to a timetable for design phases that the team established at the outset of the process and made sure the team progresses as planned.

At the level of CM^{6}s, the picture looks different. At that level, Ivan was the designer who contributed the highest proportion of critical moves: 37 percent, slightly higher than John and considerably more than his share in the general move count. Kerry again contributed the least—slightly more than one-fourth of the CM^{6}s. Both Kerry and John contributed slightly lower proportions of CM^{6}s than their share in the general move count. When we look at the distribution of <CM^{6}s and CM^{6}s>, the picture sharpens. Ivan made far more CM^{6}s> than his teammates—nearly one-half, as opposed to one-third by John and less than one-fourth by Kerry. This was at the expense of <CM^{6}s, in which Ivan trailed behind John and Kerry, who contributed an almost equal proportion of backlinking critical moves (John slightly more than Kerry). The trend here highlights what we saw at the higher level of CM^7. Ivan was very active in making new proposals, in initiating discussion topics, in asking important questions, to which the team reacted subsequently. He may have felt less of a need to sum up, repeat, or finalize decisions. John may have felt that he was the leader and that he should have the final say, which is reflected at the CM^7 level; Ivan did not share this sentiment.

A basketball team's goal is to score by shooting the ball through the net. Yet not all players try to shoot at all times; rather, they have roles, and often a player's best moves are those in which he or she passes to the player who is, at the moment, best positioned to shoot and score. The member of our design team whose (probably unofficial) role was to "score" was John, who "sealed" decisions while also making many new suggestions (for example, he was the one who first suggested the "tray" concept for the rack—a concept that, from the moment it was suggested, became the basis for a complete design solution). Ivan may have seen himself more as a shooting guard, whose role it was to let John score—in this case, to exclaim the punch line that occurs at a higher threshold level of move criticality (CM^7). Kerry's role in this session was less clear. She may have seen herself as contributing mainly detailed technical expertise, but in this session the opportunity to do so was limited by the conceptual nature of the task and by the time frame.

In the various cases presented in this chapter, we saw that with almost no background information about the designers and the particulars of the task and the design process, critical moves can tell us a fascinating story about what transpired in a design event. If we compare critical moves at different levels or between designers, we can penetrate even deeper into the situation. This further strengthens our belief that linkography in general and critical moves in particular are a very useful approach to the analysis of design thinking and processes.

6 Design Creativity

Creativity is a many-faceted phenomenon that is being researched from various perspectives in several fields. At the dawn of the era of cognitive psychology and cognitive science, Arthur Koestler (1964) was among the first authors to expose the complexity of creativity. Quite naturally, much of the relevant research is carried out in these fields. It is impossible to find a single definition of creativity that everyone agrees with, and most researchers prefer to avoid defining it (something that is not necessary for the purpose of discussing creativity). In fact, it is tenable to claim that there is no such thing as creativity, that there are only manifestations of it.[1] The literature on creativity is vast; here, let us content ourselves with the presentation of a few relevant principles before we turn to design creativity.

Creativity Research

The following five perspectives on creativity research are of the essence.

Magnitude of impact

Creative breakthroughs vary in impact. Margaret Boden distinguished between psychological creativity (P-Creativity) and historical creativity (H-Creativity), defining them as follows:

> A valuable idea is P-creative if the person in whose mind it arises could not have had it before; it does not matter how many times before other people have already had the same idea. By contrast, a valuable idea is H-creative if it is P-creative *and* no one else, in all human history, has ever had it before. (1994, 76)

Obviously there are many more instances of P-creativity than of H-creativity, although society is more concerned with instances of H-creativity that affect the lives of most of us. Radical breakthroughs under H-creativity include great works of art, important scientific discoveries and technological inventions, and influential social reforms with long-lasting effects. However, P-creativity is important to all of us in our daily lives; we value it and try to augment it in various ways. The discussion of design creativity in this chapter has P-creativity in mind.

Mode of manifestation

Since creativity as an abstract notion is elusive, most researchers prefer to study creative phenomena. One distinction that many researchers make was suggested by Howard Gardner (1988), who referred to the creative product, the creative person, and the creative process. Some researchers—among them Teresa Amabile (1983)—add the creative environment, by which they mean a social environment that fosters creativity.

A creative product, tangible or not, is usually acknowledged as a creative product only if it is both novel (original) and functional (useful), and if it is accepted as creative by the community, which may be quite small in the case of P-creativity and very extensive in the case of H-creativity. The most common method of assessing the creativity of products is judgment by experts. Most published research on design creativity treats creative products, often artifacts with enormous social, technological, and/or cultural influence.

The creative person has been studied mostly by means of case studies of individuals with extraordinary achievements and in rare cases also by attempting to profile creativity in terms of personality traits. Donald MacKinnon (1962) tried to find personality correlates of creativity among American architects by subjecting three groups of 40 architects each to a battery of personality tests. One group consisted of "most creative" architects, one of "creative" architects, and one of "regular" architects. Individual architects were assigned to these groups on the basis of a number of criteria, some of which may not be considered appropriate today. On page 3 of his 1978 book *In Search of Human Effectiveness*, MacKinnon wrote:

> To summarize, what is most generally characteristic of the creative architect . . . is his high level of effective intelligence, his openness to experience, his freedom from petty restraints and impoverishing inhibitions, his aesthetic sensitivity, his cognitive flexibility, his independence in thought and action, his high level of energy, his unquestioning commitment to creative endeavor and his unceasing striving for

creative solutions to the ever more difficult architectural problems which he constantly sets for himself.

The creative process is difficult to capture and difficult to study. There are a lot of assumptions regarding the properties of creative processes that led to the development of methods and techniques aimed at enhancing creativity in individuals and teams (e.g., brainstorming and TRIZ).

The subfield of design for which the most creativity-enhancing methods have been developed is engineering design. Behavioral studies are conducted in the laboratory and usually investigate design behavior—mostly problem solving; the problem and the experimental design usually are designed to test hypotheses, which are inferred from models of creative thinking. For example, analogical reasoning is assumed to be an important cognitive strategy in support of creativity, as it builds on abstracting the problem and thereby makes it easier to push the boundaries of the solution search space. In one study of the use of visual analogy in design, participants were asked to solve design problems under different conditions (with and without visual stimuli, and with and without instructions to use analogies based on such stimuli). Their designs were scored for creativity by naive expert judges; the scores were then assessed in light of hypotheses regarding the conditions that would yield the most creative designs (Casakin and Goldschmidt 2000). Protocol analysis is often used in such studies. In this chapter we shall look at creativity in the design process rather than at creativity in the design product or in the designer's personality.

Case studies of prominent creative people and products

Biographers and researchers have attempted to explain the extraordinary achievements of extremely creative individuals by tracing the development of their great ideas. Howard Gruber was a prominent creativity researcher, known especially for his Evolving Systems approach to creative thinking (see, e.g., Gruber 1980b; Gruber and Davies 1988). He delved into the lives of very creative individuals (including Charles Darwin and Jean Piaget) and described their breakthroughs as emanating from lifelong engagement with creative endeavors. Gruber's work was based on detailed case studies, in many of which archival materials were used. Gardner (1993) followed suit, inspecting several cases of creative individuals. His studies are less detailed than those in Gruber's monumental work, but taken together they are highly instructive. In the design literature we do not have many comprehensive case studies, but some short accounts exist (e.g., Roy 1993). Biographies and autobiographies of designers do not differ in principle from monographs on other creative and accomplished individuals in these genres; see, for example, Leibowitz 1989, in which writings by the architect Louis Sullivan are discussed. Case studies, biographies, and historical accounts are most suitable to the study of instances of H-creativity.

In addition, there have been a number of attempts to reconstruct creative processes by prominent personalities. For example, Hans König (1992) proposed a series of actions that according to him reconstruct the process of Juan Gris in the production of a famous still-life painting. Subrata Dasgupta (1994) presented a reconstruction of Maurice Wilkes' invention of microprogramming, which may be seen as an extremely creative case of design. Dasgupta's analysis, though computational in essence, is a rare attempt to see the case through a cognitive lens.

Measurements of creativity

The psychometric approach to creativity was pioneered by J. Paul Guilford, who suggested that creative achievement is commensurate with mental abilities that can be differentiated and measured, much as in studies of intelligence (see, e.g., Guilford 1956). Guilford talked mainly about productive thinking, as had the Gestalt psychologists several decades earlier. He claimed that creativity depends largely on divergent thinking, which included fluency, flexibility, originality, and elaboration. In addition, he claimed that transformations of thought, reinterpretations, and freedom from functional fixedness in deriving new solutions were essential to creativity. Guilford's Structure of the Intellect approach led to the development of creativity tests, of which there are many variants; the best-known ones were developed by E. Paul Torrance. Torrance's Tests of Creative Thinking (1974), which are still in wide use today, score abilities related to what Torrance called "skills that seem to be important in producing creative responses" (1988, 66). Criticisms of such tests question their predictive power and point out their apparent susceptibility to administration, scoring, and training effects (Plucker and Renzulli 1999).

The only specific psychometric studies of designers of which I am aware are in MacKinnon's 1962 study of architects' personalities, which used psychometric tools.

The experimental approach is not radically different from the psychometric approach. However, it usually tends to separate specific problem-solving cognitive capabilities and study them in isolation. An example may be the role of visual imagery, or the role of analogy, in creative thinking and problem solving. This type of research is most appropriate for the study of the creative process.

Neurocognitive exploration of creative thought

Neurocognitive studies of creativity center on memory activation in the brain, which displays different patterns in creative thinking than in "ordinary" thinking. The first notable trait of memory is that it is distributed (Kanerva 1988). This means that the storage of memory items is distributed across many memory locations (neurons) in a restricted region in the brain. The second important trait is that memory is content addressable (Gabora 2010). This suggests that the content of a memory item corresponds to the location (neurons) in which it is stored and from which it can be retrieved. As a result, items with related meaning are stored in overlapping or close locations.

Attention to a stimulus causes activation. The pattern of activation may be flat or spiky, depending on the type of attention paid to the stimulus and the kind of thinking it evokes. A flat pattern corresponds to a high level of activation that results from de-focused attention to a stimulus or stimuli. In this case, more overlapping memory locations are activated in the relevant region. De-focused attention is directed at the overall contemplated image and many of its details. In contrast, focused attention, wherein attention is paid to certain details of a stimulus, results in a distribution of memory locations that are farther from one another, and therefore create a spiky pattern. The spiky pattern corresponds to analytic, convergent thought, whereas the flat pattern of activation is more related to associative, divergent thought. Creativity requires variable focus, i.e., shifts between the two modes of attention. This is one aspect of memory activation that is controllable, and the ability to spontaneously widen and shrink the scope of attention and therefore the activation function is indispensable in creative thinking (Gabora 2010; Martindale 1999). Since designing involves rigorous visual thinking and representation (internal and external) and intensive use of visual stimuli of all kinds, these finding are of particular relevance to the study of design thinking and design creativity, although the explorations reported in this book are obviously not conducted in the realm of neurocognitive research. We recognize that, among other differences, the time scale of neurological activity is completely different from that of cognitive operations, and therefore no direct application of neurological data to the type of research discussed here, which is largely behavioral, is suggested. This line of research is mentioned here because the findings so far appear to support outcomes obtained in behavioral cognitive research and because the two fields are moving toward one another. This appears to offer many new research opportunities for the study of design thinking and design creativity.

Convergent and Divergent Thinking Revisited

Creativity can be studied by conducting regular behavioral experiments of the kind used to explore cognitive activity, and the linkographic experiments are seen as belonging in this category, although in most cases no hypotheses are put forth to be confirmed or refuted.

In chapter 3 it was suggested that linking moves forward and backward reflects shifts between divergent and convergent thinking. It was also stated that the creativity literature concerns itself primarily with divergent thinking, and that psychometric tests are geared to measure divergent and not convergent thinking or shifts between the two. This is also true of design research as exemplified by the recent work of Toshiharu Taura and Yukari Nagai (2013). Taura and Nagai maintain that creative design is the function of designers' ability to expand their thought space (the equivalent of the more usual term "design space") during the preliminary concept-generation phase. Taura and Nagai recognize the importance of going back and forth in thought, but they still concentrate on divergent thinking and have little to say about convergent thinking.

I take the position, supported by neurocognitive research, that creative thinking involves both divergent and convergent thinking. Support for this view is expressed by several cognition researchers. For example, David Perkins (1981) proposed that critical responses in creative thought involve an intuitive process and an analytical process, which are roughly the same as divergent and convergent processes. Perkins went on to say that these processes are usually discussed separately, but that on his view "the two strategies could occur mixed in behavior" (ibid., 105). Elsewhere he stated explicitly that "typical inventive thinking appears to demand a generous helping of both [divergent and convergent thinking]," and that "inventive people are mode shifters" (1992, 249). In a later text, Jonathan Plucker and Joseph Renzulli wrote:

Divergent thinking tests historically occupy nearly the entire creative process spotlight. Since the ability to generate ideas is only one aspect of the creative process (see, e.g., Runco and Okuda, 1988, in their discussion of the componential theory of creativity), its predominance devalues the integral role of creativity in the solving of problems. . . . Runco (1991) observes, "The evaluative component of the creative process has received very little attention. . . . This is surprising because it is a vital constituent of the creative process, and is required whenever an individual selects or expresses a preference for an idea or set of ideas. (Runco 1991, 312; Plucker and Renzulli 1999, 41)

Several methodologists have talked about divergent and convergent design phases in a prescriptive model of designing (see, e.g., Cross 1994; Fricke 1996; Pugh 1991; Roozenburg and Eekels 1995). In reaction to such talk, Ying-Chieh Liu, Thomas Blight and Amaresh Chakrabarti (2003) challenged the notion that conceptual design consists of broad phases of divergence, and then similarly extensive periods of convergence. They proposed an alternative view, "multiple divergence-convergence," that they claimed was more accurate. That approach, Liu et al. recommended, "is to carry out divergent and convergent activities in each level of solution abstraction" (ibid., 346). Regarding spoken language in design processes involving more than one person, Andy Dong wrote: "Designers routinely draw from a wide body of knowledge and experiences, personal and otherwise to establish the meaning that is assembled into the designed work. . . . Our explanation is that their language is aggregating toward a coherent design concept through cycles of convergence and divergence." (2007, 11) None of these studies reported empirical investigations at the cognitive level. Since the cognitive level is the main focus of this discourse, let us look at design creativity in terms of forelinks and backlinks of critical moves.

In chapter 3 above, it was proposed that forelinks represent divergent thinking and that backlinks stand for convergent thinking. In this chapter, special attention will be paid to forelinking critical moves. This is not to say that backlinking critical moves will be neglected or considered secondary.

Linkographs and Creativity

In his studies of the lives of very creative individuals, Howard Gruber did not conduct experiments, did not study short "live" episodes, and did not look at small-scale cognitive processes. But some of his insights into long-term creative endeavors also apply to short-term processes, just as smaller-scale neurological patterns are relevant to explorations at the cognitive scale. Gruber, who avoided overemphasizing single inspirational moments, proclaimed that "emphasis is withdrawn from the supposed single great stroke of insight and transposed to the many moments of insight that occur in the course of a creative effort" (Gruber and Davies 1988, 244). Elsewhere, Gruber stated that "interesting creative processes almost never result from single steps, but rather from concatenations and articulation of a complex set of interrelated moves" (1980a, 177).

If Gruber is right, we may conclude that the networks of links in linkographs may be useful in detecting creativity, in this case design creativity. Linkographs do not necessarily tell us everything there is to know about the creative process; referring back to the protocols may yield additional noteworthy information. For example, a protocol may reveal that a well-structured and highly interconnected linkograph describes a process involving analogical reasoning or imagistic reasoning—something that cannot be inferred from the linkograph alone. It is reasonable to assume that, at the cognitive scale at which design thinking is being dealt with in this book, design processes differ from one another in the level of creativity they exhibit. Here linkography will be used to point out these differences.

For an example, let us return to the Delft team protocol, documenting a bicycle rack design. A breakthrough was clearly identifiable when the designer John made a move in which he responded to the need to do something about the backpack's straps and suggested that the team see the bicycle rack it was designing for the backpack as a tray (unit 32, move 30):

Move 30 (John) So it's either a bag, or maybe it's like a little vacuum-formed tray kind of for it to sit in.

The tray idea was soon accepted by the other members of the team, who recognized that it addressed two aspects of the problem that were not resolved by seeing the rack as a flat plastic surface: how to contain the backpack's straps and how to protect the backpack from mud. The team immediately developed the tray idea, recognizing that it addressed all their concerns (later the production method was changed from vacuum forming to injection molding). Figure 6.1 shows the linkograph of unit 32 of the team protocol, in which all of this occurred.

Between moves 28 and 54 there is a heavily interlinked group of moves, including three webs (moves 30–37, moves 41–46, and moves 45–51) and

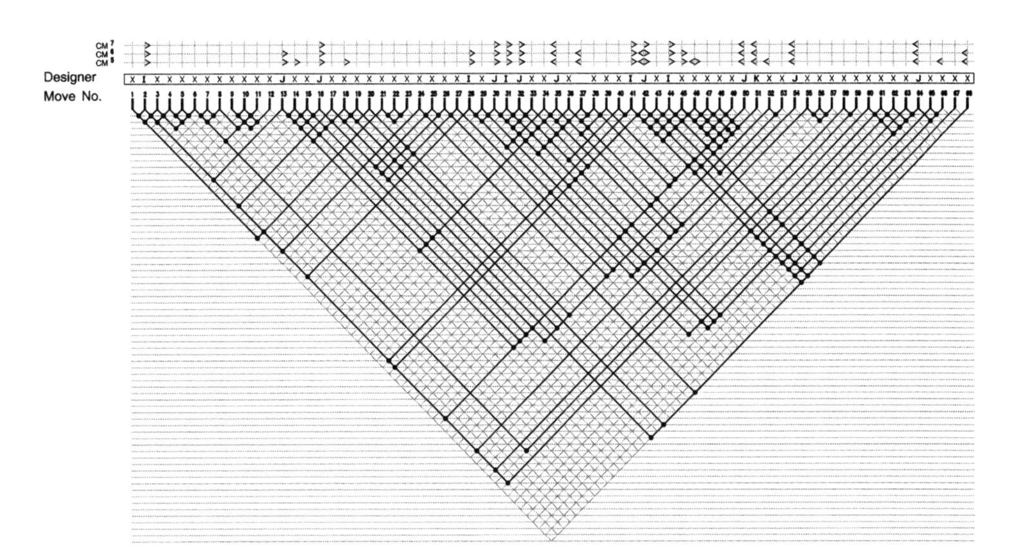

Figure 6.1
Linkograph of unit 32, Delft team protocol.

several critical moves, thirteen of which are at the threshold level of six links. Seven of these moves are CM^6s>, five are <CM^6s, and one is a <CM^6>. Let us look at these critical moves—or this "critical path," as John Habraken would call the sequence:

Move 28> (Ivan) We'll just call it that for now, er bag, put it in a bag, we're gonna need some sort of thing to do something with those straps

Move 30> (John) So it's either a bag, or maybe it's like a little vacuum-formed tray kind of for it to sit in

Move 31> (Ivan) Yeah a tray that's right OK

Move 32> (John) 'Cause it would be nice I think, I mean just from a positioning standpoint, if we've got this frame outline and we know that they're [the clients are] gonna stick with that, you can vacuum form a a tray or a

Move <35 (John) Maybe the tray could have plastic snap features in it, so you just like kkkkkk snap your backpack down in it

Move <37 (John) It's a multifunction part huh

Move 41> (Ivan) Uh uh what if your bag were big er, what if you're, you're on er, if this tray were not plastic but like a big net you just sorta like pulled it around and zipped there I dunno

Move <42> (John) Maybe it could be part, maybe it could be a tray with a, with a net and a drawstring on the top of it, I like that

Move 44> (Ivan) A tray with sort of just hanging down net, you can pull it around and and zip it closed

Move 45> (Kerry) It could be like a a a window shade so you can kinda, it sinks back in, so it just

Move <50 (John) So what we're doing right now, though is, we're coming up with like again classifications of solutions of kind of all, they're all "either or" things, I mean like we wouldn't do the net and the shade and the snap in with the tray either or any one of those will probably

Move <51 (Kerry) A net can be combined with a shade, I mean you could have a retractable net that, that's how I thought of it

Move <54 (John) I think tray is sorta a new one on the list, it's not a subset of bag, it's a kind of er yeah, but oh yeah yeah oh I see, shade straps is how do you dress the straps on the back

This is a very interesting group of moves, all generated in a little less than three minutes (between moves 28 and 54). In the first move the bag concept was seen by Ivan as a fait accompli that still required a solution to the problem of the straps. As soon as the tray concept was raised, just a few seconds later, it was contemplated in conjunction with concepts raised earlier (bag, net, shade), and attempts were made to combine all of these concepts. One could even interpret the verbalizations by Ivan and Kerry as a careful and subtle struggle to preserve ideas that they had already accepted and that they were not easily willing to discard in favor of the new idea. John, the initiator of the tray concept, insisted that the tray was a stand-alone idea that was not a subset of any of the previous concepts. All the same, as a veteran team player, he displayed openness to the possibility of a combination of ideas—hence the double-speared move 42, in which John conceded that the solution could be a tray with a net and a drawstring.

Several of the participants in the Delft protocol workshop pointed to this passage as a turning point in the design process, and this was evident in one way or another in the notations they used in their analyses of the protocol (Cross 1997). But linkography, Nigel Cross said, was "the analysis that came closest to both tracing the history of the emergence of the tray concept and indicating its important role" (ibid., 314).

For present purposes, this provides an excellent example of the birth of a new and creative idea that was not completely detached from what had happened earlier in the process, including the flat plastic rack in earlier units of the protocol. While relating to previous deliberations, this idea also affected subsequent moves in the design process. The linkograph shows that moves 60–68 are heavily linked to moves 41 and 44, and to a lesser degree also to move 42. Moves in posterior units also related to the tray concept, but this cannot be shown in the linkograph of unit 32. This short episode emphasizes the network nature of design thinking in general and creative design thinking in particular. It also shows that inventive ideas, if they are to be successful, must be developed further and must be rigorously assessed against previous work, including design decisions already made and design criteria already agreed upon (e.g., containment of straps). Therefore, we get both CMs> and <CMs in this passage—that is, both divergent and convergent thinking take place, with frequent shifts between the two modes. The high percentage of CMs in this unit is also indicative of its highly productive nature: at the level of CM^6, 27 percent of the moves are critical; of those, 58 percent are critical because of forelinks. At the level of CM^7, 19 percent of the moves are critical and of those, 62 percent are critical because of forelinks. It may also be worth noting that most of the CMs are strategically located at beginnings and endings of discernible structural components of unit 32 (see chapter 5).

We can also scrutinize the threshold level of CM^5 and compare the values found in unit 32 with those of units 37–39 in this protocol (see table 5.3). The proportion of CM^5s is 36 percent in unit 32, 24 percent in unit 37, 23 percent in unit 39, and 10 percent in unit 38. Fifty-six percent of the CM^5s in unit 32 are critical because of forelinks. We see that, despite the creative leap, the proportion of CMs> at all criticality thresholds is not overwhelming, between 56 percent and 62 percent. This means that a considerable number of critical moves are devoted primarily to assessment and evaluation, thus concurring with the theory that calls for divergent and convergent thinking in creative feats. The proportions above demonstrate that we see an increase in critical moves in a passage recognized independently as creative in the sense that it includes a breakthrough. These critical moves are rather well balanced between forelinking and backlinking, that is, divergent and convergent thinking, with frequent shifts between them.

As was discussed in chapter 5 and shown in tables 5.6 and 5.7, critical moves are in fact bidirectional. That is, although they are critical owing to their links either forward or backward, they also "dedicate" 20 percent or more of the total number of links they generate to the opposite direction. This reinforces Perkins' (1981) view that the two modes of thinking "can occur mixed in behavior." Here we ought to refer once again to Gruber, who wrote: "Insofar as divergent thinking plays some role in creative work, the system within which it occurs must regulate it, prevent it from running amok, require it to generate a well-chosen alternative." (1980b, 287–288) The required actions to which Gruber pointed can be interpreted as convergent thinking embedded in backlinking critical moves and backlinks of critical moves with mostly forelinks.

Let us return to a study, described in chapter 5, wherein Dan Tatsa looked at ideas generated by architecture students in a semester-long studio project (see Goldschmidt and Tatsa 2005). After the end of the semester the students themselves assessed their projects' ideas in terms of criticality, which meant contribution to the final outcome. In addition to a connection that was found between the level of self-assessed criticality of ideas and link indices derived from linkographs (as reported in chapter 5), the same study also looked at correlations between ideas and the final grades assigned to the students. This is of interest here because the criteria for awarding grades emphasize creativity. First Tatsa calculated the correlation between grade and the number of all ideas; this correlation was not significant. He then repeated the calculation for critical ideas only, and found a significant positive, even high, correlation between their number and the project's grade ($N = 8$; $r = 0.699$, $p < 0.5$). This confirms that processes that included a higher number of critical ideas, as assessed by the students themselves, yielded outcomes that teachers deemed higher in quality and more creative. This finding is in line with results from the Delft protocols research described in this section, namely, that creative episodes display a high proportion of critical moves.

Ideas and links

Let us now turn to another example, one derived from studies by Remko van der Lugt (2001, 2003) that do not focus on critical moves but still count links. Van der Lugt (2001) studied differences among structured idea generation meetings and the effect of sketching on the processes in these meetings. To do so he used linkography that facilitated quantitative analyses and comparisons of processes. Linkographs were constructed for design sessions that were conducted using different methods, so that the pattern of links among the ideas raised in them was revealed. A link in this case meant that an idea built on a previous idea generated in that meeting. In a final step, the participants were asked to appraise the ideas raised in the meeting in terms of their creative qualities. Later these appraisals were correlated with their "linking scores" (van der Lugt 2003). Each participant was given a number of colored stickers. The four red stickers were to be used to indicate the four most surprising ideas, then four green stickers to indicate the four most feasible ideas, and the one blue sticker to indicate the most exciting idea (the idea the participant "would be most excited about developing further"). The 192 ideas that had been generated in four design meetings were then scored by the number of stickers applied to them according to the formula

Score = green stickers + red stickers + 2(green and red stickers)
+ 4(blue stickers).

Using the scores, van der Lugt divided the ideas into two groups: ideas with a score of 7 or more and ideas with a score of less than 7. Then *t*-tests were used to check the difference between the groups in terms of the number of links among ideas as notated in the linkographs. The difference proved significant ($p < 0.05$), with 3.08 links for the high-scoring ideas and 2.13 for the low-scoring ideas. A detailed analysis of the differences between ideas that received colored stickers in any of the categories and ideas that did not receive any stickers also showed that the former had higher rates of linking. Van der Lugt concluded that there was a strong connection between "the perceived quality of an idea" and the number of links it generated (ideas it built on, and ideas that built on it). For van der Lugt "idea quality" is unequivocally related to creativity and the criteria for awarding stickers reflect this stance. However, he proposed that further research should use quality assessments by independent judges, rather than self-appraisals. Even so, this study lends further support to the notion that intense interlinking among design ideas is a prerequisite for creativity.

Expert and novice designers

Let us now return to the MIT branch library design study, in which the participants included "ordinary" architects and studio teachers, one novice student, and one prominent architect (Martin, who at the time of the

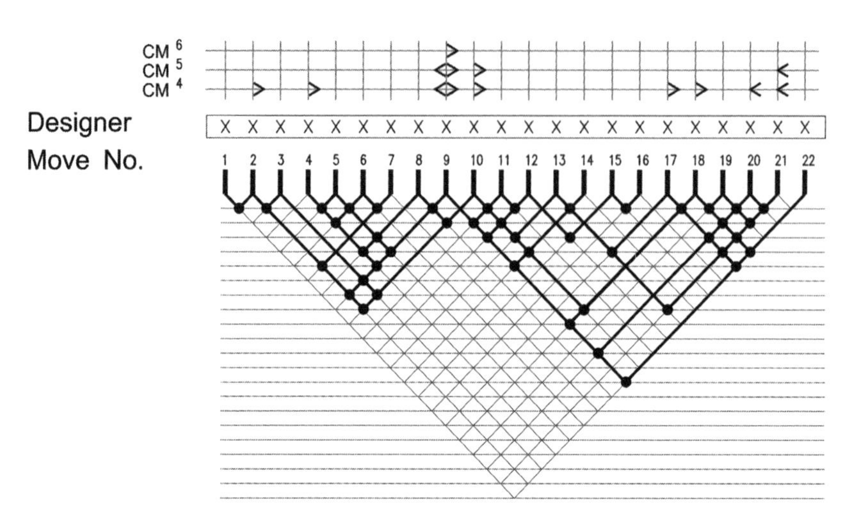

Figure 6.2
Linkograph of episode from Martin's design process, branch library design task.

experiment was internationally very famous). Martin handled the library design task easily, explaining the principles of his design theory in length and then producing a comprehensive solution within minutes. His design was by far the most complete and most creative of the designs obtained in this exercise.[2] This is not surprising—we know that experts, and certainly masters, "immediately produce higher quality options" (Björklund et al. 2013, 139) and "seem to choose a preferred option rather early on" (ibid., 140), with no need to consider many options. Figure 6.2 is a linkograph of the 22 moves in which Martin completed most of his design solution.

When the linkograph in figure 6.2 is compared with those of the processes of Gilbert, Gideon, and Glenda, who worked on the same task (see figures 5.6–5.8), it is immediately apparent that Martin's linkograph is denser in links and contains a higher proportion of critical moves. Although direct comparison is not possible, because this linkograph is considerably shorter than the other three, it appears that Martin (whose process had two distinct portions) was able to interconnect his design acts in a dense mesh—even more so than Glenda, who stood out among the three linkographs portrayed in chapter 5.

When he first saw the library's footprint, Martin complained that it lacked organization. He proceeded to explain and sketch how spatial organization might be achieved. After Martin stated that he was not able to work without any context, the researcher drew a rectangle representing a site with the library in its midst, added some trees (scattered about the site), and indicated north. Martin postponed dealing with the articulation of spaces within the library until later in the process. Let us look at Martin's critical moves at a threshold of four links:

Move 2> It's important enough because there [outdoor area shaded by trees, across from the library's entrance] one starts creating a space.

Move 4> I would make the entry—one can come through the cars [parking] here; it's the case of the other side as well.

Move <9> We start creating a hierarchy. . . . The large trees, the parking lots, the pedestrians, an entry axis.

Move 10> I would then look for a direct relationship between entrance and exterior, because here, the real edge is not this [edge of building], for me it's that [boundaries of the lot].

Move 17> So this is a way of letting elements of nature into the project. I don't like isolated buildings.

Move 18> The building needs to reach from here to here [boundaries of the lot]. I would try through this organization to make space reach until there, so it has tension, it has a prolongation. It isn't a small shed, it isn't a pavilion on the interior. There. This is a different approach, but already, these elements there have found a different organization, and beyond functions, beyond, I would say, the interior organization.

Move <20 So I will make the organization of the parking lots give force, with the trees, to this idea. I always want to take the entire, all of the land.

Move <21 I think that if there are two roads, there is already something artificial . . . drawn by man. I find it justified to master the whole. Not let the pavilion swim in the middle. So you see how the discourse becomes immediately one of exterior.

In the moves listed above, Martin did the following, while sketching continuously: First, he noticed that the trees, which cast shadows, enclosed an outdoor area adjacent to the library wall. He established an entry point into the library's footprint across from the wall facing the trees, and designated parking lots on either side of the entrance. He then reflected on the relationship between the parking lots, the entry, and the outdoor space enclosed by the trees in the "back" of the building. He declared that a hierarchy had been established among these elements through a (visual) axis that ran from the entry to the trees in the back, through a glazed back wall. He went on to emphasize the relationship between inside and outside spaces, adding that for him they were inseparable since the edges of the building were really outside, at the boundaries of the lot, and included outdoor spaces. For Martin, the hierarchy and the axis connecting the main elements of the building and its surroundings and governing the relationships among them, were the way to achieve organization, which was important to him. An examination of Martin's built works and their documentation in professional publications shows that indeed motifs of hierarchy and visual axes play a very important role in his approach to designing buildings. The emphasis on the relation of the indoor spaces with the exterior, which came up again and again in the protocol, is also a hallmark of Martin's built work (see also chapter 3).

In the linkograph of this short vignette we see that even at the threshold of five links there are three critical moves, or 14 percent of all moves. When we look at CM^4s, we find eight critical moves, or 36 percent of all moves—a high percentage, especially in comparison with the 18 percent in Glenda's protocol and the much lower percentages in the linkographs of Gilbert and Gideon. Such high rates are not typical of most episodes, with the possible exception of short passages in which a significant breakthrough is achieved, as we have seen in the case of unit 32 of the Delft team protocol. In Martin's process in this task we cannot claim a breakthrough; instead we know that a "good fit" among elements, which was quickly established, turned the ill-defined problem into an easily solvable one. Interestingly, the CM^4s include five CMs>, two <CMs, and one <CM>. The two-headed critical move, quite a rare phenomenon, is move 9, in which the all-important principles of hierarchy and axis appear.

We can compare Martin's linkograph to those of Gilbert, Gideon, and Glenda in another criterion: that of the proportion of unidirectional and bidirectional moves. In Martin's entire linkograph we find only one move that has no backlinks (move 4) and only four moves that have no forelinks (moves 7, 14, 16, and 21). This amounts to 25 percent unidirectional moves, and therefore 75 percent bidirectional moves. The percentages of bidirectional moves for the three other library designers are 67 percent for Glenda, 53 percent for Gideon, and 67 percent for Gilbert.[3] Similar values are encountered in other linkographs; for example, the proportion of bidirectional moves in the ashtray linkograph (figure 4.3), which is of similar length, is 64 percent. Bidirectionality is related to fast shifts between divergent and convergent thinking, which is typical of creative processes. Therefore, this short episode exemplifies Martin's almost simultaneous divergent-convergent thinking in a highly creative instance of designing.

Much can be learned from a comparison between Martin's high-end process and the very low-end process of Alice, another participant in the library design exercise. Figure 6.3 shows the linkograph of a portion of Alice's process. Alice, a first-year graduate student of architecture, had no design background (her undergraduate degree was in chemistry), and in the exercise she groped to make sense of the library's footprint and the consequences of entering it from each of the optional entry points. Her great discovery was that penetrating the building near the center is advantageous in terms of people's circulation in the building. In the debriefing after the exercise, when asked about possible differences between her process and the presumed process of an experienced architect, she replied as follows:

> I don't know if he would look at this [footprint] and immediately see these [implications of entry options] and wouldn't even have to draw it for himself because he can see it. I felt I had to stop and go through all of them [entry options] and actually

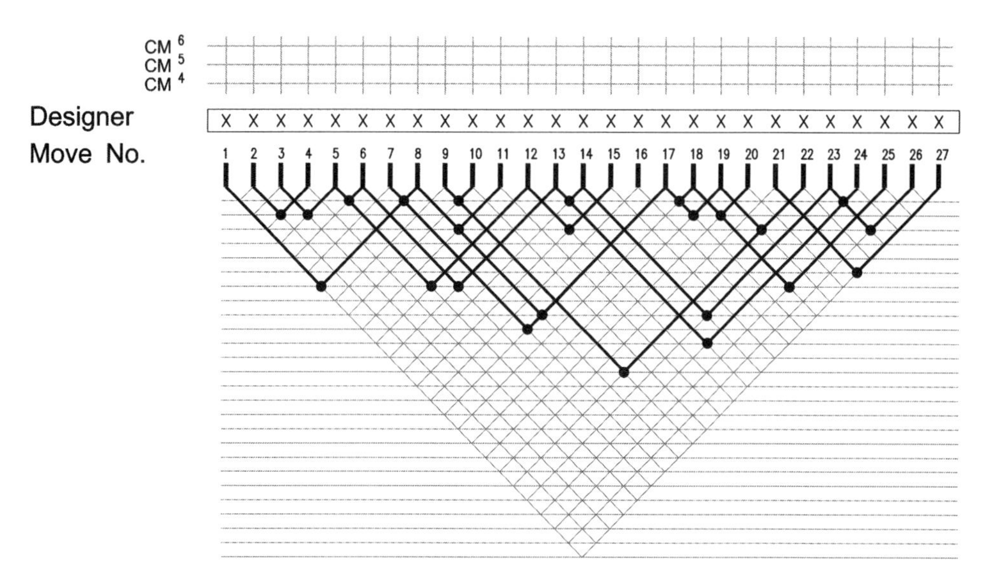

Figure 6.3
Linkograph of episode from Alice's design process, branch library design task.

draw out for myself what I'm saying in words. He might just say "this, this and this. I know what I'd prefer, or what my client would prefer." . . . He could just look at it and immediately see a lot of things I couldn't.

Alice got it right: Martin worked very rapidly, as if he could see the complete solution in his head before sketching it, much as Mozart was said to be able to hear a whole symphony in his "mind's ear."

The linkographs of the processes of Martin and Alice are similar in length (22 and 27 moves, respectively), but that is about all they have in common. Alice generated a small number of links, and no move in this stretch has more than two links either backward or forward. Therefore, there are no critical moves at all. The proportion of bidirectional moves is 40 percent, similar to Gilbert's. We also do not discern a visible structure in this process, whereas Martin's process is highly structured. Alice's process was not creative in this episode—not necessarily because she is not a creative person, but perhaps because she lacked the skills needed to handle the task and her approach was that of a layperson. Her thinking pattern was not a divergent-convergent one, and she was content with just understanding how entering at one or another point affects movement in the library. To accentuate the difference between the processes of Alice and Martin, sketches by both of them, exploring the implications of entering the library at entry point 1, are presented in figure 6.4 (for all the optional entry points, see the appendix).

Only a very experienced and creative designer with a solid design theory, and a well-developed kit of tools that allow him or her to mold any design situation so as to be manageable with those tools and according to that theory, can operate the way Martin did here. This entails moving back and forth, thinking divergently and convergently with very frequent shifts in a structured process, while generating moves that are highly interlinked, for the most part in both directions. Alice, a novice with very little domain-specific knowledge, could not possibly match such a performance.

Needless to say, there is more to design creativity than links among moves. Other important features of creative thinking—for example, prioritizing ideas, identifying opportunities, being able to use imagery or think analogically, and discerning useful information in stimuli—have not been discussed in this chapter. We have focused on the ability to connect and synthesize information, something that expert designers do well. According to Tua Björklund (2013, 152), product-development experts "accommodate

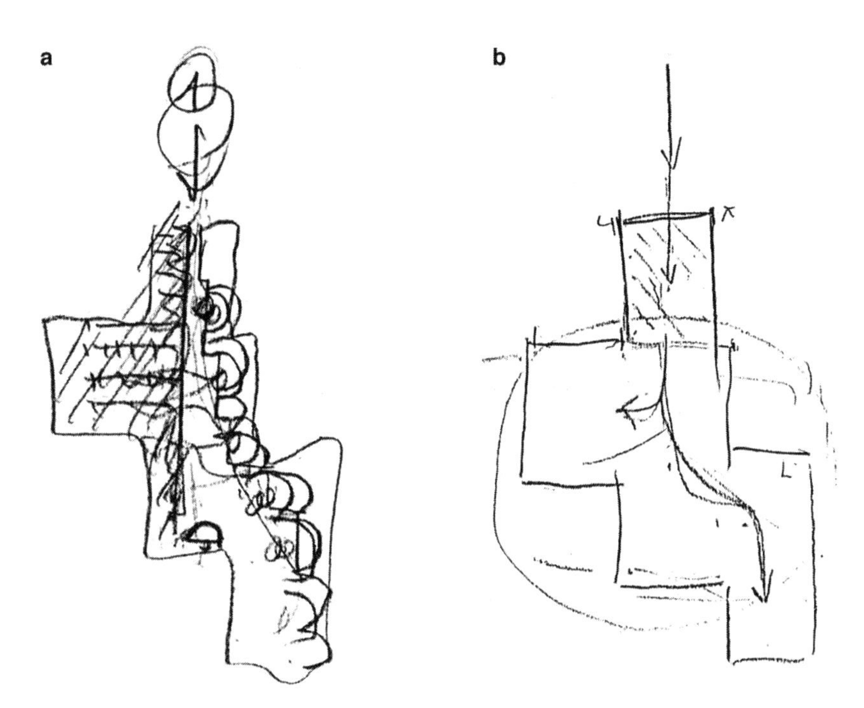

Figure 6.4
Explorative sketches of implications of entry 1, marked by arrows at the top. (a) Martin's. (b) Alice's. In these sketches the library's footprint is turned 90° relative to the original drawing (see appendix).

for a higher degree of interconnections both within the mental representations and between the problem representations and outside knowledge." Björklund has shown empirically that Alexander's (1964) "good fit" concept, according to which a successful design synthesis depends on a good fit between the solutions to subproblems into which a complex problem must be broken, is as valid as ever. The aim of this chapter, and that of the introductory comments in chapter 3, was to show that connectivity, or good fit, or a particularly successful synthesis, is a product of rapid shifting between small divergent and convergent thinking acts. The emphasis is on *small*: not only does creative design encompass divergent and convergent thinking; these modes of reasoning are so intertwined that it is hard to separate them.

Linkography proves to be capable of disentangling instances of thinking as reflected in protocols, and of showing the close relationship between these two modes of thinking and reasoning. Thus, it is not enough to ask designers to generate more ideas, or even to generate innovative ideas. A designer has to acquire the mode of thinking whereby frequent propositions are immediately followed by evaluative steps that make sure that the design holds together at every moment. It is not enough to have ideas, even many ideas; the ideas have to be good, and to be good they must be perfectly integrated and interlinked.

7 Further Insights

In this chapter, insights from thirteen studies in which linkography was used (for a variety of purposes) are reported. In some of them, linkographs of the original kind were used; in others, the linkographs were modified somewhat to suit the needs of specific research goals, and in one study, linkography was evoked as a metaphor. The reports are not meant to be critical; rather, they are meant to be impartial and faithful to the works they represent. The intent is to offer a glimpse at wide applicability options for linkography, beyond what has been dealt with in the previous chapters. In a few instances, I add a minor comment expressing my own view.

Design Problem-and-Solution Spaces

Kees Dorst (2003) was interested in the structure of design problems, which, he claimed, had not been studied sufficiently. Alongside the design process and the designer, the design problem is of great importance in the development of design strategies and methodologies. As was noted in chapter 2, design problems are considered to be ill-structured and even wicked. Dorst described the two major approaches to dealing with such problems, as exemplified in the writings of Herbert Simon and Donald Schön.

Simon (1973), who had developed a theory of problem solving for well-structured problems, recognized the difference between well-structuredness and ill-structuredness of problems. The differences notwithstanding, he thought that in principle both kinds of problems are subject to rational problem solving. Such problem solving takes place within a designated problem space (in which problem-related knowledge is represented) and a solution space (in which solution-related knowledge is represented). In this view, the problem space of an ill-structured problem is too large;

consequently, the problem solver works within only part of the problem space, and the ensuing solution is therefore *satisficing* (sufficiently satisfying; good enough)—it need not be optimal. This approach is called *technical rationality*.

For Schön (1983), technical rationality is the wrong paradigm for the treatment of ill-structured problems, which are frequently encountered in practice, including design practice. Departing from a constructivist point of view, Schön advocated *reflective practice*, which is seen not as a way to solve problems but as a way to frame and reframe problematic, even "messy" situations, until they become malleable. In the case of design, this happens in a design space (rather than problem space). Schön's approach resembles the Gestalt approach to solving novel problems in that it requires productive (as opposed to reproductive) thinking. The reflective practitioner uses experience and a repertoire of previously mastered solutions to see a messy situation in a new light wherein professional intervention is both possible and fruitful.

Dorst maintained that neither Simon nor Schön paid sufficient attention to the structure of a problem (or a situation). He believed that problems differ, some likely to fall into the rational paradigm and others into the reflective paradigm, and that the two approaches can be combined. Combining them, he thought, would lead to a definition of design tasks as situated problems, the structure of which Dorst wished to study by "describ[ing] the behavior of designers as operations on the design problem." Dorst hoped to achieve this by using linkography. He opted for the matrix version, and proposed to use three different linkographs to record three different types of links between problem elements and solution elements that would be extracted from protocols, as follows:

Linkograph I would link among problem elements, ignoring solutions.

Linkograph II would link among solution elements, ignoring problems.

Linkograph III would link among problem and solution elements.

From these three linkographs Dorst expected to learn about different structures of design problems, as related to the paradigms of technical rationality and reflective practice. He predicted that in rational problem solving, the design activity would focus first on the problem(s) and not on solutions, and that because to this focus there should be many links among problem elements (linkograph I). The solution would be tackled only later in the process (linkograph II). He also estimated that the reflective practice paradigm should yield many links among problems and solutions, starting early in the process (linkograph III). Dorst proposed that the complete pattern of problem-solution connections that would be imposed on the problem and the solution would be a *frame* and the actual linking of problem and solution would accordingly be the activity of framing.

Conceptual Dependency Links and Chunks

Masaki Suwa and Barbara Tversky (1997) were interested in architects' interpretations of their own sketches. They conducted a two-phase experiment with two experienced architects and seven advanced architecture students as subjects. In the first phase, each designer was asked to design a museum and its surroundings in a 45-minute session, which was videotaped. In the second phase, each participant was asked to articulate, while viewing the corresponding videotape, the thoughts he or she recalled having at the time each sketch was made. The verbalizations were recorded and transcribed into protocols, so this method falls into the category of retrospective protocol analysis. The protocols were parsed into segments (resembling design moves), which then were encoded by means of a category scheme that included four major categories, each further divided into subcategories. On the basis of the encoded protocols, Suwa and Tversky were able to point at a number of differences in the ways experienced architects and students used their sketching activities to develop design solutions.

Later, Suwa and Tversky looked at links among protocol segments. Rather than produce linkographs per se, they established what they called "conceptual dependencies" among segments, on two levels. What they characterized as a conceptual dependency between a segment and a previous segment was identical to what I call a backlink. They soon discovered that "the entire design process includes many blocks of contiguous segments" (1997, 392). These blocks were called "dependency chunks," a chunk being a small unit typically consisting of two or three segments. What Suwa and Tversky mean by "chunk" is very different from what I mean by the same term (see chapter 4). Links among adjacent segments within a chunk are reminiscent of a sawtooth track pattern. Suwa and Tversky interpreted such links as representing in-depth, detailed explorations of a design topic akin to what Vinod Goel (1995) called "vertical transformations." The same

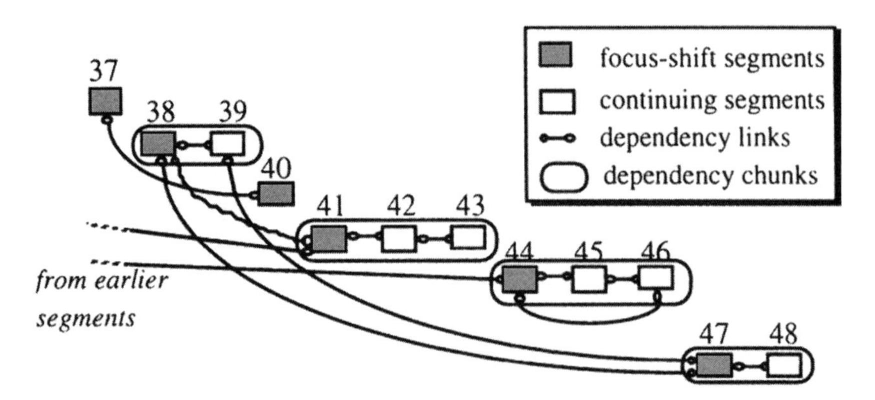

Figure 7.1
Conceptual dependencies. Source: Suwa and Tversky 1997, 394. Reprinted with permission.

segments may, however, also display links to more remote previous segments, which are not included in the same chunk. Goel called such links "lateral transformations." There are also stand-alone segments that do not belong to chunks.

Figure 7.1 is a schematic representation of dependency chunks comprising twelve segments and dependency links among them in a small portion of Suwa and Tversky's analysis. The first segment of a new chunk (or a stand-alone segment) was taken to represent a shift in focus. Suwa and Tversky found that the architects in their study had "remarkably more continuing segments" (within chunks) than the students. This led them to conclude that the architects had shifted focus less often. According to Suwa and Tversky (1997, 395), the difference stemmed from the architects' ability to "'read off" more different types of information from their sketches." Suwa and Tversky concluded their paper by recommending that a design-support tool that is intended to replace paper sketches should be able to evoke new ways of "reading off" information from sketch-like depictions.

Topic Shifts in Design

David Botta and Robert Woodbury (2013) were interested in design histories and especially in topic shifts. They developed a model that used an algorithm and linkographs to predict the locations of topic shifts. Their findings indicated that the rate of success of the predictions was reasonably high in large series, or data sets, but poor in small series, when compared to an independent human assessment of topic shifts in the same data sets. Botta and Woodbury posited two hypotheses: that "a linkograph that is constructed from finer-grained design moves than topical segmentation can be used to predict topical segmentation" and that "the topical segmentation can provide a dynamic granularity by which to filter transitive links" (ibid.).

Botta and Woodbury's data consisted of protocols of eleven instructional design meetings, each two to three hours long, in which a team worked to develop a broad first-year university course in design thinking. The first two meetings were exploratory, and Botta and Woodbury used them for a pilot study; the data obtained from these meetings were the notes of an observer. The subsequent nine meetings were audiotaped and then transcribed into protocols, which were segmented into units of one sentence each. A linkograph was generated for each meeting. No initial breakdown of the meeting into separate units according to subject matter of the conversation was attempted (quite on the contrary, performing this breakdown mechanically was one of the goals of the study). Figure 7.2 shows an example of the linkographs produced in this study.

After all links had been notated, Botta and Woodbury felt that only links between segments that were remote in time (which they called "deep links") should be considered; therefore they developed rules for filtering out links they considered to be transitive. If segment n linked back to segment $n - 3$ and to segment $n - 6$, the link to $n - 3$ was filtered out because it was considered insufficiently deep. Botta and Woodbury called this "the *skip three segments* rule." A mathematical model (an algorithm) that was based on the first two exploratory meetings looked at the contribution of links to a measure of a topic shift. Contributions varied between 0 and 1 per link and were calculated separately for the sum of forelinks and the sum of backlinks. The algorithm was calibrated by trial and error to suit the more detailed data of the subsequent nine meetings.

The model succeeded in predicting topic shifts in long series, with a success rate greater than 0.6. Any discrepancies between the predictions by the model and human assessment were attributed mainly to the fact that a human tends to choose the first sentence in a group of interlinked sentences as the initiation of a topic while the model relies on a linking

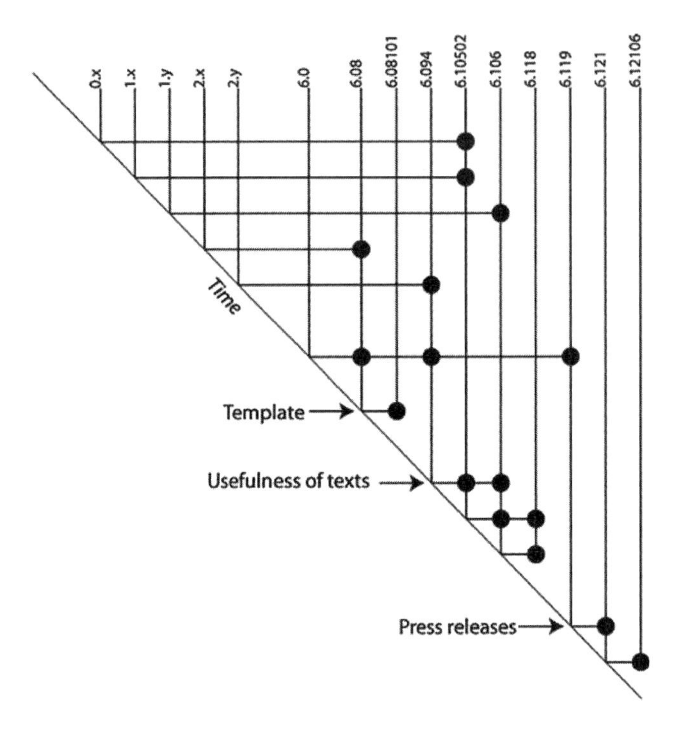

Figure 7.2
An extract from the linkograph of meeting IV. Source: Botta and Woodbury 2013, 249. Reprinted with permission.

measure that is sometimes higher for subsequent nearby sentences in the discussion, which expose the meaning of the topic more forcefully. When the method of interpreting the topic-shift measure was somewhat relaxed, a higher prediction rate (0.8) was achieved. The relaxation allowed the link-contribution measures of a few subsequent sentences to be added to the lead sentence, in case the measure of the initial sentence was significant but below a predetermined threshold. The number of added measures could be varied. Other relaxations included repetitions and redundant material: paragraphs that covered a lot of material, and frequent reminders of recent issues of the "just said" and "incessant" kind, were omitted from the count. The purpose was to achieve "thick descriptions." The results roughly matched the predictions of topic shifts made using the "skip three segments" rule. Other cases of relaxation included segments with mainly transitive links in a text that was considered a "calling text," defined as having at least one deep (i.e., not transitive) link. These and other relaxations made for a sufficiently dynamic model that could adapt itself to local circumstances of various portions of a design process.

Botta and Woodbury concluded that the results they obtained, although encouraging, were rather weak in predictive power, especially for short series. However, they expressed hope that further development would be able to increase the rate of success, especially if an automated system for the construction of linkographs could be devised. Botta and Woodbury asserted that knowing the locations of topical shifts in a design history helps to bridge the gap between conversation and visual representations.

Extended Linkographs

Hui Cai, Ellen Yi-Luen Do, and Craig Zimring (2010) explored the effect of inspiration sources on the design process, which may be positive if they enhance idea generation or negative if they cause fixation. For their empirical study, Cai et al. developed an extended version of the linkograph. Their desire to treat relatively long protocols ruled out the use of moves as units of analysis, as there would have been too many of them. Participating designers were asked to sketch in response to given visual stimuli, and their sketches were taken to reflect the influence of the sources of inspiration (the stimuli). Accordingly, the sketches were chosen as units of analysis. Each sketch was examined for its links with previous sketches and with the original stimulus.

The links among sketches were seen as transformations. In line with the terminology of Goel (1995), they were classified as lateral transformations (LTs) or vertical transformations (VTs). A lateral transformation is a slightly different or alternative idea; a vertical transformation is an elaboration or detailing of a previous idea.[1] This distinction is notated in an extended linkograph, as shown in figure 7.3. The links can be counted separately, L_{LT} representing lateral transformations and L_{VT} representing vertical ones. Cai et al. asserted that the division into two types of transformation is relevant to the impact a stimulus has, and is also indicative of creativity: Along with a larger number of webs and chunks, vertical transformation represent a bolder detachment from the stimulus. A separate link-density index (the equivalent of link index) can also be calculated for the two types of links. Figure 7.3 illustrates the process of a participant who produced four sketches

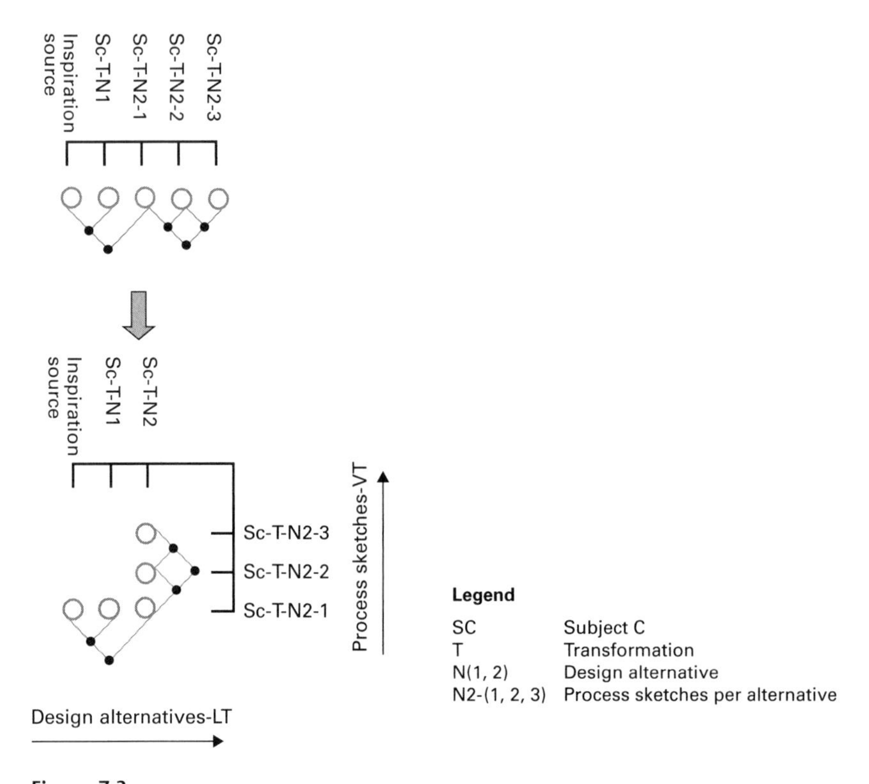

Figure 7.3
From linkograph to extended linkograph. Source: Cai et al. 2010, revised. Reprinted with permission.

for two alternative solutions (solutions T-N1 and T-N2). T-N1 consisted of only one sketch, whereas T-N2 included three sketches. The links among these sketches are notated in a regular linkograph and in an extended linkograph that breaks the linkograph into two perpendicular sublinkographs.

Refining the Function-Behavior-Structure Ontology

A coding system for design protocols called the FBS (Function, Behavior, Structure) ontology, advanced by John Gero and associates, was mentioned in chapter 2. Introduced in a 1990 paper by Gero, it has undergone development ever since then. This ontology is designed to overcome difficulties stemming from the use of custom coding schemes. The use of such schemes "limits the applicability of the results obtained" (Kan and Gero 2009a, 228) because they are too particular to the case in hand. Function, behavior, and structure (and their subcategories) are independent of design domains and cases, as well as of the number of designers, and are claimed by Gero and associates to be a generally applicable coding basis.

In order to refine the system, Gero and his associates (Kan 2008; Kan and Gero 2009a; Pourmohamedi and Gero 2011) applied linkography to the FBS coding system. They started with a basic coding scheme comprising the following main categories and subcategories: Function (F), Structure (S), Expected behavior (Be), Behavior derived from structure (Bs), and Documents (design description) (D). The relationship between elements thus coded represents the following design activities: formulation (inferring expected behaviors from functions and requirements), analysis, synthesis, evaluation, documentation, and three levels of reformulation (changing the space of possible designs by changing the structures, behaviors and functions). Two additional categories are requirements (R) and others (O). The latter may be taken out of the analysis later on. The protocol Kan and Gero (2009a) analyzed was of a session of an engineering project in which a two-person team worked on a new thermal printing pen. The session was selected because of the many analogies the designers evoked, which interested the researchers. The protocol was divided into segments that are precisely equivalent to moves. After they were coded, a linkograph was constructed in order to determine links among segments of different codes. Figure 7.4 shows a portion of the linkograph.

By comparing the percentage of segments of each code with the percentage of links generated by segments of the same code, the researchers were able to compare the frequencies of the codes with the linking evidence and found that linking rates were above the frequency levels for segments coded S and Be; other codes displayed a slight drop in linkage rates compared to their frequencies (except R, which remained unchanged). The conclusion was that S and Be segments were more influential. Next the researchers determined which codes linked to same and other codes. After consolidating codes into groups representing design activities, they were able to look at frequencies of transformations. They found that the most prominent type of transformation was from S to S (notated S>S), which was translated into level 1 reformulation. Next in prominence were analysis (S>Bs), evaluation (Be<>Bs), and synthesis (Be>S), in a descending order of occurrence and percentage. Kan and Gero (2009a) went on to refine their analysis by making

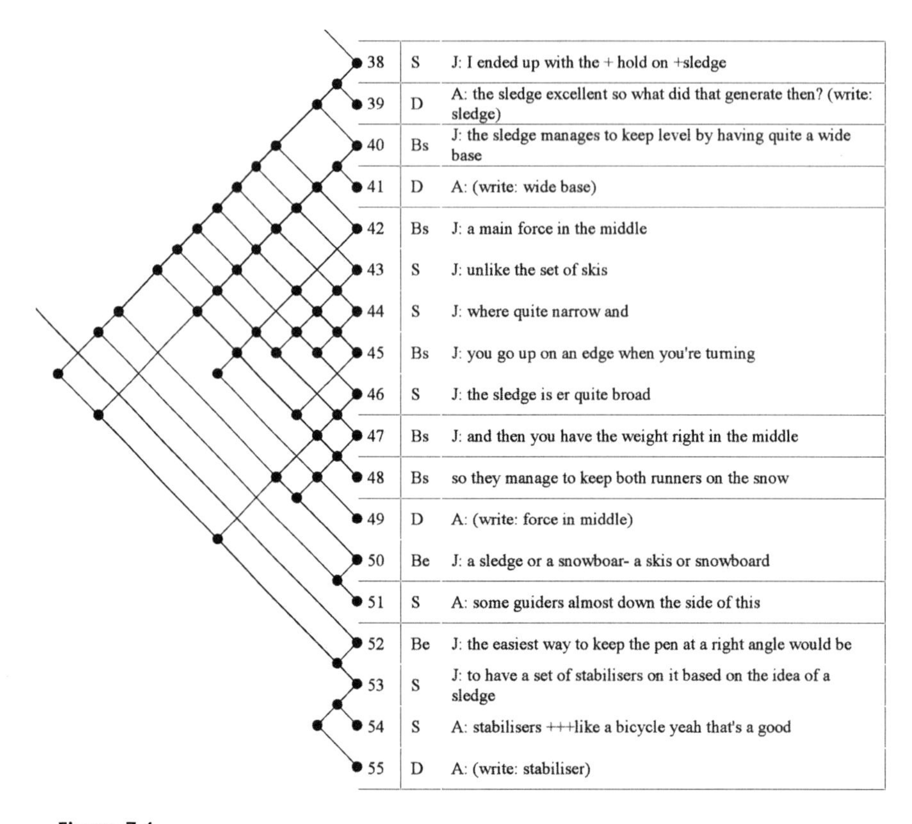

Figure 7.4

Partial linkograph with protocol segments by designers A and J, coded according to the FBS scheme. Source: Kan and Gero 2009a, 218. Reprinted with permission.

some further distinctions within a "situated FBS framework" in which they introduced interactions among external, interpreted, and expected "worlds of design." They repeated the previous analytic procedures to determine frequencies of transformations, based on links. Kan and Gero concluded that "the links not only provide a structural view of the processes but also locate the dominant codes and the frequency of each design transformation process" (ibid., 228). The combination of linkography and the FBS ontology gives a sharper view of the network of acts in designing.

To facilitate the analysis of FBS-based linkographs, Pourmohamedi and Gero (2011) developed a software system called lincoder.[2] Once a protocol is parsed using the FBS codes, the program automatically draws the corresponding linkograph and analyzes it in accordance with a number of built-in quantitative parameters. In addition to the calculations performed by Kan and Gero (2009a) regarding distributions and frequencies of codes, these parameters include first-order and second-order Markov models and entropy calculations. The system is also capable of "fractioning," "windowing," and "trimming" linkographs; all these operations are aimed at isolating a portion of a linkograph in order to analyze it and perhaps compare it with other portions of the same or another linkograph. Pourmohamedi and Gero say they hope to further develop this program with open coding possibilities instead of the current restriction to the FBS ontology. They are also ready to rise to the formidable challenge of automating the coding and linking stages of protocol analysis and linkograph construction, which they rightly claim requires a lot of labor when done manually.

Problem Framing in Different Design Settings

Thomas Kvan and Song Gao (2006) set out to explore the important activity of problem framing by design teams in digital and paper-based settings. Problem framing was adopted from Schön (1983, 165) as the initial phase in ill-defined problem solving wherein problem solvers "determine the features to which they will attend, the order they will attempt to impose on the situation, the directions in which they will try to change it. In this process, they identify both the ends to be sought and the means to be employed." In this study an experiment was carried out in which participants solved a simple design problem in three different settings: online remote (chat-line-based textual communication and digital drawings), online co-located, and paper-based co-located. Six teams of two student designers each were assigned to each of the settings. The sessions were recorded and protocol analysis was employed. The protocols were parsed into moves, which then were coded using a scheme (adopted from Schön 1983) that had three categories: framing, moving, and reflecting.

The count of the categorized moves showed a significant difference between the online remote setting, which had a low number of activities, and the two co-located settings, which yielded a much higher number of overall activities. The frequency of each activity category in the three settings was inspected, and it was found that the online remote setting had the highest percentage of framing (almost 45 percent), and the lowest percentage of moving (less than 25 percent). No significant differences were found between the other two settings, and the proportion of reflecting was similar in all settings (about 33 percent).

Next, linkographs were constructed for each of the teams, and were divided into components. A component was defined as "one unit in which all design units are inter-linked" (Kvan and Gao 2006, 251), which is reminiscent of the term "chunk" as introduced in this book. The average number of components was highest in the paper-based setting and lowest in the online remote setting. The latter setting had the highest average link index, somewhat higher than the average for the other two settings. Kvan and Gao then singled out the largest components in each setting and compared them on diameter ("the number of linked design moves"; in our terms—link span) and depth ("the largest number of nodes linking two discrete design actions in a component"). The online remote setting had the greatest depth and the smallest diameter; the online co-located setting had the lowest depth and the largest diameter.

The rest of the study focused on the largest component of each setting, for which two ratios were calculated: R1 (the ratio between the number of activities in the largest component divided by the number of activities in the entire protocol) and R2 (the ratio between the greatest depth in the largest component divided by the number of activities in the entire protocol). The highest R1 and R2 values were found in the remote online settings. Figure 7.5 shows the linkograph of one of those remote online protocols.

The linkographs of the components with the highest R1 values in the other settings were much shorter. The percentage of framing activities in them was considerably lower; the R2 values were also much lower. For both ratios the components in question were poorly or not at all interlinked with adjacent components that preceded and followed the component under investigation.

Kvan (2013) concluded that the findings suggest that digital tools are not detrimental to problem solving in conceptual design, that they do not interfere with framing, and that in fact they may support framing. This conclusion was surprising and counterintuitive, especially since it stands in contrast to designers' subjective reports and to findings in some other research projects. It was acknowledged that the sample was too small to allow general conclusions to be drawn, and that the quality of the resultant designs played no role in this study. Kvan (ibid.) explained that the insights gained from the study suggested that multiple representations in different

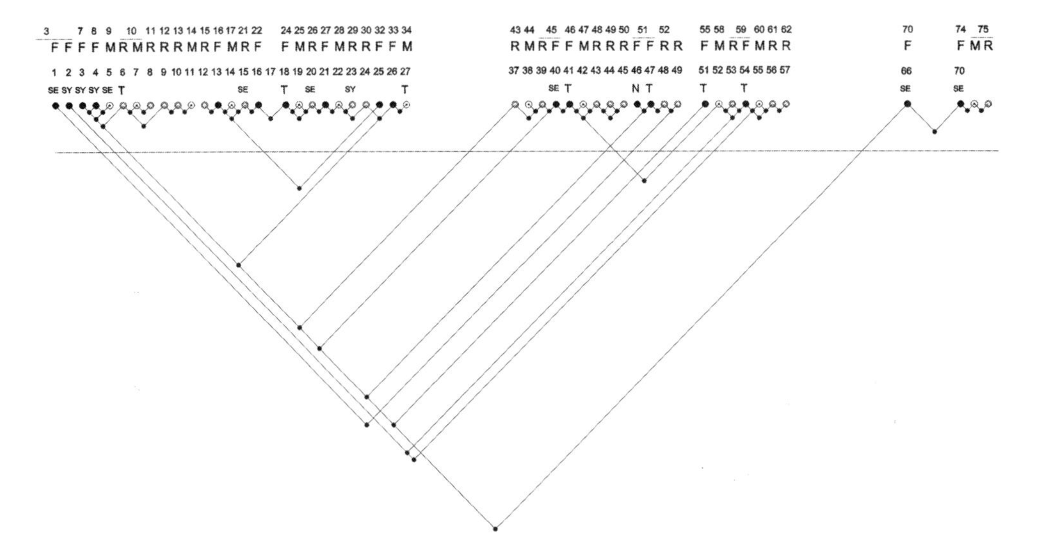

Figure 7.5
Linkograph of an online remote setting. Source: Kvan 2013, 78–79. Reprinted with permission.

modes (including textual communication) are always advantageous. He believes that diagramming (sketching) is essential in designing; digital tools, especially in a remote collaboration, enable higher levels of abstraction, which in turn enhances interpretative activity, which leads to framing and reframing. This may explain the results obtained in this experiment.

Entropy and Productivity

In a number of papers (Gero 2011; Kan 2008; Kan and Gero 2005, 2008, 2009b; Kan, Bilda, and Gero 2007), John Gero and associates explored the use of entropy measurements based on linkographs to assess the productivity of design processes. According to the notion of entropy they used, which was taken from information theory (Shannon 1948), "the amount of information carried by a message or symbol is based on the probability of its outcome" (Kan and Gero 2005, 52). Entropy is the amount of information that is missing before reception, or before communication is achieved. Kan and Gero applied this notion to the design process and claimed that a link between moves is information—the link is considered ON. Where there is no link between two moves, the link is considered OFF. If all moves

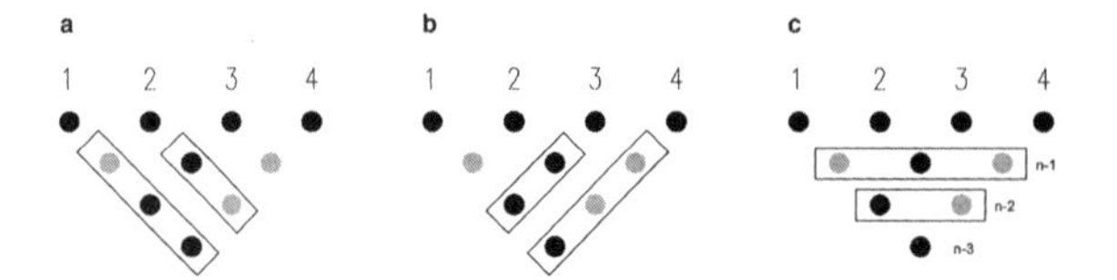

Figure 7.6
Entropy measured by rows: (a) rows of forelinks; (b) rows of backlinks; (c) rows of horizon links. Source: Kan 2008, 30. Reprinted with permission.

are linked to all other moves in a linkograph, that is, if they are all ON, the linkograph is saturated. Shannon's theory looks at the relationship between ON and OFF nodes in a selected set of symbols to calculate the set's entropy. Maximum entropy (H) is achieved when that relationship is unpredictable, because this situation is diversified and allows for surprise and further development. The maximum value, which is $H = 1$, occurs when half the nodes are ON and the other half are OFF. In a linkograph of n moves, the potential number of links is $n(n - 1)/2$ and therefore the highest entropy is achieved when the number of links is $n(n - 1)/4$. When the linkograph is either empty or fully saturated, the entropy is at its lowest level, $H = 0$.

The linkograph sets chosen by Gero and his associates for entropy calculations are diagonal rows of backlinks that measure enhancement and confirmation, diagonal rows of forelinks, measuring the new idea-generation opportunities, and the "horizonlinks," the links along horizontal rows that measure cohesiveness and incubation. Figure 7.6 shows these rows. Entropy is calculated for each row separately according to a probability algorithm devised by Shannon. A mean value can then be calculated for each of the three types of rows.

According to Jeff Kan, John Gero, and their associates, entropy is a yardstick for measuring productivity. High entropy is indicative of a productive process; the researchers maintained that when the proportion of ON links is between 0.35 and 0.65, then $H > 0.93$. In other words, if the rate of linking is between one-third and two-thirds of all possible links, the process is productive and we should expect a good outcome.

Kan and Gero (2005) and Kan (2008) provided the preliminary theoretical basis for design entropy measurements. In work that was reported in further publications, the researchers tested actual cases. Kan et al. (2007) looked at one of the findings of Bilda et al. (2006): that blindfolded architects who had successfully completed a 45-minute design session using imagery only showed a decrease in cognitive activities after about 20 minutes. Kan et al. (2007) asked whether this drop corresponded to a drop in entropy. They constructed linkographs of twelve design sessions undertaken by six participants in the experiment. Each participant completed two sessions: one in which sketching was allowed and one in which the designer was blindfolded. Entropies were calculated for the first 20 minutes, and for the remaining time (approximately 25 minutes) of each session. Values were normalized by dividing the sum of entropies of each segment by the number of segments; this was done for the three types of entropy described above. Entropy was found to have decreased in the second half of the session in all but one of the sketching sessions. In the blindfolded condition, results were mixed: half the participants showed similar trends in both session types; in the other half entropy values increased in the second half. This meant that the decrease in cognitive activities did not necessarily lead to a decrease in the generation of new ideas in the blindfolded sessions. When dynamic entropy charts were plotted to represent the entire linkographs, an interesting finding emerged. The plots were overlaid with quadratic (second-degree) polynomial fit curves. These may take one of three shapes: linear, ∪, and ∩. According to Kan et al. (2007, 373), "the ∪ shape trend suggests that the entropy values are climbing toward the end of the session indicating a well-integrated process, whereas the ∩ shape trend suggests the opposite." In these plots the trend remained the same for each participant across conditions, which may be related to individuals' cognitive styles. Another observation was that the three sessions that scored the highest qualitatively all had ∪-shaped curves, whereas the three sessions that scored the lowest all had ∩-shaped curves. This may suggest that high entropy toward the end is, by and large, a sign of a productive session.

In Kan and Gero 2009a, the authors extended the argument that linkographic entropy indicates productivity to claim that it is also a hallmark of creativity. They conducted an experiment in which they compared the processes of two teams, each consisting of two architects, that were charged with producing a conceptual design for an art gallery on a given site with a given brief. A qualitative assessment ranked one of the sessions as more creative; the other session was considered pragmatic. First Kan and Gero calculated text entropies based on the protocols. Although the more creative session boasted almost twice as many words as the pragmatic session, the relative entropy and the text entropy were identical or almost identical in both cases. In the next stage Kan and Gero used WordNet to construct linkographs of the two sessions. The linkographs were based on at least four common "synset IDs." A synset is a cognitive synonym that can be used to group words into sets of similar meaning. Words with the same synset share the same ID. Linkographs constructed with this automated method showed semantic links among verbalizations (nouns only) in the protocols. Since the numbers of segments in these linkographs differed, they were divided into 5-minute "windows"; the mean entropy of these windows was then calculated. In this calculation a difference of about 15 percent was found in favor of the creative session. Kan and Gero also showed that the windows with the highest entropy were the most productive in terms of number of ideas generated and number of sketches produced.

In yet another study, Gero (2011) used design entropy inferred from linkographs to measure design fixation. The premise was that entropy should be lower during fixation than during the rest of the process. In an empirical study in which fixation could be qualitatively detected, a protocol was parsed and coded according to the FBS coding scheme (introduced earlier in this chapter); then a 116-segment linkograph was constructed. Entropy was calculated for portions of the linkograph, including twelve segments that appeared to display moments of fixation; this entropy was termed "dynamic entropy." The exercise was repeated three times for three different local fixation instances. In each of these cases the entropy value at the point of fixation was the lowest in the sequence of entropy values measured for the series of twelve segments. Figure 7.7 shows a portion of the linkograph and one graph of dynamic entropy.

In several publications (e.g., Kan and Gero 2008), Kan and Gero also suggested looking at links in a linkograph as nodes in a plane defined by x and y axes. Each link can then have an x value (its distance from move 1) and a y value that corresponds to its link span. The x and y values can be calculated for each move, and a mean value called the *centroid* can be established. "A higher mean value of x," Kan and Gero wrote, "implies that more nodes appear at the end of a session and a lower value suggests that more nodes are present in the beginning of the session. . . . A higher mean value of y indicates longer linking lengths [spans]." (ibid., 324) This gives a very rough indication of distribution of links; however, as Kan and Gero noted,

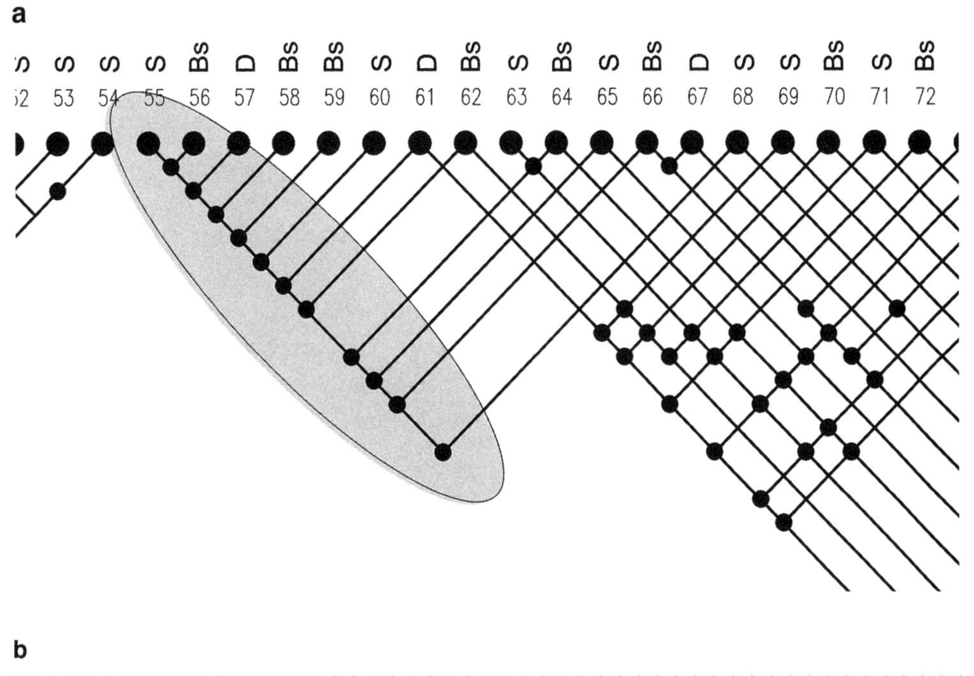

Figure 7.7
(a) A portion of a linkograph of a design session in which fixation was detected, culminating in move 55. (b) A graph of dynamic entropy values. Lowest values correspond to instances of fixation, culminating in move 55. Source: Gero 2011, 112. Reprinted with permission. Note that parts a and b of this figure are not at the same scale.

it does not reveal anything regarding the spreading of the links. Therefore, they also calculate the standard deviations, "which suggest how concentrated the nodes are clustered around the means" (ibid., 324).

Linkography and Space Syntax

Tamer El-Khouly and Alan Penn (2012) sought to relate linkographs and graphs of urban systems used in Space Syntax studies. Such systems are very complex, and the authors investigated and measured properties of linkographs in order to shed light on certain characteristics that are also found in urban systems, such as access to locations via road networks. Two perspectives (seen here as discrete theories) illuminated the study: that of information theory and that of entropy theory. The main hypothesis of the paper was that "in multi-level complex systems high orderliness tends to become less complex overall, and therefore a highly linked node delivers few choices and probabilities" (ibid., 3). A further hypothesis was that "complexity is created in different scales in the graph system from the local subgraph to the whole system" (ibid., 1). In this graph system a node corresponds to a move in the terminology of this book.

The backward and forward links and "no-links" (that is, empty spots on a link line, where there are no links to other moves) of each node (move) are listed in a separate subgraph. This is noted in a combination of a backlinks string and a forelinks string, where a link is notated as 1 and its absence is notated as 0. The forelinks string follows the backlinks string, separated by a dot. The string is considered to be a "string of information" that represents the complexity of the particular subsystem. Figure 7.8 shows a linkograph and the compilation of the strings of information for node 15.

As in Kan and Gero 2008, the premise in El-Khouly and Penn 2012 was that to achieve complexity high entropy is needed, which means a combination of ones and zeroes in strings. An "empty" string of zeroes only (no links) and a "saturated" string of ones only (each node is linked to every other node) have an equally low entropy—in fact, the entropy is zero—meaning a low probability for complexity.

Later in the paper, El-Khouly and Penn compared three types of measures extracted from linkographs—integration, complexity, and entropy—for two sets of linkographs: ordered and structured linkographs. The former are saturated, the latter are not. Then they looked at the degree of

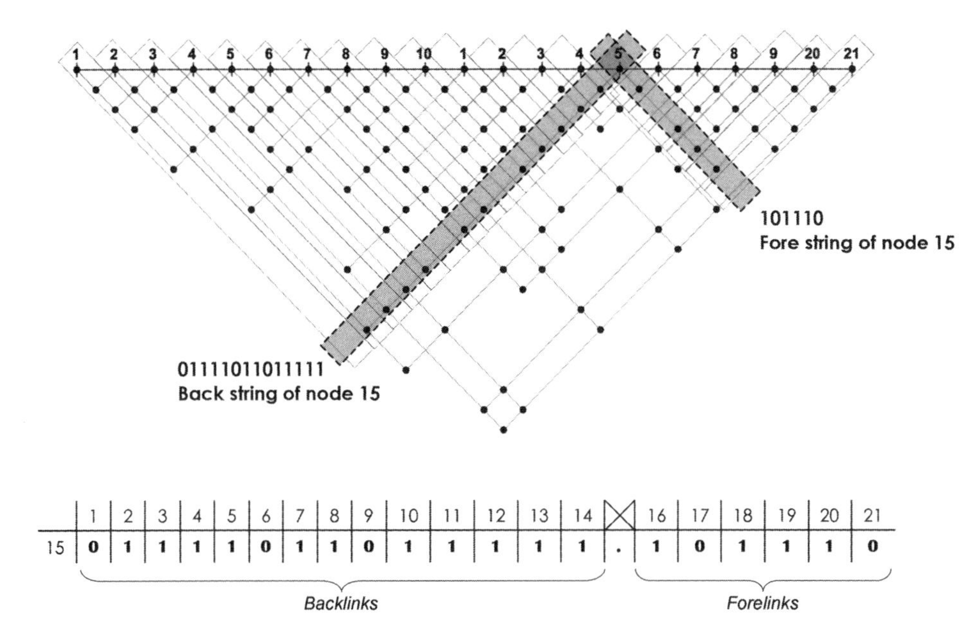

Figure 7.8
Extracting a string for node 15 in a linkograph: **01111011011111.101110**. Source: El Khouly and Penn 2012, 10. Reprinted with permission.

correlation of entropy, complexity, and integration. Complexity and entropy are "dynamic"; that is, they vary along the system, as each node has a different value. Many of the correlations between integration and complexity and between integration and entropy were found to be negative, and when positive they were mostly low. Correlations between complexity and entropy were positive but low. The linkographs in question were short, comprising 21 nodes, and the authors found that measures for short sequences were inadequate. Therefore they set out to look at correlations in two much longer linkographs that consist of hundreds of nodes. First, using syntactical methods, they identified the most integrated nodes and looked at similar correlations as in the short linkographs, supplemented by a few other correlations that pertain to properties that are of interest in the urban context: closeness, centrality, and betweenness. All the correlations were found to be positive, and most to be quite high. The authors concluded that "the more a node is connected to the surroundings, the less predictable the information, and therefore low string complexity results" (ibid., 19), which confirmed their main hypothesis. This result has implications for the structures of cities; for instance, when a piazza is highly accessible from the surrounding areas, navigation is clear and easy and therefore complexity is low. The combination of linkography and Space Syntax seems promising.

The Linkograph as a Visualization Tool in Project Risk Management

Kilian Gericke, Björn Kleinod, and Lucienne Blessing (2009) were interested in how risk management could be used to ensure that an engineering project remained on track. Their goal was to minimize the costs incurred when failures occur in a particular work package (a discrete phase). Such failures may also affect subsequent work packages; in fact, they may not be detected until their effects on a later work package are discovered. The aim of Gericke et al. was to easily and visually communicate the predicted failure risks such that special attention could be paid to sensitive work packages in an effort to prevent later failures. The linkograph was chosen as the means of representation. This was a theoretical study in which the units of analysis were not brief moves but rather were planned work packages along the life span of the project. In contrast with a standard linkograph, the time line on which they were indicated was time scaled.

A linkograph was generated, the planned work packages were notated, and forelinks were established between each work package and all subsequent work packages that, according to the plan, were to be affected by that work package. The cost to the affected work package if something were to go wrong in the earlier package was calculated. A choice among three cost concepts—minimum, maximum, and average cost—was offered. This cost was indicated in the linkograph next to the appropriate link. Work packages that were to be executed in parallel were notated in a column, one on top of the other. The equivalents of critical moves ("critical" has a different connotation in this study; see below) were "milestone packages"; these too were pre-determined and indicated in the linkograph. Backlinks in this notation were divided into two types. Type I backlinks were simply the links that had been established as forelinks, but in the reverse direction. Type II backlinks "represent a planned iteration in the process" (ibid., 5). To distinguish them from backlinks Type I, backlinks Type II were notated above the move, or work package line, as shown in figure 7.9.

Gericke et al. argued that "the later the failure is detected, the greater the failure costs" (ibid., 5). Therefore, the distance of a link (in the terminology

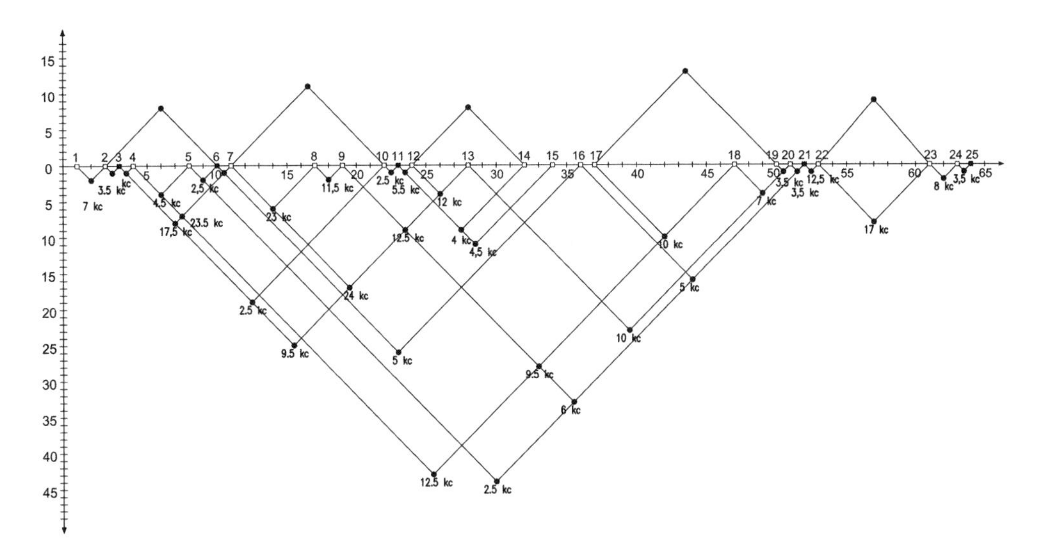

Figure 7.9
Linkograph by Gericke, Kleinod, and Blessing (2009, 7). Reprinted with permission.

of the present book, a link span) is important. To facilitate its representation on the linkograph, a vertical axis to the left of the network was added, with distance marks in both directions: down, in the field of the forelinks/backlinks Type I, and up, in the field of backlinks Type II.

Gericke et al. used the word "criticality" to indicate the predicted impact resulting from failure in a work package. A conceptual and dimensionless criticality index can be computed for every work package and can be used to assess the importance of monitoring it closely. The criticality index is the product of the duration and the cost of each work package divided by chosen affected units. The results are to be assessed by experts to ensure their validity. Gericke et al. asserted that the linkographic representation is easy to produce and easy to read, and that it offers a qualitative and quantitative basis for systematic risk management.

Comparison between Solving and Designing of Well-Defined Problems

The cognitive psychologists Geert Wissink and Saskia Jaarsveld (2002) were interested in differences in cognitive activity between designing and solving of well-defined problems, and between the first and second halves of such processes. Their assumptions were that more reliance on ideas generated earlier in the process occur in a designing task than in a solving task, that more different cognitive activities take place in a designing task than in a solving task, that more links among consecutive activities are apparent in a solving task than in a designing task, and that in both a designing task and a solving task the second phase (which is more exploratory and evaluative than the first) is characterized by more links among activities.

To investigate these assumptions, Wissink and Jaarsveld carried out an empirical study in which two different but related tasks were given to psychology students who were instructed to "think aloud" while executing them. The study yielded 21 usable protocols. The first solving task to be administered was Raven's Standard Progressive Matrices (SPM),[3] including three different tests. In the designing task, participants were asked to design a test item similar to the ones in the solving task. The sessions were recorded, and the ensuing protocols were parsed into five-second segments. These protocols were the basis for linkographs (the matrix version) of the designing and solving processes. The assumptions above were translated into assumed linkographic patterns and statistics as follows:

- more unlinked segments (akin to orphan moves) in the solving task than in the designing task
- more unlinked segments in the first half of the linkographs of both tasks
- more critical segments (equivalent of critical moves) in the designing task than in the solving task
- higher link indices in the designing task than in the solving task
- higher link indices in the second halves of the linkographs of both tasks
- more webs and chunks and less sawtooth tracks in the designing task than in the solving task

A one-way analysis of variance was employed to check for possible differences among the three solving tasks in the mean numbers of segments, of links, and of link indices. Because no significant differences were found, the mean values could be compared with the values obtained in the designing task. The first comparison pertained to the number of segments. Significant differences were found between the tasks (the designing task took considerably longer and involved more segments). The distribution of links within each task was quite uneven, but with a normal overall distribution. The following results were obtained:

Unlinked segments The assumptions that there would be more unlinked segments in the solving task and more unlinked segments in the second halves of both tasks were not confirmed. The only significant differences were found in a comparison between the first and second halves of both tasks: for both halves the proportion of unlinked segments was smaller in the solving task.

Critical segments Critical segments were checked at the threshold level of five links. A small number of critical segments was found in the linkographs of both tasks, and especially in the solving task. I propose that the reason is most probably that the threshold level was too high for these tasks and possibly for well-defined problem-solving protocols in general.

Link index The assumption that the link indices of the second halves of both sets of linkographs would be higher than those of the first halves of those linkographs was confirmed for both the solving and the designing tasks. However, the main assumption that the mean L.I. of the designing task would be higher than that of the solving task was not confirmed. The reason may be that the number of links in these linkographs is quite low to begin with, in part because of a relatively high proportion of unlinked segments, but possibly also because of the way a link may have been established. The L.I. values that were obtained in this study are particularly low: the means vary between 0.43 and 0.72.

Sawtooth tracks and chunks Contrary to the assumption, more sawtooth tracks were found in the designing-task linkographs than in the solving-task linkographs. In accordance with the assumptions, more chunks were found in the linkographs of the designing task than in those of the solving task, although the difference is not statistically significant. The number of chunks was low, especially in the solving-task linkographs. No webs were found in any of the linkographs.

Link depth The mean link depth (link span) was measured for the two sets of linkographs. The designing task boasted a significantly higher link depth than the solving task, meaning that segments were more frequently linked to segments farther away in time in the designing-task than in the solving-task.

Although many of the assumptions were not confirmed in this study, it did reveal certain differences between the solving tasks and the designing tasks. The more significant indicators were link index, critical segments, unlinked segments, and link depth. In addition to questioning the theoretical basis of the assumptions, we may question the logic of segmentation by time units, especially since in this study segments were also assigned to periods with no verbal activity, thus reducing the number of links and the resultant link index. We may also question the usefulness of linkography for the study of well-defined problem solving, in which the search for a solution involves a fixed routine. The importance of calibration (what is considered a segment, a link, what threshold should be used for criticality measures, and so on) is a major lesson to be drawn from this study.

Comparison of Modes of Representation at the Front Edge of the Design Process

To compare the cognitive effects of three different modes of representation in the early phases of designing, Benay Gürsoy and Mine Özkar (2010) conducted an experiment in which three designers of equal experience solved three different short design problems of similar complexity. For each problem they were allowed only one representational mode, which varied across problems. The modes were freehand sketching, a matchbox model (later developed into a cardboard model, but that phase was not analyzed), and a digital model. The designers were asked to think aloud. The taped verbalizations yielded nine protocols (three per designer and three per representation mode). The protocols were parsed into moves ranging in length from 5.9 to 40 seconds. The total time per task, which was not restricted, also varied greatly across designers, the longest task being at least twice as long as the shortest one. Linkographs were generated for all nine design sessions.

Because they were interested in design productivity, Gürsoy and Özkar calculated link indices. They found considerable differences among representational modes and amid designers, and no coherent pattern. Next they derived from the linkographs lateral and vertical transformations, a distinction based on work by Goel (1995). Gürsoy and Özkar assumed that there was a correlation between the number of lateral transformations and the level of ambiguity of the design representation mode. That is, higher lateral transformation values should be obtained for the physical models and freehand sketching than for the digital model.

The criterion for a distinction between the modes of transformation was based on the distribution of links: "dense clusters of links correspond to vertical transformations while scattered links denote lateral transformations" (Gürsoy and Özkar 2010, 7). Dense clusters of links were demarcated in the linkographs as triangles, each of which was considered to represent one lateral transformation. Unlinked moves ("orphan" in our terminology) were added to this count, as they too were considered to be lateral transformations. The total sum of triangles and unlinked moves was the number of lateral transformations. According to Gürsoy and Özkar, vertical transformations were harder to determine. They adopted the idea of a Vertical Transformation Value (that is, the depth of the process defined as the mean distance of links from the *x* axis) from Kan and Gero 2008.

The assumption that ambiguous representation modes would yield a larger number of lateral transformations was not supported by the results, as each of the designers achieved the highest number of lateral transformations in a different modality. There were no specific assumptions concerning the vertical transformations, but they allowed Gürsoy and Özkar to determine how well developed each design solution was in each representational mode. In two cases the highest values were achieved in the sketching mode; in the third case they were achieved in the physical model mode.

The inconclusiveness of the results from this study may be attributable to several methodological difficulties. First, the small number of participants may have been restrictive, as the authors acknowledged. Second, the grain of the analysis was quite coarse, the number of moves was restricted, and the variation in their length may have been too large. Third, at least one participant was not fluent using the software that was provided for digital modeling, which must have affected that participant's performance. In addition, the use of matchboxes for the physical model mode is questionable; restriction to a fixed single component is very strict; in "regular" physical modeling, any number of components may be used. It is reasonable to assume that if the experiment were repeated with these methodological difficulties addressed, the use of linkography might reveal differences among the modes of representation.

Effectiveness of Modes of Representation

Rosario Vidal, Elena Mulet, and Eliseo Gómez-Senent (2004) conducted a relatively large-scale study that had goals quite similar to those of the aforementioned study by Gürsoy and Özkar. Vidal and her associates were interested in the effect of what they called "means of expression" on the effectiveness of ideas generated in design brainstorming. Three variants of brainstorming were defined: sentential brainstorming (verbal, although later writing was included); visual brainstorming (sketching), and objectual brainstorming (in which participants prototyped their ideas using Meccano components). Twelve groups, each made up of five first-year industrial design students, were asked to design, at a conceptual level, an inexpensive tiltable drafting table that would take up minimal space when not in use. The sessions, each lasting an hour, were recorded, and a list of ideas that were generated was prepared for each session. All measured variables were expressed as means across participating groups for each variant of brainstorming. Links among ideas were established and notated in Excel matrix linkographs, in accordance with van der Lugt's (2001) precedent; a linkograph was constructed for each session. The unit of analysis was termed a "global idea," meaning an idea of pronounced significance. ("Global ideas" were chosen instead of all ideas because of the large size of the data set.)

To measure effectiveness (which was contingent on how valid an idea was relative to the requirements), Vidal et al. used a coding scheme with three levels: valid, rejected, and not related. The significant values the researchers were interested in were the number and percentage of valid ideas. The link density (that is, the ratio between the number of links and the number of global ideas—equivalent to our link index) was calculated for each linkograph. The higher the link density, the more developed the idea was considered to be. The ratio between the total number of ideas and the number of global ideas was also calculated, to indicate how focused the process of idea generation was.

The findings of this study affirmed that in functional design, at least when it is performed by novice designers, there are differences in the effectiveness of the design process that are related to the mode of representation used in brainstorming, or in preliminary design sessions. The objectual mode emerged as the mode with the highest proportion of valid ideas, the highest link density, and the highest ratio of global ideas to all ideas. On the other hand, the sentential mode had a much higher score than the other modes in the number of global ideas generated. Vidal et al. concluded that the classic sentential variant should be used if the goal is a wide range of ideas, regardless of their applicability. If, however, more integrated and plausible ideas are sought, the objectual variant gives the best results. The sketching mode was somewhere between the two other variants on almost all counts.

Linkograph as Metaphor

Hyo-Jeong Kwon, Hwa-Sei Lee, Doo-Heon Song, and Chee-Yong Kim (2008) were interested in specifying an appropriate search and navigation system for social networks and similar Web 2.0 interfaces. They claimed that a visual search that uses memory and visualization tools is more satisfactory to users than a search based on text, thumbnail icons, and screen shots. Visual search of a website, they wrote, is "a searching method using visual navigation factors where search results are arranged in a visual connection, a visual relation and a visual shape" (ibid., 379). Their claim was that since this type of search takes into account emotional factors, a visual search is most effective and popular in social network service and similar sites. Kwon et al. claimed that this kind of visual search is "a good example of linkography design web navigation" (ibid., 379). In their view, the linkograph is an example of a visual representation of information structure that combines a visual model with "attention and elucidation" factors. Therefore, they advanced the concept of "linkography design" for web navigation, where "linkography" is used "as a metaphor of web structure analysis" (ibid., 378).

Epilogue

Design is like a trip. As a novice, one travels to uncharted territories, to new and unfamiliar lands where everything is to be discovered. As an expert, one often travels to a place one has visited before, yet there are always new sights and landscapes, some of them unexpected, that invite further exploration. It takes a while to put the pieces of the puzzle together, to gain an appreciation of the whole picture, to decipher patterns, to understand relationships, and to become aware of one's blind spots. At its best, design thinking research is quite similar: an experienced researcher is able to point to gaps in our knowledge, and this leads to new insights, questions, and prospects. Such was my trip in the lengthy preparation of this book.

At the outset, most of what I knew about design thinking was based on observation and personal experience. I had to turn to psychology to make sense not only of what experience had taught me but also of the questions that began to emerge. After all, psychology tries to explain mental phenomena, and design thinking is a mental phenomenon.

Linkography emerged as a key, or rather one of the keys to a better understanding of the design process and design thinking. Undoubtedly there are other keyholes that linkography does not open—we need a set of several different keys. For example, the very significant and special contribution of visual thinking may not be unveiled by linkography, and therefore it is important to acknowledge what linkography cannot do. Like any other methodology, linkography is good for certain things, and expectations for its use should be shaped accordingly. Nevertheless, linkography has been successful in imposing some structure on what is known about design thinking and framing it in a coherent way, allowing it to be inspected in structural and quantitative terms. Moreover, measurements have permitted qualitative interpretations and insights regarding the observed state of affairs. Creative and agile researchers have also been able to employ linkographs in other design-related explorations, not necessarily cognitive ones, and similar uses in disciplines other than design may also be anticipated.

More important to me is the theoretical basis for linkography, which has been built up gradually. The theory was developed in an inductive manner; that is, as evidence from empirical studies piled up, generalizations and conjectures were proposed. Experimental data could then be used to test the conjectures. A specific proposition that is raised in this book for the first time is the correspondence between forward and backward linking and divergent and convergent thinking, respectively. This notion is offered to cognitive psychology, which is the appropriate framework in which to further advance this idea. It seems to me that the study of creativity begs for a more fundamental inspection of this issue, and it is high time that we engage in it.

Linkography, its study and its usage have been an exciting trip that is not over yet. As I write these lines, a mathematical treatment of linkographs as complex networks is being initiated. But since the book could no longer wait to get out into the world, the first two decades of the trip are herewith concluded. I hope that the coming years will see linkography grow and develop, with numerous creative researchers making it their own and taking it in directions we may not be able to anticipate at present. Chapter 7 begins to suggest the wide range of explorations for which linkography may prove useful. To me this would be a most rewarding outcome of this endeavor.

Appendix: Sources of Data

The linkographic studies in this book are based on data derived from several empirical studies. In each of these studies, protocols of design sessions (or their equivalent) were generated and linkographic analyses were conducted by the author or by other researchers. The number of studies based on protocols in which linkographs have been used is significantly larger than can be reported here (see chapter 7 for more on various uses of linkography); the eight studies featured here are the main sources for the empirical analyses in this book. They are listed in chronological order, highlighting those aspects that are relevant to linkography.

Ming-Hung Wang and N. John Habraken, 1982

Source: Wang and Habraken 1982

In the fall of 1982, John Habraken and his PhD student Ming-Hung Wang set out to study the basic operations that they believed are sufficient to carry out designing, based on decisions that are being taken during the design process. They suggested six such operations. In an empirical study, they asked a designer to arrange furniture in a living and dining space in a student's apartment, and then listed the sequence of design decisions that had been made from the beginning to the end of the design session. A report was generated, consisting of a list of 35 decisions, achieved in 24 steps, each employing one operation. Next the operations that were carried out more or less at the same time were consolidated into a single step, resulting in a reduction of the number of steps to twelve. The decisions were subsequently coded using the six operations as the scheme of categories (the coding scheme, although it was the main goal of the study, is not relevant here). They also graphed the decisions across the given form variants, which were nine furniture "sites" (e.g., dining, working, TV, blind, long drape). The results proved that the six operations are necessary and sufficient to encompass all design decisions.

Branch library study, MIT, 1986–87

Source: eight protocols of design sessions

The Branch Library study was initiated in 1986 by Donald Schön and William Porter of the School of Architecture and Urban Planning at the Massachusetts Institute of Technology.[1] Its primary purpose was to study how designers make sense of design problems, which Schön and Porter regarded as under-defined and under-structured in most cases. It was a grounded theory study: there were no predefined research questions and it was assumed that such questions would arise from analyses of the experimental data. In keeping with the study's goals, Schön and Porter invented the "Branch Library Footprint" design task, which was intentionally poorly defined and poorly structured. The task called for commentary on six optional entry points into a branch library, indicated on a given outline plan referred to as "footprint" (figure A.1). Participants were asked to think

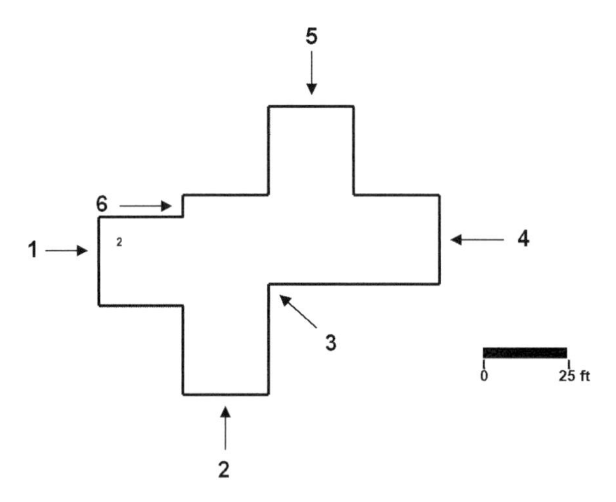

Figure A.1
"Footprint" of library. Numbered arrows indicate optional entry points.

aloud about the consequences of choosing a specific entry point while proposing preliminary design concepts for the library. Transcriptions of audio recordings and sketches produced during the sessions were used to prepare protocols.

The assignment instructions were given to participants orally and were not formalized in writing; the following is a reconstruction:

An association that builds and operates branch libraries in suburban areas (in the USA) has a standard "footprint" for its libraries, which are single floor buildings. Because of changing site conditions the entry point may vary; there are six alternative points at which the entry could be positioned that are indicated in the given drawing [figure A.1]. Could you please help the Library Association by commenting on the design implications of the different optional entry points?

Eight designers volunteered to participate in the experiments. Each of them undertook the assignment alone, in the presence of an experimenter (three researchers served as experimenters). There was no time limit. The participants spent between 30 minutes and 70 minutes completing the assignment. Six of the participants were affiliated with MIT. Most of them were full-time or part-time design teachers with different amounts of design experience, one was a visitor, and one was a first-year graduate student with an undergraduate education in chemistry. The remaining two participants were highly experienced, well-known European architects. Two of the protocols were not analyzed and are therefore not featured here.

In a follow-up task, called "branch library II," six designers were asked to design a library for a site in a clearing with several low walls. Only two of the protocols were analyzed and are featured here. The two participants were experienced architects who were pursuing PhD degrees at MIT.

Table A.1 summarizes the data about the participants in the two library design tasks.

Delft protocol workshop, 1994

Sources: two protocols transcribed by Anita Clayburn Cross; Cross et al. 1996

The Delft protocol workshop was initiated by Nigel Cross, Kees Dost, and Henri Christiaans in the Faculty of Industrial Design Engineering at the Delft University of Technology. The idea was to have a group of experienced

Table A.1
Participants in the branch library experiment.

Participant	Background	Moves in linkograph
Alice	First-year graduate student	27
Franz	Experienced architect; senior faculty	22
Glenda	Architect; visiting faculty	50
Ronna	Architect; graduate student and teaching assistant	37
Tim	Architect; graduate student and teaching assistant	23
Martin	Prominent European practicing architect	45
Gideon[a]	Experienced practicing architect; part-time faculty and graduate student	64
Gilbert[a]	Architect; graduate student	63

a. Gideon and Gilbert undertook the task "branch library II."

design researchers analyze a set of design protocols, and then to bring them together "to discuss the state of the art in protocol research" (Cross et al. 1996, 4). The task Cross, Dost, and Christiaans came up with called for the design of "a fastening device that should allow a given backpack to be fastened onto a mountain bike" (ibid., 5). The experiment took place in 1994 at Xerox PARC (now called the Xerox Research Center) in Palo Alto. The eight participants (two of whom worked individually and six in two three-person teams) were all experienced industrial designers. The bicycle and the backpack were in the room in which they worked. The subjects were asked to think aloud, and the sessions were videotaped. They worked under the same conditions for two hours, after which they were debriefed for ten minutes.

One team's protocol and one individual's protocol were selected (on the bases of clarity and completion of data) for analysis. These protocols, sketches produced during the sessions, and the video tapes of the sessions were sent to 19 invited design researchers (and research groups) with experience in protocol analysis. Later in 1994 they presented their work at what came to be called the Delft protocol workshop. Papers from the workshop were published in a book (Cross et al. 1996) and in a special issue of the journal *Design Studies* (volume 16, issue 2, 1995). Today researchers continue to use the "Delft protocols" in various studies.

Table A.2
Data on Delft protocols.

Designers	No. Participants	Analyzed portion	Moves in linkographs
Individual	1 (Dan)	32 minutes (6 units)	191
Team	3 (John, Ivan, Kerry)	46 minutes (14 units)	624

Table A.2 summarizes the data about the Delft protocol workshop used in this book.

Remko van der Lugt, 2001

Source: van der Lugt 2001

In his PhD research in industrial design engineering at the Delft University of Technology, Remko van der Lugt studied various methods of conducting idea-generation meetings at the outset of product-development tasks. The methods studied were all variants of brainstorming. In some sessions, the participants sketched; in others, only the facilitator sketched; in yet others, there was no sketching at all. Groups of advanced design students then were given two series of industrial design tasks that were facilitated according to the brainstorming variants. From the protocol of each session, van der Lugt extracted a list of ideas, which he then used as the units of analysis for an Excel-based linkograph. The linkographs allowed him to compare the groups regarding the number of links, the level at which team members built on each other's ideas, and more.

The linkograph from van der Lugt's study that is used in this book (see figure 4.9) pertains to a session in which a team of five designers generated 72 ideas in about 90 minutes. The task was to propose an accessory kit for a family car that would keep children in the back seat busy during a ride.

Dan Tatsa, 2004

Sources: Tatsa 2005; Goldschmidt and Tatsa 2005

Dan Tatsa's study, done in the course of his graduate work, is a "real world" study rather than a laboratory study. Tatsa was interested in the dynamics of idea generation in an undergraduate studio class in architecture. Assuming that such a setting is highly conducive to idea generation, he attended all sessions of a second-year undergraduate studio class for a semester and documented in detail the development of projects by eight students, listing the ideas raised by each student, by the teacher, and by fellow students. The assignment was to design a museum on the seashore of Tel Aviv.

At the end of the semester, Tatsa presented each student with a list of all ideas related to his or her project that had been communicated in the studio and asked the student to assess the impact of those ideas on the final design. There were five levels of impact, from "major contribution" to "negative impact." The two highest assessments were "contribution" (later changed to "critical") and "major contribution (later changed to "very critical"). Table A.3 presents the data.

Later Tatsa engaged in two rounds of linkograph generation. First he drew an Excel-based linkograph for each student. Since the lists of ideas were lengthy, this was a formidable task, and the results were used only for a general characterization of each student's process. In the second round, he constructed linkographs only for the "critical" and "very critical" ideas in each student's project. The latter process was repeated for two projects after links had been determined by two additional judges. Values extracted from these linkographs were correlated with the students' semester grades.

Table A.3
Participants in Tatsa's experiment.

Participant	All ideas	Self-assessed critical ideas	Self-assessed very critical ideas
Yoav	233	135	NA[a]
Noa	275	143	NA
Ronen	177	39	10
Sam	272	158	NA
Meirav	158	95	23
Liron	246	66	NA
Shirly	139	67	NA
Amit	92	25	NA

a. not applicable

Michal Daum-Cohen, 2005

Source: Daum-Cohen 2008

Michal Daum-Cohen was interested in the arguments designers use for decisions they contemplate and eventually make. In other words, she wanted to explore designers' reasoning in the early conceptual design phase. In particular, she wanted to compare novice and experienced designers in order to explore the know-how of the latter, which the former appear to not yet possess. As part of her graduate work, she conducted an experiment with ten novice (first-year) and ten more experienced (fourth-year or fifth-year) undergraduate architecture students. Each student was individually presented with the same design task, which called for the redesign of a small vacation house.[2] The student was given 25 minutes to perform the task and was asked to think aloud.

Daum-Cohen analyzed the first part of each protocol (about 8 minutes) which she parsed into design moves. The number of moves within this time frame varied significantly among participants. Later she generated Excel-based linkographs for each of these portions of the protocols. Figure A.2 shows the drawing that was given to each participant with this explanation of the task:

> You have inherited a small lot with a small house on it. The house is old and in poor condition and you can pull it down and build a new vacation house for yourself instead. As was the case in the past, building laws enable single-floor construction on 2/3 of the lot's area. When the house was built there was a requirement for a one-meter clearance between the property line and any construction. The law has since been eased and today building right to the property line is allowed. Openings are allowed anywhere in the house's perimeter, provided the 3 meter high party walls between your lot and adjoining lots remain intact.

Table A.4 presents the relevant data.

Daum-Cohen assumed that a higher positive correlation between values extracted from the linkographs and an independent evaluation of the quality of the design outcomes would be achieved by the advanced students. Her findings indicated that although this was the direction of the results, no statistically significant difference was found between advanced and novice students. Two possible explanations were offered. The first was that the difference in expertise between the two groups of students was not sufficiently pronounced: advanced students are still beginners and not

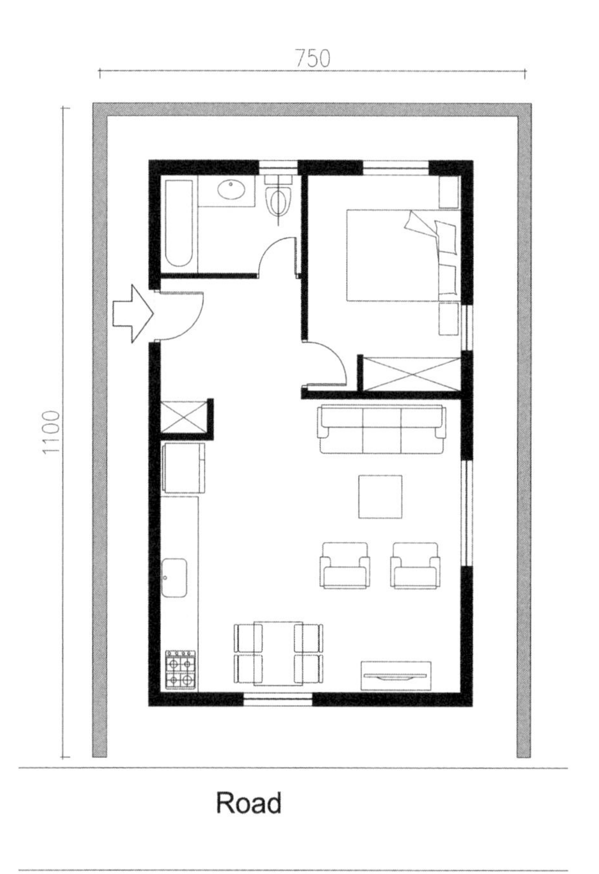

Figure A.2
Plan of small lot with old house used by Daum-Cohen.

experts. The second was that the initial part of the process (the eight minutes that were analyzed) may not be sufficiently indicative of the entire process.

André Neumann, 2006

Sources: protocol generated by Andre Neumann as part of his PhD work; Neumann 2012

In his PhD research at the Delft University of Technology, André Neumann investigated shared mental models in design teams: the extent to which they exist, the forms they take, and their effects. In a preliminary empirical

Table A.4
Participants in Daum-Cohen's experiment.

	Moves in linkograph
First-year students	
Anat	36
Barak	45
Dana	38
Inbal	47
Nimrod	59
Orit	33
Roni	25
Sharon	53
Fifth-year students	
Hadar	56
Iris	55
Liat	25
Noa[a]	50
Ronit	37
Ruth	70
Shahar	62
Yaniv	48

a. Not the individual of the same name who participated in Tatsa's study.

study, he asked seven three-person teams of advanced industrial design students to come up with conceptual designs for a movable ashtray. The task was described as follows:

> Since there is no suitable disposal system, cigarette stubs are an environmental problem in outdoor areas where many people gather for an event. You are asked to design a mobile ashtray (not fixed to the ground or attached to an object) that can be used in outdoors events such as a concert or a village fair.

After the task was introduced, each team member worked alone for 15 minutes and developed one or more ideas. In the next 50 minutes, members of the team worked together. In the next 10 minutes, they wrote down ideas individually. They then re-convened for 30 minutes and synthesized a joint solution. A short debriefing followed. The total working time, excluding the debriefing, was 120 minutes.

In this book, one vignette from one of Neumann's protocols is used. Taken from the stage in which members of the team worked together

Table A.5
Verbalizations across crits, Hochman and Dafni.

Crit	Total no. of verbalizations	% verbalizations by student	% verbalizations by teacher
Mani and teacher	65	41.5	58.5
Alona and teacher	63	58.7	41.3
Yoav[a] and teacher	90	50	50

a. Not the individual of the same name who participated in Tatsa's study.

before they had reached a final solution, it comprises 27 moves (this is referred to as the "short version"). An extended vignette from the same protocol, comprising 47 moves, was also linkographed (referred to as the "long version") and is sometimes used—see table 4.1.

Hagay Hochman and Itay Dafni, 2006

Source: Goldschmidt et al. 2010

Hagay Hochman and Itay Dafni were interested in the dynamics of the design critique ("crit"), a conversation between a student and a teacher about the student's project in progress. Hochman and Dafni documented three "crits" in three different second-year architecture studio classes and produced protocols. The protocols were parsed into verbalizations by turn taking of the conversants (student and teacher), regardless of their lengths (see table A.5). Linkographs were then prepared from the protocols.

Hochman and Dafni then produced a second set of linkographs, including only links between verbalizations by the student and the teacher and omitting links between verbalizations by the same party. They compared the resultant revised linkographs in terms of the communication dynamics. Next, they extracted critical verbalizations from each linkograph and calculated the percentage generated by each party. The results were compared with the participants' self-assessments (collected separately by means of questionnaires) regarding the question "Who raises important issues in studio crits?"

Notes

Chapter 2

1. http://pinker.wjh.harvard.edu/lectures/Rediscovery_Labels_revised.pdf.

2. "Stirling in Germany, The Architects' Report," *Architectural Review* 160, no. 957 (1976): 289–296; James Stirling and Partner, Landesgalerie Nordrhein-Westfalen, Düsseldorf, James Stirling and Partner with Werner Kreis, Robert Livesey, Russ Bevington, Ueli Schaad, The Wallraf-Richartz Museum in Cologne, *Lotus International* 15 (1977): 58–67 and 68–79 respectively; *Architectural Design* 47, no. 9–10 (1977): xx–61.

3. Letter to the author, May 12, 2000.

4. http://www.psy.fsu.edu/faculty/ericsson/ericsson.proto.thnk.html.

Chapter 3

1. Excluding those who study the brain rather than the mind and approach the topic from a neurocognitive or even a purely neurological point of view, which necessitates completely different research methods.

2. Milne's informal calculation yielded a value of about 7 seconds (personal communications, August 2010 and January 2012). Baya's results ranged from 6.9 seconds to 7.4 seconds in a number of studies (the equivalent term to "move" that Baya used, and Milne adopted, was "information fragment"). Kan and Gero found in one study that the average duration of a segment, which is the equivalent of a move, was 6.6 seconds. Goldschmidt reached a value of 6.9 seconds per move in one study.

3. http://www.thefreedictionary.com.

4. Previous attempts to automate this process were unsuccessful because they were based entirely on word similarity, which is not enough to express actual thought processes.

Chapter 4

1. The move line is a non-scaled time line, as the duration of moves varies.

2. The protocol was recorded by André Neumann in 2006 as part of his PhD research in the Faculty of Industrial Design Engineering at the Delft University of Technology (see appendix).

3. The 10–12% proportion was found, by trial and error, to yield the clearest picture regarding the structure of a process, but in short linkographs this proportion tends to be higher.

4. The slight difference between experienced and novice designers is interesting. One possible explanation is that experienced designers tend to make moves in a more integrated way, so that a high number of links is distributed among more moves and therefore the top 10% are responsible for a slightly lower number of links, with more links associated with the next percentiles.

5. The term "link span" should not be confused with the term "degree of separation," which is used in network theory. In this book, span is an adjacency measure in a sequentially ordered series. "Degree of separation" refers to the number of links needed to connect between pre-designated nodes in a network (e.g., a social network). Adjacency is inconsequential.

6. The percentage increases to 80.9 if we ignore Daum-Cohen's architecture students, whose link-generation pattern is a little different (see figure 4.8). For information about the processes that originated these calculations, see the appendix.

7. We do not attempt to inspect link percentages at L.S. levels higher than 7, as those vary significantly across cases.

Chapter 5

1. Since the operation typology is not our focus here, the operation types described by Wang and Habraken are omitted from the current discussion.

2. A threshold of three links yields seven critical moves, more than we would normally choose to inspect if adhering to the 10–12% rule of thumb, which would be achieved at a threshold of four links. The lower threshold was chosen because it yields the appropriate number of critical moves for a comparison with Wang and Habraken's critical path, which includes eight moves. This is a good example of the benefits of a flexible threshold setting.

3. The percentage of self-assessed critical ideas is very high in this study. The ideas that were classified as "very critical" yield a more appropriate percentage according to linkography theory. However, this is not relevant to the point made here regarding the increase of interlinking with the (independently measured) significance of the ideas to the designers.

4. *Move 21* and then er in this tray, if we assume the tray could be injection molded, 'cause that seems to be within our cost targets.

5. See also figure 4.6, in which this linkograph was chosen to exemplify a poorly structured process.

6. The proportion of CM^6s is rather high. For most analyses of the Delft protocols the threshold was seven links, but in this case we wanted to test a somewhat larger sample and therefore the link count was conducted at a lower threshold.

7. The 80/20 proportion should not be confused with the "80/20 principle" (Pareto principle), which stipulates that in many phenomena 80% of attained results are attributable to 20% of investment or effort (see, e.g., Koch 1998).

Chapter 6

1. This is a paraphrase of a dictum by the architect Louis Kahn, who maintained that there is no such thing as architecture; there are only works of architecture.

2. Since the task was very ill-defined, some of the participants were satisfied to comment on various aspects of it and did not attempt a complete solution.

3. In calculating the percentage of bidirectional moves, the total number of moves is taken to be $n - 2$, as the first and last moves are unidirectional by definition.

Chapter 7

1. A similar distinction was made by Rodgers et al. (2000), who used the scale at which sketches were drawn as a yardstick for transformation type (same scale—lateral transformation; larger scale—vertical transformation). The question of scale does not come up in the study by Cai et al.

2. The name first chosen for the program was Linkographer. Since this is the name of our linkographing software, developed earlier, Pourmohamedi and Gero changed the name of their system to lincoder. However, the change was not yet reflected in the referenced paper.

3. A Standard Progressive Matrices (SPM) test is a 3 × 3 design: three columns of three figures each, with the ninth figure absent. The progression from the top to the bottom figure of each column is governed by a different rule. The task is to deduce the rule for the third column and complete the missing figure (to be selected from eight given possibilities).

Appendix

1. The study was supported by the National Science Foundation under grant 8611357-DMC.

2. I devised this task for a 1988 Design Seminar session at MIT.

References

Akin, Ö. 1978. How Do Architects Design? In *Artificial Intelligence and Pattern Recognition in Computer Aided Design*, ed. J. Latombe. North-Holland.

Akin, Ö. 1986. *Psychology of Architectural Design*. Pion.

Alexander, C. 1964/1971. *Notes on the Synthesis of Form*. Harvard University Press.

Alexander, C., S. Ishikawa, and M. Silverstein. 1977. *A Pattern Language*. Oxford University Press.

Amabile, T. M. 1983. *The Social Psychology of Creativity*. Springer.

Anderson, L. B. 1979. Foreword. In *Plan No. 10, Process in Architecture: A Documentation of Six Examples*. School of Architecture and Planning, Massachusetts Institute of Technology.

Archea, J. 1987. Puzzle-Making: What Architects Are Doing When No One Is Looking. In *Computability of Design*, ed. Y. Kalay. Wiley-Interscience.

Arnheim, R. 1954. *Art and Visual Perception: A Psychology of the Creative Eye*. University of California Press.

Arnheim, R. 1969. *Visual Thinking*. University of California Press.

Asimow, M. 1962. *Introduction to Design*. Prentice-Hall.

Basadur, M. S. 1995. Optimal Ideation-Evaluation Ratios. *Creativity Research Journal* 8 (1): 63–75.

Baya, V. 1996. Information Handling Behavior of Designers During Conceptual Design: Three Experiments. PhD dissertation, Department of Mechanical Engineering, Stanford University.

Baya, V., and L. J. Leifer. 1996. Understanding Information Management in Conceptual Design. In *Analysing Design Activity*, ed. N. Cross, H. Christiaans, and K. Dorst. Wiley.

Bayazit, N. 2004. Investigating Design: A Review of Forty Years of Design Research. *Design Issues* 20 (1): 16–29.

Best, G. 1969. Method and Intention in Architectural Design. In *Design Methods in Architecture*, ed. G. Broadbent and A. Ward. Lund Humphries.

Bilda, Z., J. S. Gero, and T. Purcell. 2006. To Sketch or Not to Sketch? That Is the Question. *Design Studies* 27 (5): 587–613.

Björklund, T. A. 2013. Initial Mental Representations of Design Problems: Differences between Experts and Novices. *Design Studies* 34 (2): 135–160.

Boden, M. A. 1994. What Is Creativity? In *Dimensions of Creativity*, ed. M. Boden. MIT Press.

Botta, D., and R. Woodbury. 2013. Predicting Topic Shift Locations in Design Histories. *Research in Engineering Design* 24 (3): 245–258.

Broadbent, G. 1973. *Design in Architecture*. Wiley.

Broadbent, G., and A. Ward eds. 1969. *Design Methods in Architecture*. Lund Humphries.

Buchanan, R. 1992. Wicked Problems in Design Thinking. *Design Issues* 8 (2): 5–21.

Bruner, J. S., J. J. Goodnow, and G. A. Austin. 1956. *A Study of Thinking*. Wiley.

Cai, H., E. Y.-L. Do, and C. M. Zimring. 2010. Extended Linkography and Distance Graph in Design Evaluation: An Empirical Study of the Dual Effects of Inspiration Sources in Creative Design. *Design Studies* 31 (2): 146–168.

Casakin, H., and G. Goldschmidt. 2000. Reasoning by Visual Analogy in Design Problem-Solving: The Role of Guidance. *Journal of Planning and Design: Environment and Planning B* 27: 105–119.

Chai, K.-H., and X. Xiao. 2012. Understanding Design Research: A Bibliometric Analysis of Design Studies (1996–2010). *Design Studies* 33 (1): 24–43.

Chase, W. G., and H. A. Simon. 1973. Perception in Chess. *Cognitive Psychology* 4 (1): 55–81.

Chermayeff, S., and C. Alexander. 1963. *Community and Privacy: Toward a New Architecture of Humanism*. Doubleday.

Coyne, R. D., M. A. Rosenman, A. D. Radford, M. Balachandran, and J. S. Gero. 1990. *Knowledge-Based Design Systems*. Addison-Wesley.

Cross, N. 1984. *Developments in Design Methodology*. Wiley.

Cross, N. 1994. *Engineering Design Methods—Strategies for Product Design*. Wiley.

Cross, N. 1997. Creativity in Design: Analyzing and Modeling the Creative Leap. *Leonardo* 30 (4): 311–317.

Cross, N. 2006. *Designerly Ways of Knowing*. Springer.

Cross, N. 2010. Editorial. *Design Studies* 31 (1): 1–2.

Cross, N. 2011. *Design Thinking*. Berg.

Cross, N., and A. Clayburn Cross. 1995. Observations of Teamwork and Social Processes in Design. *Design Studies* 12 (2): 143–170.

Cross, N., H. Christiaans, and K. Dorst, eds. 1996. *Analysing Design Activity*. Wiley.

Dasgupta, S. 1994. *Creativity in Invention and Design*. Cambridge University Press.

Daum-Cohen, M. 2008. Structure in Architectural Design Processes: A Comparison between Novice and Advanced Students. MSc thesis, Technion.

Davies, S. P. 1995. Effects of Concurrent Verbalization on Design Problem Solving. *Design Studies* 16 (1): 102–116.

de Groot, A. D. 1965/1978. *Thought and Choice in Chess*. Mouton.

Dillon, M. R. 2010. Dynamic Design: Cognitive Processes in Design Sketching. *Indiana Undergraduate Journal of Cognitive Science* 5: 28–43.

Do, E. Y.-L., and M. D. Gross. 1995. Drawing Analogies: Finding Visual References by Sketching. In Proceedings of Association of Computer Aided Design in Architecture, Seattle.

Dong, A. 2007. The Enactment of Design through Language. *Design Studies* 28 (1): 5–21.

Dorst, K. 2003. Exploring the Structure of Design Problems. In Proceedings of the Fourteenth International Conference on Engineering Design, Stockholm.

Dorst, K., and N. Cross. 2001. Creativity in the Design Process: Co-Evolution of Problem-Solution. *Design Studies* 22 (5): 425–437.

Duncker, K. 1926. A Quantitative (Experimental and Theoretical) Study of Productive Thinking (Solving of Comprehensible Problems). *Pedagogical Seminary* 33: 642–708.

Duncker, K. 1945. On Problem-Solving. *Psychological Monographs* 58: 1–114.

Eastman, C. M. 1970. On the Analysis of Intuitive Design Processes. In *Emerging Methods of Environmental Design and Planning*, ed. G. Moore. MIT Press.

El-Khouly, T., and A. Penn. 2012. Order, Structure and Disorder in Space Syntax and Linkography: Intelligibility, Entropy, and Complexity Measures. In Proceedings of Eighth International Space Syntax Symposium, Santiago.

Ericsson, K. A., and H. A. Simon. 1984/1993. *Protocol Analysis: Verbal Reports as Data*. MIT Press.

Field, M., S. Gordon, E. J. Peterson, R. Robinson, T. F. Stahovich, and C. Alvarado. 2010. The Effect of Task on Classification Accuracy: Using Gesture Recognition Techniques in Free-Sketch Recognition. *Computers & Graphics* 34 (5): 499–512.

Finke, R. A., T. B. Ward, and S. M. Smith. 1992. *Creative Cognition: Theory, Research, and Application.* MIT Press.

Fodor, J. 1975. *The Language of Thought.* Crowell.

Frankenberger, E., and P. Badke-Schaub. 1998. Modeling Design Processes in Industry—Empirical Investigations of Design Work in Practice. *Automation in Construction* 7 (2–3): 139–155.

Fricke, G. 1996. Successful Individual Approaches in Engineering Design. *Research in Engineering Design* 8 (3): 151–165.

Gabora, L. 2010. Revenge of the 'Neurds': Characterizing Creative Thought in Terms of the Structure and Dynamics of Memory. *Creativity Research Journal* 22 (1): 1–13.

Galle, P., and L. B. Kovács. 1996. Replication Protocol Analysis: A Method for the Study of Real-World Design Thinking. *Design Studies* 17 (2): 181–200.

Gardner, H. E. 1988. Creativity: An Interdisciplinary Perspective. *Creativity Research Journal* 1 (1): 8–26.

Gardner, H. E. 1993. *Creating Minds: An Anatomy of Creativity as Seen Through the Lives of Freud, Einstein, Picasso, Stravinsky, Eliot, Graham, and Gandhi.* Basic Books.

Gericke, K., B. Kleinod, and L. Blessing. 2009. Analysis and Visualization of Project Structure Using Linkography: Focusing Project Risk Management. In Proceedings of ASME IDETC/DTM 2009: International Design Engineering Technical Conference and International Conference on Design Theory and Methodology, San Diego.

Gero, J. S. 1990. Design Prototypes: A Knowledge Representation Schema for Design. *AI Magazine* 11 (4): 26–36.

Gero, J. S. 2011. Fixation and Commitment While Designing and its Measurement. *Journal of Creative Behavior* 45 (2): 108–115.

Gero, J. S., and U. Kannengiesser. 2011. Design. In *Encyclopedia of Creativity*, second edition, volume 1, ed. M. Runco and S. Pritzker. Academic Press.

Goel, A., and S. Bhatta. 2004. Design Patterns: A Unit of Analogical Transfer in Creative Design. *Advanced Engineering Informatics* 18 (2): 85–94.

Goel, V. 1995. *Sketches of Thought.* MIT Press.

Goldschmidt, G. 1990. Linkography: Assessing Design Productivity. In *Proceedings of the Tenth European Meeting on Cybernetics and Systems Research*, ed. R. Trappl. World Scientific.

Goldschmidt, G. 1991. The Dialectics of Sketching. *Creativity Research Journal* 4 (2): 123–143.

Goldschmidt, G. 1994a. Development in Architectural Designing. In *Development and the Arts: Critical Aspects*, ed. M. Franklin and B. Kaplan. Erlbaum.

Goldschmidt, G. 1994b. On Visual Design Thinking: The Vis Kids of Architecture. *Design Studies* 15 (2): 158–174.

Goldschmidt, G. 1995. The Designer as a Team of One. *Design Studies* 16 (2): 189–210.

Goldschmidt, G. 1996. The Designer as a Team of One. In *Analysing Design Activity*, ed. N. Cross, H. Christiaans, and K. Dorst. Wiley.

Goldschmidt, G. 2001. Is a Figure-Concept Binary Argumentation Pattern Inherent in Visual Design Reasoning? In *Visual and Spatial Reasoning in Design II*, ed. J. Gero, B. Tversky, and T. Purcell. Key Centre of Design Computing and Cognition, University of Sydney.

Goldschmidt, G. 2012. A Micro View of Design Reasoning: Two-Way Shifts between Embodiment and Rationale. In *Creativity and Rationale: Enhancing Human Experience by Design*, ed. J. Carroll. Springer.

Goldschmidt, G., H. Hochman, and I. Dafni. 2010. The Design Studio 'Crit': Teacher-Student Communication. *Artificial Intelligence for Engineering Design, Analysis and Manufacturing* 24 (3): 285–302.

Goldschmidt, G., and D. Tatsa. 2005. How Good Are Good Ideas? Correlates of Design Creativity. *Design Studies* 26 (6): 593–611.

Goldschmidt, G., and M. Weil. 1998. Contents and Structure in Design Reasoning. *Design Issues* 14 (3): 85–100.

Grabow, S. 1983. *Christopher Alexander: The Search for a New Paradigm in Architecture*. Oriel.

Gregory, S. A., ed. 1966. *The Design Method*. Butterworth.

Grice, H. P. 1975. Logic and Conversation. In *Syntax and Semantics*, volume 3, ed. P. Cole and J. Morgan. Academic Press.

Grobman, Y. J., and E. Neuman, eds. 2011. *Performalism: Form and Performance in Digital Architecture*. Routledge.

Gross, M. D. 1994. Recognizing and Interpreting Diagrams in Design. In *Proceedings of Workshop on Advanced Visual Interfaces*. ACM.

Gruber, H. E. 1980a. Afterword. In D. H. Feldman, *Beyond Universals in Cognitive Development*. Ablex.

Gruber, H. E. 1980b. The Evolving Systems Approach to Creativity. In *Towards a Theory of Psychological Development*, ed. S. Modgil and C. Modgil. NFER Press.

Gruber, H. E., and S. N. Davies. 1988. Inching Our Way Up Mount Olympus: The Evolving-Systems Approach to Creative Thinking. In *The Nature of Creativity*, ed. R. Sternberg. Cambridge University Press.

Gryskiewicz, S. S. 1980. A Study of Creative Problem Solving Techniques in Group Settings. PhD dissertation, University of London.

Guilford, J. P. 1956. Structure of Intellect. *Psychological Bulletin* 53 (4): 267–293.

Günther, J., E. Frankenberger, and P. Auer. 1996. Investigation of Individual and Team Design Processes. In *Analysing Design Activity*, ed. N. Cross, H. Christiaans, and K. Dorst. Wiley.

Gürsoy, B., and M. Özkar. 2010. Is Model-Making Sketching in Design? In Proceedings of Design Research Society International Conference on Design and Complexity, Montreal.

Heath, T. 1984. *Methods in Architecture*. Wiley.

Heims, S. J. 1991. *The Cybernetics Group*. MIT Press.

Herbert, D. M. 1988. Study Drawings in Architectural Design: Their Properties as a Graphic Medium. *Journal of Architectural Education* 41 (2): 26–38.

Herbert, D. M. 1993. *Architectural Study Drawings*. Van Nostrand Reinhold.

Howard-Jones, P. A., and S. Murray. 2003. Ideational Productivity, Focus of Attention, and Context. *Creativity Research Journal* 15 (2–3): 153–166.

Hubka, V., and W. E. Eder. 1982. *Principles of Engineering Design*. Butterworth-Heinemann.

Hubka, V., and W. E. Eder. 1996. *Design Science: Introduction to Needs, Scope and Organization of Engineering Design Knowledge*. Springer.

Jacob, R. J. K., and K. S. Karn. 2003. Eye Tracking in Human Computer Interaction and Usability Research: Ready to Deliver the Promises. In *The Mind's Eye: Cognitive and Applied Aspects of Eye Movement Research*, ed. J. Hyona, R. Radach, and H. Deubel. Elsevier Science.

Jones, J. C. 1969. The State-of-the-Art in Design Methods. In *Design Methods in Architecture*, ed. G. Broadbent and A. Ward. Lund Humphries.

Jones, J. C., and A. G. Thornley, eds. 1963. *Conference on Design Methods*. Pergamon.

Kahneman, D. 2011. *Thinking, Fast and Slow*. Farrar, Straus and Giroux.

Kalay, Y. 2004. *Architecture's New Media: Principles, Theories and Methods of Computer-Aided Design*. MIT Press.

Kan, J. W. T. 2008. Quantitative Methods for Studying Design Protocols. PhD dissertation, University of Sydney.

Kan, J. W. T., and J. S. Gero. 2005. Design Behaviour Measurement by Quantifying Linkography in Protocol Studies of Designing. In *Human Behavior in Design '05*, ed. J. Gero and U. Lindemann. Key Centre of Design Computing and Cognition, University of Sydney.

Kan, J. W. T., and J. S. Gero. 2008. Acquiring Information from Linkography in Protocol Studies of Designing. *Design Studies* 29 (4): 315–337.

Kan, J. W. T., and J. S. Gero. 2009a. Using the FBS Ontology to Capture Semantic Design Information in Design Protocol Studies. In *About: Designing. Analysing Design Meetings*, ed. J. McDonnell and P. Lloyd. CRC Press.

Kan, J. W. T., and J. S. Gero. 2009b. Using Entropy to Measure Design Creativity. In Proceedings of International Conference of the International Association of Societies of Design Research, Seoul.

Kan, J. W. T., Z. Bilda, and J. S. Gero. 2007. Comparing Entropy Measures of Idea Links in Design Protocols. *AIEDAM* 21 (4): 367–377.

Kanerva, P. 1988. *Sparse Distributed Memory*. MIT Press.

Koch, R. 1998. *The 80/20 Principle: The Secret to Success by Achieving More with Less*. Doubleday.

Koestler, A. 1964. *The Act of Creation*. Huchinson.

Kolarevic, B., and A. M. Malkawi, eds. 2005. *Performative Architecture: Beyond Instrumentality*. Spon.

Kolodner, J. L., ed. 1988. *Proceedings of Workshop on Case-Based Reasoning*. Morgan Kaufmann.

König, H. G. 1992. The Planar Architecture of Juan Gris. *Languages of Design* 1 (1): 51–74.

Kvan, T. 2013. Conversations With Ideas: A Micro View of Design. In *Designing the Dynamic*, ed. J. Burry. Melbourne Books.

Kvan, T., and S. Gao. 2006. A Comparative Study of Problem Framing in Multiple Settings. In *Design Computing and Cognition'06*, ed. J. Gero. Springer.

Kwon, H.-J., H.-S. Lee, D.-H. Song, and C.-Y. Kim. 2008. Toward a Linkography Design Visualization Tool on Web 2.0 Social Network Type Interface. In Proceedings of IEEE/WIC/ACM International Conference on Web Intelligence and Intelligent Agent Technology.

Lawson, B. 1980/2005. *How Designers Think: The Design Process Demystified. Oxford.* Butterworth.

Lawson, B. 1994. *Design in Mind.* Butterworth-Heinemann.

Leibowitz, H. 1989. Reveries of an "Incorrigible Romanticist": Louis Sullivan's the autobiography of an Idea. In *Fabricating Lives: Explorations in American Autobiography.* Knopf.

Linhares, A., A. Freitas, A. Mendes, and J. Silva. 2012. Entanglement of Perception and Reasoning in the Combinatorial Game of Chess: Differential Errors of Strategic Reconstruction. *Cognitive Systems Research* 13: 72–86.

Liu, Y.-C., T. Blight, and A. Chakrabarti. 2003. Towards an 'Ideal' Approach for Concept Generation. *Design Studies* 24 (4): 341–355.

Longuet-Higgins, H. C. 1987. *Mental Processes: Studies in Cognitive Science.* MIT Press.

Luckman, J. 1969. An Approach to the Management of Design. In *Design Methods in Architecture,* ed. G. Broadbent and A. Ward. Lund Humphries.

MacKinnon, D. W. 1962. The Personality Correlates of Creativity: A Study of American Architects. In *Proceedings of the Fourteenth Congress on Applied Psychology,* volume 2, ed. G. Nielsen. Munksgaard.

MacKinnon, D. W. 1978. *In Search of Human Effectiveness: Identifying and Developing Creativity.* Creative Education Foundation.

Maher, M. L., M. B. Balachandran, and D. M. Zhang. 1995. *Case-Based Reasoning in Design.* Erlbaum.

Mark, E., M. Gross, and G. Goldschmidt. 2008. A Perspective on Computer Aided Design after Four Decades. In Proceedings of eCAADe08 on: Architecture 'in Computro': Interacting Methods and Techniques, University College of Antwerp.

Martindale, C. 1999. Biological Bases of Creativity. In *Handbook of Creativity,* ed. R. Sternberg. Cambridge University Press.

Mednick, S. 1962. The Associative Basis of the Creative Process. *Psychological Review* 69 (3): 220–232.

Mesarović, M. D. 1964. *Views on General Systems Theory.* Wiley.

Miller, G. A. 1956. The Magical Number Seven, Plus or Minus Two: Some Limits on Our Capacity for Processing Information. *Psychological Review* 63 (2): 81–97.

Miller, G. A. 2003. The Cognitive Revolution: A Historical Perspective. *Trends in Cognitive Sciences* 7 (3): 141–144.

Naisberg, E. D. 1986. Non Continuous Steps in Architectural Design: Examination of Design Processes, First Year Students. MSc thesis, Technion.

Neisser, U. 1967. *Cognitive Psychology.* Prentice-Hall.

Neumann, A. 2012. Designerly Ways of Sharing: The Dynamic Development of Shared Mental Models in Design Teams. PhD dissertation, Delft University of Technology.

Newell, A. 1980. Human Problem Solving. http://garfield.library.upenn.edu/classics1980/A1980KD04600001.pdf.

Newell, A., and H. A. Simon. 1972. *Human Problem Solving*. Prentice-Hall.

Page, J. K. 1963. A Review of the Papers Presented at the Conference. In *Conference on Design Methods*, ed. J. Jones and A. Thornley. Pergamon.

Pahl, G., and W. Beitz. 1984/1996. *Engineering Design: A Systematic Approach* (second edition with K. Wallace). Springer.

Perkins, D. N. 1981. *The Mind's Best Work*. Harvard University Press.

Perkins, D. N. 1992. The Topography of Invention. In *Inventive Minds: Creativity in Technology*, ed. R. Weber and D. N. Perkins. Oxford University Press.

Piaget, J. 1971. *Structuralism*. Harper Torchbooks.

Plucker, J. A., and J. S. Renzulli. 1999. Psychometric Approaches to the Study of Human Creativity. In *Handbook of Creativity*, ed. R. Sternberg. Cambridge University Press.

Pourmohamadi, M., and J. S. Gero. 2011. Linkographer: An Analysis Tool to Study Design Protocols Based on FBS Coding Scheme. In Proceedings of the Eighteenth International Conference on Engineering Design, Copenhagen.

Pugh, S. 1991. *Total Design: Integrated Methods for Successful Product Engineering*. Addison-Wesley.

Purcell, T., J. S. Gero, H. Edwards, and T. McNeill. 1996. The Data in Design Protocols: The Issue of Data Coding, Data Analysis in the Development of Models of the Design Process. In *Analysing Design Activity*, ed. N. Cross, H. Christiaans, and K. Dorst. Wiley.

Putnam, H. 1975. Brains and Behavior. In *Mind, Language, and Reality: Philosophical Papers*, volume 2. Cambridge University Press.

Pylyshyn, Z. W. 1986. *Computation and Cognition*. MIT Press.

Reitman, W. R. 1964. Heuristic Decision Procedures, Open Constraints, and the Structure of Ill-Defined Problems. In *Human Judgments and Optimality*, ed. M. Shelly and G. Bryan. Wiley.

Rittel, H. W. J., and M. M. Webber. 1973. Dilemmas in a General Theory of Planning. *Policy Sciences* 4 (2): 155–169.

Robertson, L. C. 1986. From Gestalt to Neo-Gestalt. In *Approaches to Cognition: Contrasts and Controversies*, ed. T. Knapp, and L. Robertson. Erlbaum.

Rodgers, P. A., G. Green, and A. McGown. 2000. Using Concept Sketches to Track Design Progress. *Design Studies* 21 (5): 451–464.

Roozenberg, N. F. M., and J. Eekels. 1995. *Product Design: Fundamentals and Methods*. Wiley.

Roy, R. 1993. Case Studies of Creativity in Innovative Product Development. *Design Studies* 14 (4): 423–443.

Runco, M. A. 1991. The Evaluative, Valuative and Divergent Thinking of Children. *Journal of Creative Behavior* 25 (4): 311–319.

Runco, M. A., and S. M. Okuda. 1988. Problem Finding, Divergent Thinking, and the Creative Process. *Journal of Youth and Adolescence* 17 (3): 211–220.

Schön, D. A. 1983. *The Reflective Practitioner*. Basic Books.

Schön, D. A. 1984. Problems, Frames and Perspectives on Designing. *Design Studies* 5 (3): 132–136.

Schön, D. A. 1992. Designing as Reflective Conversation with the Materials of a Design Situation. *Knowledge-Based Systems* 5 (1): 3–14.

Shannon, C. E. 1948. A Mathematical Theory of Communication. *Bell System Technical Journal* 27 (4): 397–423.

Simon, H. A. 1973. The Structure of Ill Structured Problems. *Artificial Intelligence* 4 (1): 181–201.

Simon, H. A. 1982. *The Sciences of the Artificial*, second edition. MIT Press.

Skinner, B. F. 1974. *About Behaviorism*. Vintage.

Sloman, S. A. 1996. The Empirical Case for Two Systems of Reasoning. *Psychological Bulletin* 119 (1): 3–22.

Suwa, M., T. Purcell, and J. S. Gero. 1998. Macroscopic Analysis of Design Processes Based on a Scheme for Coding Designers' Cognitive Actions. *Design Studies* 19 (4): 455–483.

Suwa, M., and B. Tversky. 1997. What Do Architects and Students Perceive in Their Design Sketches? A Protocol Analysis. *Design Studies* 18 (4): 385–403.

Swerdloff, L. M., and Y. E. Kalay. 1987. A Partnership Approach to Computer-Aided Design. In *Computability of Design*, ed. Y. Kalay. Wiley.

Tatsa, D. 2005. Ideas in Students' Projects in the Architectural Studio: Their Sources, Development, Roles and Assortment. MSc thesis, Technion.

Taura, T., and Y. Nagai. 2013. *Concept Generation for Design Creativity: A Systematized Theory and Methodology*. Springer.

Torrance, E. P. 1974. *The Torrance Tests of Creative Thinking: Technical-Norms Manual*. Scholastic Testing Services.

Torrance, E. P. 1988. The Nature of Creativity as Manifest in its Testing. In *The Nature of Creativity: Contemporary Psychological Perspectives*, ed. R. Sternberg. Cambridge University Press.

Ullman, D. G. 1992. *The Mechanical Design Process*. McGraw-Hill.

van der Lugt, R. 2001. Sketching in Design Idea Generation Meetings. PhD dissertation, Delft University of Technology.

van der Lugt, R. 2003. Relating the Quality of the Idea Generation Process to the Quality of the Resulting Design Ideas. In Proceedings of the 14th International Conference on Engineering Design, Stockholm.

van Someren, M. W., Y. F. Barnard, and J. A. Sandberg. 1994. *The Think Aloud Method: A Practical Guide to Modeling Cognitive Processes*. Academic Press.

Vidal, R., E. Mulet, and E. Gómez-Senent. 2004. Effectiveness of the Means of Expression in Creative Problem-Solving in Design Groups. *Journal of Engineering Design* 15 (3): 285–298.

Visser, W., and M. L. Maher. 2011. The Role of Gesture in Designing. Guest Editorial. *Artificial Intelligence for Engineering Design, Analysis and Manufacturing* 25 (3): 213–220.

Vygotsky, L. 1986. *Thought and Language*. MIT Press.

Wang, M. H., and N. J. Habraken. 1982. Notation of the Design Process: The Six Operations. Unpublished research paper, Massachusetts Institute of Technology.

Watts, R. D. 1966. The Elements of Design. In *The Design Method*, ed. S. Gregory. Butterworth.

Wertheimer, M. 1923/1938. Laws of Organization in Perceptual Forms. In *A Source Book of Gestalt Psychology*, ed. W. Ellis. Routledge and Kegan Paul.

Wertheimer, M. 1945/1971. *Productive Thinking*. Harper Torchbooks.

Wissink, G., and S. Jaarsveld. 2002. Solving and Designing of Well-Defined Problems: A Structural Analysis of Cognitive Tasks Using the Linkograph System. Unpublished research paper, University of Amsterdam.

Woodbury, R. F., and A. L. Burrow. 2006. Whither Design Space? *Artificial Intelligence for Engineering Design, Analysis and Manufacturing* 20: 63–82.

Wrede, S. 1986. *Mario Botta*. Museum of Modern Art.

Zeisel, J. 1981. *Inquiry by Design: Tools for Environmental-Behavior Research*. Brooks/Cole.

Index